A KID'S GUIDE TO
NATIVE AMERICAN HISTORY

More than 50 Activities

YVONNE WAKIM DENNIS AND
ARLENE HIRSCHFELDER

CHICAGO
REVIEW
PRESS

Library of Congress Cataloging-in-Publication Data

Dennis, Yvonne Wakim.

A kid's guide to native American history : more than 50 activities / by Yvonne Wakim Dennis and Arlene Hirschfelder.

p. cm.

Includes bibliographical references and index.

ISBN 978-1-55652-802-6 (pbk.)

1. Indians of North America—History—Juvenile literature. 2. Indians of North America—Alaska—History—Juvenile literature. 3. Hawaii—History—Juvenile literature. 4. Handicraft—Juvenile literature. 5. Cookery—Juvenile literature. 6. Games—Juvenile literature. I. Hirschfelder, Arlene B. II. Title.

E77.4.D46 2010

970.004'97—dc22

2009015832

Interior design: Scott Rattray

Cover and interior illustrations: Gail Rattray

Published by Chicago Review Press, Incorporated

814 North Franklin Street

Chicago, Illinois 60610

ISBN: 978-1-55652-802-6

Printed in the United States of America

19 18 17 16 15 14 13 12

❖ Contents ❖

◈ Acknowledgments ◈

We are filled with gratitude for all the amazing folks who grace these pages.

Linda Coombs of the Wampanoag Indian Program of Plimoth Plantation for her time and expertise. Adriana Ignacio and Berta Welch for sharing their Wampanoag heritage. Michael Courlander for his generosity. Kim LaFlame for telling his story and for his resolve to save the American Indian Dog breed. Deborah Harry and all the activists who give back to the community when they could be having an easier life. We wish there was a chapter for each of them! Cody, Nick, and Travis and the rest of the March Point crew could have been doing a million other things teens do, and instead they gave the world a wonderful documentary—we are grateful to all the young Native people who take up the cause. We would love to have Ray Young Bear in every book we ever write!

Thanks to all the elders and scholars who keep Native languages alive. We are particulary grateful to Dr. William H. Wilson (Pila) of the 'Aha Punana Leo Board of Directors for taking time to critique the Hawaiian words; to Aquilina (Debbie) Lestenkof of the St. Paul Tribal Government Ecosystem Conservation Office for once again sorting out the Unangan language for us; and to Barbara Delisle, from the Kahnawake community in Canada and a graduate of McGill University's first program for Mohawk language teachers, for translating all that we asked of her.

Arlene's wisdom, knowledge, fairness, compassion, attention to detail, and commitment to teaching the true history of the First Nations make her an incredible writing partner. I am honored to be friends with such a beautiful, righteous person! Thanks, Arlene!

Yvonne is a colleague and friend extraordinaire who has enriched my life beyond measure.

We really appreciate our husbands, who take care of us when we are doing the "deadline dance."

We appreciate the Rattrays' ability translating our activities into illustrations and for their cooperation in making sure each region was appropriately represented.

Michelle Schoob, thanks so much for tightening up the prose and making it sing.

And thank you, Cynthia Sherry, for believing that young children have the capacity to understand what really happened to Native peoples and making a place for this book at CRP.

◈ Note to Readers ◈

Long before the rest of the world even knew this part of the globe existed, millions of people lived in the western hemisphere. They had distinctive cultures, territories, religions, housing, transportation, foods, and traditions. In fact, there was incredible diversity in North America. Native peoples have a rich past full of art and inventions. They also have histories of interacting with each other through trade, negotiations, organizations like the current United Nations, and sometimes war. The independent governments formed alliances and agreements with each other like countries in other parts of the world.

There is not enough room in this book to contain the entire history of even one Native nation, so it would be impossible to include them all. The time line on the next page starts a mere 500 years ago, and it represents a very short period of time in the history of hundreds of separate nations. But the last 500 years have been the most destructive and life changing for the original peoples. Native peoples initially welcomed Europeans as guests and trading partners. For most nations, it was customary to be hospitable and curious about new cultures. However, the newcomers did not always come with open minds and open hearts. They disliked Native religions, traditions, governments, clothing, houses, and languages, and they tried to erase Native cultures across the United States. The time line covers the impact the past 500 years have had on Native peoples.

◈ Time Line

circa 900 | The Five Nations (Iroquois) Confederacy was founded.

1607 | The British Virginia Company established a colony at Jamestown in the territory of the Powhatan Chiefdom.

1620 | Wampanoag people helped English colonists survive their first winter in Plymouth, Massachusetts.

1626 | Carnarsee Indians who occupied the southern end of Manhattan island sold it to Peter Minuit, governor of the Dutch colony of New Netherland.

1680 | The Pueblo Indians of New Mexico unified and successfully expelled the Spanish from their land.

1692 | The Spanish returned and reconquered Pueblo villages in New Mexico.

1787 | The United States Constitution gave Congress the power to make treaties, the supreme law of the land, with Indian nations.

1830 | President Andrew Jackson signed into law the Indian Removal Act.

1849 | Congress transferred the Bureau of Indian Affairs from the War Department to the newly created Department of the Interior.

1864 | Some 8,000 Navajos were rounded up and forced to make the "long walk" from their Arizona homeland to a prison-like location in New Mexico.

1867 | The United States purchased Alaska from Russia and assumed control over Athabascan Indians, Yup'ik and Iñupiat, and Aleut peoples.

1871 | Congress ended treaty making with American Indian tribes, but some 370 treaties remained in effect.

1879 | Carlisle Indian (boarding) School founded in Pennsylvania.

1887 | The Dawes Act opened up millions of acres of reservation lands to non-Indian ownership.

1924 | Congress granted citizenship to all Indians who were not yet citizens. Although Indians could then vote in national elections, some states prohibited Indians from voting in state elections.

1934 | The Indian Reorganization Act (IRA) repealed the Dawes Act and introduced a federal program essential to Native survival.

1948 | The Arizona Supreme Court held that Indians had the right to vote in Arizona.

1952–1957 | The federal relocation program moved Indians far from reservations to cities such as Chicago, Denver, and San Francisco.

1953 | A congressional resolution called for the termination (end) of the special relationship between the federal government and Indians, without their consent.

1968 | The Navajo Community College, on the Navajo Reservation in Arizona, became the first two-year college established and controlled by an Indian tribe. Today it is called Diné College.

1971 | The Alaska Native Claims Settlement Act was passed.

1978 | The American Indian Religious Freedom Act was passed.

1988 | Congress ended the termination policy of 1953.

1990 | The Native American Languages Act was enacted.

1990 | The Indian Arts and Crafts Act was enacted.

2001 | Congress awarded gold and silver medals to Navajo Code Talkers for their heroism during World War II.

2002 | John Bennett Herrington, a member of the Chickasaw Nation of Oklahoma, blasted into space aboard the space shuttle *Endeavour*. He is the first Native American astronaut and the first Native person to perform a space walk.

2004 | The Smithsonian's National Museum of the American Indian opened in Washington, D.C.

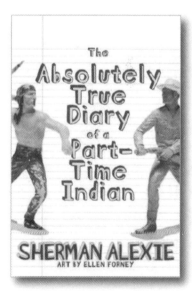

◆ Introduction ◆

Boston Red Sox player Jacoby Ellsbury stole so many bases that he became the 2008 American League Stolen Base Leader. In 2002 NASA astronaut John Bennett Herrington strolled in space thousands of miles above Fenway Park. CBS national news correspondent Hattie Kauffman reports stories like these on the *Early Show*. What do all these events have in common? They were all carried out by American Indians, or Native Americans. And they were all firsts in their fields. Although Ellsbury is not the first American Indian ballplayer, he is the first Navajo to play in major league baseball. Herrington (Chickasaw) is the first American Indian astronaut, and Emmy Award winner Kauffman (Nez Perce) is the first Native American to report on the national news. They have received national acclaim for doing their jobs well, but all over the United States there are countless other, non-famous, Native people involved in every aspect of American society, from politics to music to sports to science. *A Kid's Guide to Native American History* is about history, but it is also about real Native people today.

What comes to mind when you think about First Nations or American Indians? Most people think about feathered headdresses, tipis, or canoes. Books and movies rarely show the many different customs and cultures of Native people. Seldom do you see anything about modern or contemporary Native people. This gives the impression that the original peoples of this country are all the same or that they do not even exist today. Children sometimes play at "being Indian" by making drums, clothing, or masks. It is as if Indian cultures and peoples are toys. Imagine being an American Indian student and not learning anything accurate or positive about your group in school. This doesn't hurt only Native people. Other Americans miss the chance to know about the original cultures of this land and who Native people are today.

There are several terms used to describe the original inhabitants of the United States: American Indians, Native Americans, First Nations, Amerindians, Indians, Natives, Native peoples, and indigenous peoples. Most of these names are not very accurate—the original people of this hemisphere

NATIVE AMERICAN QUICK FACTS

- According to the 2000 United States Census, there are 4.1 million Native Americans living in the United States, which is 1.5 percent of the total population.
- The 10 U.S. states with the largest Native populations are, in order, California, Oklahoma, Arizona, Texas, New Mexico, New York, Washington, North Carolina, Michigan, and Alaska.
- In 2000 the state with the highest percentage of Native people was Alaska. Nearly 20 percent of Alaska's residents identify as Alaska Native.
- The 10 largest tribal groupings are, in order, Cherokee, Navajo, Latin American Indian, Choctaw, Sioux, Chippewa, Apache, Blackfeet, Iroquois, and Pueblo.
- Almost half of the Native population (43 percent) lives in the west.
- In 2000 the population of Native people in Honolulu, Hawaii, came in just behind that of Los Angeles, California.

were here centuries before there was an "America." *America* is not a Native word and *Indian* refers to people from India, a country Christopher Columbus thought he had reached after sailing to the western hemisphere quite by mistake. Before Europeans came to this part of the world, hundreds of separate nations, each with its own language, dress, customs, religion, communities, and homelands, had their own names and were never lumped together. A *nation* is a tightly knit group of people who share a common culture and are united under one government. Most Native nations have treaties with the United States; a nation does not make treaties with tribes, but only with other nations. The correct way to refer to people whose ancestors have always been in the lands now called the United States is to use the name of their nation, like Cheyenne, Wampanoag, or Yurok, to name just a few. Some Native people prefer the term First Nations when referring to

Native Names

Names of Native nations can be confusing. That's because, over the centuries, many tribes have been named by others. Today a number of nations prefer to use their original names for themselves, even if those names are difficult for others to spell or pronounce. We use the names of nations that, because of custom, are familiar. But we hope you take the time to learn some of the original names that Native people now call themselves.

Names for people who originally called themselves Anishinaabe (a-NI-shi-NO-ba) have included Ojibwa, Ojibway, Ojibwe, and Chippewa. They all refer to the same group. In this book we use Ojibway except when referring to a person who designates his or her nation as Chippewa.

The Fox, who share a reservation with the Sauk (also spelled Sac) people in Iowa and Oklahoma, originally called themselves Meskwaki. In Alaska, native people are often referred to as Eskimo. The people in southwestern Alaska prefer to be called Yup'ik, and people in northwest Alaska are the Iñupiat.

People commonly called Iroquois prefer to call themselves Haudenosaunee, their original name. Their neighbors, the Delaware, were originally called the Lenni-Lenape, and some still use the name today.

Some people referred to as the Sioux prefer to call themselves Lakota, Nakota, or Dakota, their original names.

Although many Navajo routinely call themselves Diné, their traditional name in their own language, the group also continues to call itself the Navajo Nation.

In 1984 the Papago of Arizona officially changed back to their original name, Tohono O'odham. Papago was the name the Spanish called them.

In 1994 the Winnebago of Wisconsin officially renamed themselves the Ho-Chunk, their traditional name for themselves. The Winnebago of Nebraska have not made the change.

the hundreds of nations together. In this book, individual names of nations are used whenever possible. You will also see the terms American Indian, Native American, Native, and Indian used interchangeably throughout the book.

Although First Nations make up a small percentage of the U.S. population, they represent half of the languages and cultures of the United States. In this book, you will get a sense of how many differences there are among the peoples who make up the First Nations. The activities give you a chance to make everyday items with a Native twist. We have not included activities that feature ceremonial objects or clothing, as we do not encourage "playing Indian." This can be very offensive to Native people.

We grouped the cultures into nine different geographical areas because people from the same region often share similar climates and natural resources. But within each region there are many differences among Native groups. It is our hope that, by organizing the book in this way, we will help you to begin

to understand how some Native people think and to learn about some of the values important to the various Native communities today as well as long ago.

The book is filled with sidebars of interesting facts about Native peoples and communities. You'll find biographies of scientists, authors, educators, artists, athletes, and others who have made the world a better place. Each chapter starts with an overview and a map of the region and then introduces the rich heritage of the First Peoples in that area. The resource section features information on books, Web sites, museums, and festivals that will help you learn more.

Traditions and values that have been handed down for generations are still vital to Native peoples and can teach everyone a lot about living in a healthy way. Native science holds some answers to today's challenges, such as preserving forests, creating wildlife habitats, and restoring rivers for fish. We invite you to begin an exploration of Native American history.

✦ 1 ✦

Who Are Native People?

James ran to catch the bus and jumped on just before the doors closed. It was after 6 P.M., and he had to get home and have dinner before his school friends came over to work on their class history project. He hadn't had time to change from his ribbon shirt into his street clothes. That afternoon, he and other students at the Native American Education Program had posed for pictures in their regalia. James only wore his Native clothing on special occasions, like powwows and ceremonies.

"Are you an Indian?" an elderly white lady asked, her booming voice echoing throughout the bus.

"Yes," James answered in a quiet voice, trying not to draw any more attention to himself.

"Why's an Indian riding a bus instead of a horse? Indians aren't supposed to be in New York City. Don't you belong in a tipi on a reservation?"

Twelve-year-old James felt everyone's eyes on him. He wasn't sure what to do. His family taught him to be respectful to elders, but what if they were disrespecting you?

Finally James answered in a firm but polite voice. "Indian people live everywhere in this country. After all, it is our country. And I live in an apartment building, like other New Yorkers. In fact, my people never lived in tipis. There are all kinds of Native people and we are all different, but today more Indians live in cities than on reservations."

People began to cheer at his response to the rude woman. But this just embarrassed James even more. He was relieved when the bus reached his stop and he could get off.

Stereotypes of Native People

Native American people often have to deal with these kinds of uncomfortable encounters. Native people are from this country, but others are often surprised to meet them and know little about them. One reason is that books and movies often do not present the truth about Native peoples. Some make it seem as if they have all vanished. Others present all Native people as if they were all the same. When people believe that every person in a group is the same, it is called a stereotype. It is also a stereotype if people believe something untrue about an entire group of people. Stereotypes are hurtful and damaging about any group.

A way that stereotypes can be hurtful is the way Native images are used for sports teams' logos or mascots. Using these images gives the impression that Native people are objects, not real human beings. Today, many school sports teams have changed their "Indian" mascots and names to less controversial ones, making sports more enjoyable for Native people, too.

Here are some stereotypes and truths about Native people.

Stereotype	Truth
All Native people ride horses.	Today some Native people ride horses at times, but all Native people use modern transportation.
All Native people live in tipis.	At one time, some Native people lived in tipis, while others lived in longhouses, earth lodges, hogans, or other types of houses. Today, most Native people live in houses, like other Americans.
Indians are hostile and warlike, and they don't fight fairly.	In historical times, Native people were defending their homelands against invaders. Some of the most famous peacekeepers in the world are American Indian.
All Native people wear feathered war bonnets.	Some people, like the Lakota, wore beautiful headdresses—and they still do on special occasions. However, there are many different types of clothing and headdresses among Native nations.
All Native people look the same and speak the same simple language, like "ugh" or "how."	There are more than 500 different Native nations, cultures, and languages. Native people come in all shapes, colors, and sizes. "Ugh" and "how" are not real Native words.

Stereotype	Truth
Native people were simple and didn't know much until Europeans taught them.	Native cultures were and are very complex. Native people have contributed and continue to contribute much to the world in language, medicine, music, architecture, agriculture, government, and science.
Native people came from somewhere else, like India or Asia.	Christopher Columbus thought he was in India, so he called the people he met "Indian." Native peoples have their own accounts of how the western hemisphere was populated.
Native people are not alive anymore—or, if they are, they live the same way they did hundreds of years ago.	Native people live in every state and do most of the same things as other Americans. Many, but not all, still practice their traditional religions and customs. Like other Americans, Native people do not live the same way their ancestors did, but their history and culture is connected to the country now called the United States.
All Native people go to a medicine man and smoke the peace pipe.	Many Native people observe their traditional religions, which may include a sacred pipe ceremony. Many Native people are also Catholic, Baptist, or Presbyterian.
You can become Native by wearing an Indian "costume."	One can only be born a Native person. Traditional Native clothes are hard to make and are never called costumes.
Native people are braves, papooses, chiefs, or squaws.	Native women should just be called women, not squaws. Men are just men, not braves, and babies are not papooses. Not every leader was or is a chief.
Native people only eat corn, and they did not have a financial system.	Tomatoes, potatoes, cassava, and zucchini are just some of the thousands of foods developed by ancient Native scientists that have made their way around the world. Native peoples made tools, foods, and other inventions to trade for other items all over the Americas. Native contributions of democracy, ecology, and healthy living are as important today as they were in the past, and modern scientists study these ancient ideas for solutions to modern problems.

CHARLENE TETERS, SPOKANE (1952–)

When Charlene Teters was a graduate student in fine arts at the University of Illinois, she took her two children to a basketball game for a fun night. But it was anything but fun. The University of Illinois team mascot, Chief Illiniwek, did a fake "Indian" dance to a made-up "Indian" song on the basketball court. He was dressed in a beautiful Native outfit decorated with fringe and feathers. His face was painted and he pretended to be fierce and "warlike." The mascot represented many stereotypes about Native people. Teters and her children were angry, embarrassed, and sad. One of only three Native students at the school, Teters began to protest the hurtful image. She created an art exhibit called "It Was Only an Indian: Native American Stereotypes," which identified Native American stereotypes in the movies and television. Many non-Indian people were outraged. Some people even threatened her, but others stood up for her. Teters helped found the National Coalition on Racism in Sports and Media, an organization that has helped stop sports teams from using mascots that offend Native people. Today Teters is a professor at the Institute for American Indian Arts in Santa Fe, New Mexico. *In Whose Honor?* is a film about Teters and her work. Some call Teters the Rosa Parks of Native Americans because she stood up for what she thought was right.

Native Powwows

Many different American Indian communities and organizations hold powwows, which are social gatherings. Usually social dances, not religious dances, are featured. Many powwows have dance competitions in different categories for men, women, children, and even tiny tots. Native artists and businesspeople add to their income by selling jewelry, books, CDs, food, and art. Powwows are a chance for people to catch up with friends and spend a day enjoying Native culture. Because Native people live all over the United States, you may have the opportunity to attend a Native event like a powwow in your area. The Resources section of this book lists Native American festivals and powwows across the country. You can also check online for a powwow in your area and plan a visit. It's important to be a polite guest and observe proper manners at a powwow.

Powwow Manners

- Don't wear "fake" Indian clothes or go barefoot. Do not wear swimsuits or clothing that bares the midriff.
- Don't use bad words or speak loudly. Do not make "whoops" or other sounds that have been used in movies to portray Indian people.

- Don't take the seats around the arena, as these are for dancers only. Bring your own seating, and ask permission before you set up your chair or blanket.
- Donate money to the Drum group, which is referred to as just the "Drum" during a blanket dance. Dancers dance around the arena with a blanket or lay it on the ground to collect donations. The money covers travel expenses for the musicians.
- Listen to the master of ceremonies for important information. Stand and remove your hat during special songs like the Grand Entry, when all the dancers enter the arena, during veteran songs, or any other time that the master of ceremonies announces a special song.
- Do not take pictures of dancers, people in regalia, or the dance arena unless you ask permission.
- Do not litter. Be responsible for your belongings.
- You can ask people questions, but don't interrupt their dancing or take up too much of their time. Do not walk across the dance arena or join in a dance unless you are invited. Guests are usually asked to dance during a round dance, or friend-ship dance.
- Have a good time, and be a polite guest!

LARGEST POPULATIONS OF FIRST NATIONS

Reservations are all that indigenous peoples own of their original territories, but only about 34 percent of Native peoples live on reservations. Many tribes still struggle to get back their lands, which were taken away illegally. Some California and Maine nations have been successful in gaining the rights to some of their original territories. Most Native people live with other Americans in cities, towns, and rural areas across the country. Indigenous peoples living in urban areas have founded Indian centers and other organizations where they can attend cultural events and be with other Native people. Below is a list of the 10 cities with the largest Native populations in 2000:

New York, New York
Los Angeles, California
Phoenix, Arizona
Tulsa, Oklahoma
Oklahoma City, Oklahoma
Anchorage, Alaska
Albuquerque, New Mexico
Chicago, Illinois
San Diego, California
Houston, Texas

Learn a Round, or Friendship, Dance

Almost every powwow features a round, or friendship, dance. Guests are invited to join the circle—it represents the circle of life, which has no beginning and no end. It is a social dance, and it's one of the few where men and women dance together. It is easy to learn and lots of fun. There are variations of the dance, but it usually starts off with the dancers going clockwise or from left to right, holding hands. Sometimes the head dancer reverses the circle for a time. Often at the end of the dance, everyone dances to the middle, still holding hands, and then back into a circle. The tunes vary and are sung in a Native language, English, or vocables. Vocables are syllables, sung to a tune, that have no meaning, like "tra-la-la." Borrow a round dance or powwow CD from the library, order one from Canyon Records (see Resources), or find a song online. You can also sound out the beat as you dance.

What You Need

Friends   Music

Open area

What You Do

1. Join hands in a circle.
2. Repeat the beat, "BOOM, boom," for a few seconds. When you feel that you have the beat, start with your feet together and step to the left on the "BOOM." Bring your right foot next to the left on the soft "boom." Keep going round and round. Think about all the good things in your life, like good friends or a sunny day.
3. After going round and round, change direction. Now step to the right on the "BOOM," and bring your left foot next to the right on the little "boom." Think of some sad or frustrating things in your life, like when you forgot to do your homework or scraped your knee. Life is full of both good and bad times.
4. Quick! Think of some good times again and change the direction to the right, the way you began.

◆ 2 ◆
Northeast

Checking, cradling, dodging, and cutting moves make the lacrosse playing field vibrate. Young Iroquois (IR-uh-kwoy) teammates charge through the game their ancestors played for centuries before Europeans came to North America. Lacrosse has been a way of life for the Iroquois. Since ancient time, Iroquois men have played this fast-paced ball-and-stick game that requires speed, stamina, and precision. Called Tewaaraton (little brother of war) in Mohawk, it was often played as a way to train for war. To the Iroquois, lacrosse is a sacred game from the Creator that heals and rejuvenates individuals and communities. It is also a competitive game, played both on the field (field lacrosse) and in enclosed arenas (box lacrosse). As a sport, lacrosse has grown increasingly popular among non-Iroquois. Across the United States and Canada boys, girls, men, and women play in high schools, colleges, and in youth and professional leagues.

Many Iroquois children receive their lacrosse sticks as soon as they can walk. At the age of three, they begin to play the game, just like their fathers, grandfathers, and great-grandfathers before them. They even carry their curled hickory sticks around with them when they are not practicing. Some grow up to become members of the Iroquois Nationals lacrosse team, a sports organization that not only competes, but also teaches the history and skill of the game to young children. It is the only Native national sports team in international competition.

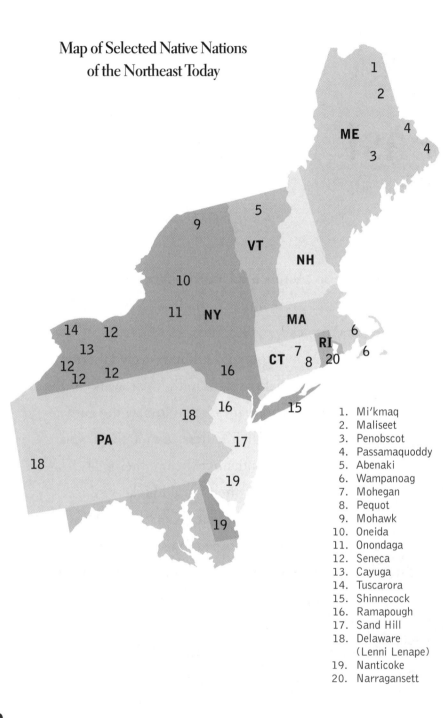

Map of Selected Native Nations
of the Northeast Today

1. Mi'kmaq
2. Maliseet
3. Penobscot
4. Passamaquoddy
5. Abenaki
6. Wampanoag
7. Mohegan
8. Pequot
9. Mohawk
10. Oneida
11. Onondaga
12. Seneca
13. Cayuga
14. Tuscarora
15. Shinnecock
16. Ramapough
17. Sand Hill
18. Delaware
    (Lenni Lenape)
19. Nanticoke
20. Narragansett

The Northeast Region

The Northeast spreads from the Atlantic Ocean to the Mississippi River. The enormous area includes New England, the Ohio Valley and Great Lakes, and the Atlantic states as far south as Virginia. The area also includes the present-day Canadian provinces of Nova Scotia, New Brunswick, and Prince Edward Island, plus parts of Quebec and Ontario. The Northeast is sometimes called the Woodlands area because of its huge forests of birch, elm, hickory, maple, oak, and willow. The region includes lakes, rivers, and mountain ranges. Because the area is so big, the climate and geography differ in some parts. In general, most of the Northeast has warm-to-hot summers and cold, snowy winters.

The Iroquois

The huge, complex woodland region of the Northeast has been home to dozens of First Nations for thousands of years. Most of the tribes spoke either Iroquoian or Algonquian (al-GON-kwee-in). The Iroquoian-speaking tribes lived in what are now parts of Quebec and Ontario in Canada and upstate New York and Pennsylvania in the United States. Many tribes spoke the Iroquois language, but the Seneca (SEN-eh-ca), Onondaga (OWN-ah-DA-ga), Oneida (oh-NI-da), Mohawk (MO-hawk), and Cayuga (ki-YOU-ga) peoples are the best known. These five nations originally called themselves the

Haudenosaunee (hoe-de-no-SHO-nee), which means "People building an extended house." They are more commonly referred to as "People of the Long House." Their name symbolizes the fact that, long ago, Iroquois lived in large, permanent longhouses. Some were as long as 200 feet and housed several families under one bark roof. Iroquois villages were made up of many longhouses belonging to related families.

Iroquois were great farmers. During the spring and summer, people worked the soil with bone, antler, and wooden tools. They called their three main crops, corn, beans, and squash, "the three sisters." Important religious festivals honored corn as well as other plant foods. In the fall and winter, Iroquois men, who were master boatmen, made long river journeys far from home to hunt. The canoes were made from large logs that they hollowed out and covered with birch, elm, or spruce bark.

Iroquois Corn Husk Dolls

There are several different accounts as to why Iroquois corn husk dolls do not have faces. Some say it is because only the Creator can create a face. Others say it is so children can learn a lesson about not being vain. This story is based on an Oneida explanation.

☀ ONEIDA TRADITIONAL ACCOUNT

A long time ago, children were getting into trouble or getting hurt because the adults were busy and not watching them every second. The Creator fashioned a beautiful doll from corn husks to watch over the children. Corn Husk Doll was not only beautiful, she could walk and talk, and she seemed like a real person. She took good care of the children and taught them many things. She entertained them with stories, played games with them, and sang them to sleep.

One day after a very heavy rainfall, Corn Husk Doll took the children outside to play. She spied her reflection in a puddle and was quite struck with her beauty. From then on, she only wanted to make herself even prettier. She stopped doing her chores and was only interested in having beautiful clothes and looking at herself in the water. She became lazy, vain, and selfish. The children were getting into trouble again because no one was watching them. The Creator warned her, but still she only thought about her looks. Finally, the Creator sent Owl to take away her face and her powers to walk and talk.

Today, the Oneida and other Iroquois people make corn husk dolls without faces so children can be reminded to think about other people and to chip in with chores and other responsibilities. Most of the dolls are dressed in beautiful clothing of a particular nation and many are prized by collectors all over the world.

Make a Corn Husk Doll

Children around the world have many different kinds of dolls. A long time ago, many Indian children had dolls made of corn husks.

What You Need

5 or 6 dried corn husks (available in craft or Mexican grocery stores)

Bucket of water

Waterproof work surface

String

Scissors

What You Do

1. Soak the corn husks for at least 20 minutes. Don't take them apart until they are softened and pliable. Separate 5 husks and shake off the excess water.

2. Lay them out on a waterproof work surface. Line up three husks on top of each other. Fold them in half.

3. Tie a string one inch from the fold to form a head and neck.

4. Stack two more husks on top of one another. Tie a string half an inch from each end to make hands.

5. Slide the arms underneath the top three husks of the body. Push them up to the string you tied for the neck. Tie a string around the body underneath the arms to form a waist and to hold the arms in place.

6. For a boy doll, form pants by cutting the husks below the waist into two pieces to ½ inch below the waist. Tie a string ½ inch from the bottom of each leg to form a foot. Trim the strings.

If you'd like to dress your doll, you can sew or draw clothes. Research traditional Iroquois corn husk dolls for ideas.

12

The Iroquois Confederacy and the Great Law of Peace

Long ago, the Iroquois groups of the Northeast were often at war with each other. Sometime around 900 (the precise historical date is uncertain), a great man from the Huron nation came to the Iroquois with a message of peace, friendship, and unity. At first the people did not want to listen to him because he was an outsider, and his ideas were foreign to them. He and his helper traveled among the Iroquois, healing old grudges and teaching them how to settle differences without anger and hatred. He proposed that the five nations in present-day New York and Ontario unite to form a confederacy. It took quite a while for the Iroquois to accept his teachings, but they finally did and united, vowing to never be at war with each other again. The Huron leader was so respected that to this day it is considered disrespectful to his memory to speak his name aloud except on special occasions. He is lovingly called the Great Peacemaker.

The five (later six) Iroquois groups have lived under the Great Law of Peace for centuries. It was first written down in English in the 19th century. It is a constitution that spells out rules for governing. Each nation of the Iroquois Confederation is independent and governs its own internal affairs. The Great Law of Peace established the Grand Council, with members representing all of the member nations, to deal with problems that affect all of the nations within the confederacy.

The Grand Council consists of 50 male leaders called chiefs in English. In the Iroquois language, they are called *Hoyaneh*, which means "Caretakers of the Peace." Although men make up the Grand Council, women elders, called Clan Mothers, help choose them. They look for a male who is honest, kindhearted, knowledgeable about Confederacy laws, and capable of upholding the Great Law. Women have the power to remove the men if they violate the Great Law.

It is required that all the chiefs be of one mind in making decisions of importance to the confederation, such as going to war, peacemaking, and treaty making. A unanimous decision ensures that all the chiefs become committed to the decision and that no one feels left out. The Grand Council does not vote, and majority rule is not practiced. If the chiefs disagree with one another, they meet over and over to work through their differences and reach a decision that everyone agrees to. Each person has the right to express himself and be listened to, even if the person does not have good speaking skills. Sometimes reaching a unanimous decision takes many days. If all efforts to reach such a decision fail, the Grand Council puts the issue aside, and each of the six nations chooses its own way.

European Americans were impressed by this democracy. Among them was Benjamin Franklin, one of the authors of the U.S. Constitution. He was the most vocal of the

19th-century leaders who admired the Iroquois form of government. In 1754 Franklin proposed the creation of a colonial grand council. He challenged the colonists to create a united government similar to the Iroquois representative form of government. One of the good ideas Ben Franklin learned was that each person should be able to speak without being interrupted. Some historians believe that the Great Law of Peace influenced the development of the U.S. Constitution.

The Iroquois Confederacy and the American Revolution

Although the members of the confederacy pledged not to fight wars against one another, they fought together against neighboring Algonquian and other Iroquoian tribes. The confederacy became a political and military power in the Northeast. But when the American Revolution broke out between the British and the American colonists, the Six Nations could not reach a unanimous agreement on which side to support. The Onondaga, Seneca, and Cayuga supported the British. The Oneida and Tuscarora, the sixth nation that joined the confederacy around 1722, fought with the Americans. For the first time in the confederacy's history, these Iroquois were at war with one another. The division of allegiance ended the confederation's military strength. After the American Revolution, the United States took over much of the Iroquois land in New York State.

Thanksgiving Address

For thousands of years, First Nations across North America have observed ceremonies and rituals to give thanks to a higher power. The Iroquois nations have a Thanksgiving Address, a traditional prayer delivered by a speaker at the beginning of each day and at ceremonial and governmental gatherings. In the prayer, people greet each morning by giving thanks to all living things, from the Earth upward to the Creator. The address dates back to the formation of the Great Law of Peace.

The Thanksgiving Address is a way to remember to thank all living things that share our world and to not take anyone or anything for granted. A part of it is printed on the U.S. passport so that all Americans, as well as people around the world, can appreciate the thoughtfulness of the Six Nations people.

CORNPLANTER, SENECA (1732–1836)

A chief among the Seneca, Cornplanter was a brilliant war leader and negotiator. He wanted the Seneca to remain neutral during the Revolutionary War, but out of obligation to the wishes of others in his clan, he agreed to support the British. Although the Seneca came to their aid, the British did not support the Seneca in return during the rest of the American Revolution. After the colonists won the war, Seneca lands and crops were destroyed by the U.S. military as punishment for siding with the British. The Seneca, along with other Iroquois, were driven away from their homes. Cornplanter looked for ways to keep Seneca lands and agreed to help the United States in the war of 1812. Because he was a skilled diplomat and fought for the Americans, he was able to negotiate a peace settlement with the Supreme Executive Council of Pennsylvania and Governor Thomas Mifflin. His people were granted lands in northwestern Pennsylvania, right on the New York State border. The state of Pennsylvania was so grateful for Cornplanter's assistance in negotiating with other Indian nations that it not only gave him the land, but it also erected a monument in his honor, the first dedicated to an American Indian.

However, in 1961 the U.S. Army Corps of Engineers built the Kinzua Dam on the Allegheny River and flooded about one third of the Seneca Allegany Reservation. The dam destroyed Seneca houses, hunting and fishing grounds, a longhouse (*ceremonial building*), and a school. It forced the removal of nearly 600 Senecas from the area. The Seneca Indian cemetery, home to Cornplanter's grave, was moved to higher ground just across the border in New York State. Today, Pennsylvania does not recognize any American Indian groups despite its promise to Chief Cornplanter.

Make a Family "Thank You" List

"Thank you" is a phrase used to show appreciation for a thoughtful deed or a present. Most people say thank you on a holiday like Thanksgiving or when receiving a birthday gift. But many forget about giving thanks at other times. Think about the many situations in which you say thank you to your family, friends, or people who help you in a store, library, or restaurant. Remember the times when people thanked you. Think about thanking the earth, trees, plants, and water that help us by giving us gifts of oxygen so we can breathe, food so we can eat, and a planet we can call home. Make a thank-you list to show appreciation for all the ways you and your family help each other and are helped.

What You Need

White poster board

Magnets to attach paper to refrigerator (you might want to use another door in the house)

String or yarn

Markers

Tape

What You Do

1. Talk with your family and talk about the importance of giving thanks.
2. Attach the poster board to the refrigerator with magnets. Tie markers onto one end of the string, and tape the other end to the poster.

3. Ask everyone to give thanks at least once every day by writing down on the poster something for which they are thankful. Include the earth, water, fresh air, birds, animals, and food. Drawings can be used, too.

4. When the paper is filled up, discuss it with your family. Then flip the poster board over and hang it back up on the refrigerator. This time write down ways to *show* thanks. Maybe you can recycle more, hold doors open for people, adopt and clean up a stream, or make art with used objects.

Iroquois Today

In the United States, the Great Law of Peace is very much alive. The traditional form of government of the Iroquois Confederacy still exists. The Grand Council meets regularly at Onondaga, the capital of the confederacy, near Syracuse, New York. It operates in the same way it did hundreds of years ago.

Today many Iroquois live in cities like New York, Buffalo, and Syracuse in New York State. They also live on reservations (called reserves in Canada). There are reservations and communities located in New York State, Wisconsin, Oklahoma, and Canada.

Just as most Americans today no longer live in log cabins or sod houses, neither do Iroquois people live in their tradi-

SAY IT IN MOHAWK

The Mohawk alphabet has 12 letters: a, e, h, i, k, n, o, r, s, t, w, and y.

There are three different dialects in the Mohawk language. The words below are from Canada's Kahnawà:ke Reservation near Montreal.

Hello	*she': kon*	(say gon)
Good-bye	*ó:nen*	(oh nen)
Thank you	*niá:wen*	(neea wen)

Here is how you count to five in Mohawk:

One	*énska*	(ens-KA)
Two	*tékeni*	(tee-kee-ni)
Three	*áhsen*	(ah-sen)
Four	*kaié:ri*	(ka-ee ri)
Five	*wisk*	(whisk)

tional elm longhouses. They live in houses, mobile homes, and apartment buildings, like other Americans, and they work as teachers retail clerks, lawyers, nurses, and construction workers and in many other professional occupations. They work hard to hold on to their distinct laws, language, and customs.

Wabanaki

It is said that the Wabanaki (WAH-beh-NOCK-ee) see the sunrise long before anyone else in the United States. In fact, Wabanaki means "people of the dawn." The Wabanaki include the Algonquian-speaking Passamaquoddy (PASS-ah-ma-QUOD-dee), Penobscot (Pa-NOB-scot), Mi'kmaq (MICK-mahk), and Maliseet (MAWL-eh-seet) tribes in Maine and the Abenaki (ab-NAH-kee) in Vermont. They have always lived in Maine and neighboring areas in Canada.

Since tribes like the Penobscot and Abenaki lived further north than the Iroquois, they had a harder time. The weather was colder, and the snow was deeper during winter. People had to travel a long way to hunt deer, moose, and other animals. Tracking large animals was easier in deep snow because hunters could pursue them on snowshoes and the animals could not travel as fast or as far. If there was little or no snow, people likely went hungry. Some farming was practiced in Maine, but the Wabanaki did not depend on it. The growing season was usually too short to produce many crops but, weather permitting, they raised corn, beans, and squash, like the Iroquois did.

The Wabanaki Confederacy

The tribes united in the Wabanaki Confederacy. It is believed that it formed before 1700. Wabanaki leaders joined together to defend themselves against enemies, especially the English and, later, American colonists. By 1800 the Wabanaki nations were reduced to a fraction of their original strength. Indians did not have immunities to measles, chicken pox, and other European diseases. When European fishing crews, traders, and colonists carrying these diseases met the Indian people, the sicknesses swept through the villages, killing entire families. Warfare with the English and the American colonists also reduced the tribal populations.

From the beginning of European settlement, the Wabanaki had befriended the French, then the English, and then the American colonists. They signed treaties with the

English colonists with the understanding that the land they occupied would be shared. But the English and, later, the American colonists believed they had bought the land. They said the Wabanaki had no legal claim to the area.

Beginning in the 1800s, the state of Maine greatly reduced the land and governing powers of the Wabanaki tribes, severely limiting the power of the confederacy. There were few opportunities to make a living in their homelands, so some Native people moved away to find work in cities or other parts of the United States.

In the 1960s the tribes discovered that portions of their land were sold or leased by the state of Maine without U.S. government consent. The 1790 Indian Trade and Intercourse Act prevented the states from purchasing Indian lands without federal approval. This discovery set off a legal battle in the 1970s. The Passamaquoddy and Penobscot peoples claimed nearly two thirds of the state of Maine. The claim was settled by the Maine Indian Claims Settlement Act in 1980. The act provided money for the Passamaquoddy, Penobscot, and Maliseet to purchase land that had been illegally taken in 1794, 1796, and 1818. The act also gave the nations the ability to purchase a cement company, blueberry farms, and other businesses, which meant people could get jobs. In return, the tribes gave up claims to 12.5 million acres of their traditional lands.

The Wabanaki Today

The Wabanaki now comprise about 1 percent of the population of Maine. The Wabanaki are working together to stop factories from dumping waste into rivers because it makes the fish unsafe to eat and the water unsafe to swim in or drink. On the Passamaquoddy reservation, people keep track of the health of the moose herds by keeping an eye on them from airplanes. Some Wabanaki schools teach their language and culture as part of a regular school program. On National Indian Day, non-Indian children are invited to the Indian Island School to learn about Penobscot culture.

JOANNE SHENANDOAH, ONEIDA

(Contemporary)

Tekaliwah-kwa (She Sings) is Joanne Shenandoah's Oneida name. And sing she does! She has won a Grammy Award plus 11 Native American Music Awards. Her songs are a rich mix of traditional Indian, pop, folk, and classical music. She has been featured on soundtracks of both television shows and movies, and she is also an actress.

Fashion a Penobscot Basket

Penobscot Designs

Penobscot artists use birch and other kinds of bark to fashion wonderful watertight baskets. Birch bark is never taken from a live tree; it is only gathered from fallen ones. Stripping bark off a living tree will kill it. You can make paper look like birch bark and create a basket. And if you ever see paper-thin birch bark laying on the ground by a dead tree, you can use that, too.

What You Need

Newspaper

12-inch-square heavyweight
　watercolor paper

3 paintbrushes (1 wide,
　1 medium, and 1 fine tip)

Cup of water

Roll of toilet paper

Ruler

Finepoint black marker

Scissors

Gray, light rust, and
　black paints

Glue

3 feet of brown twine
　or yarn

What You Do

1. Cover your work surface with newspaper and place the watercolor paper on it. Dip the wide-tip paintbrush in the water and stroke the water over the watercolor paper, making sure it is completely wet.

2. Tear off pieces of toilet paper and lay them across the wet watercolor paper. It will crumple up and stick to the paper. Cover all of the paper with toilet paper pieces.

3. While the paper is wet, very carefully paint small areas with gray and light rust colors, leaving other areas white. Let the paper dry.

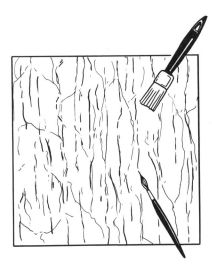

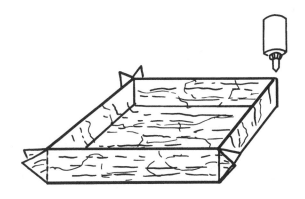

4. Paint fine lines across the paper with black paint to look like birch bark. Let dry completely.

5. With the ruler, measure 1½ inches from the edge of the paper and make a dot. Do this 2 times on each of the four sides. Draw a line on each side connecting the two dots. These are your fold lines.

6. Draw a line from the point of each corner to where the lines cross at each corner. Cut along this line, but do not go past the fold lines.

7. Fold up the long sides first. Then fold up the short sides. At each corner leave one triangular tip on the outside of the basket and fold the other to the inside of the basket. Glue all the 8 tips down.

8. Decorate your basket with Wabanaki designs by gluing brown twine or yarn on the edges to look like sweetgrass decoration.

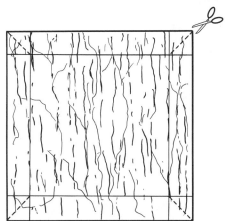

Louis Sockalexis, Penobscot (1871–1913)

Louis Sockalexis, the first American Indian pro-league baseball player, was Penobscot. He was so strong he could throw a baseball across the Penobscot River! He had a great season for the Cleveland Spiders in 1897, often hitting balls right out of the park. Even though Sockalexis was one of the best ballplayers in the league, he cut his career short. Fans and other ballplayers bullied and disrespected him by spitting at him, calling him names, and making fun of him because he was Indian. Sockalexis became very depressed by this harassment and finally left the sport in 1899. When the Cleveland Spiders changed their name to the Cleveland Indians, team officials said it was in tribute to Sockalexis. But the Sockalexis family and the Penobscot Nation find "Chief Wahoo," the cartoon mascot of the Cleveland Indians, racist and insulting. At one time, the Penobscot community of Old Town, Maine, had a 2,500-seat Sockalexis Ice Arena, named after Louis, where Indian Island youth learned the joy of sports.

PLAY WALTES, A DICE GAME

Most Native tribes have some form of a dice game. Waltes is played by the Mi'kmaq people. The name comes from the Mi'kmaq word *waltestaqn* (wall-tess-stah-ahn), which is the name for the circular dish used in the game. The game sets have beautiful, hand-carved wooden bowls and caribou bone dice. Dice are domed with decorations on the flat side. Their rounded shape makes it harder to land with the flat side up, which is the way to score. Waltes can be a very long game with many phases, and it is usually only played by grown-ups. Try your hand at this simpler version.

What You Need

6 large buttons or wooden disks (available at craft stores)

Markers

26 bamboo skewers

Scissors

4 craft sticks

Shallow wooden bowl or heavy metal pie plate

Towel

What You Do

1. Make the dice by decorating one side of each button with the markers. You can use any design you like, but use the same design for each button. The Mi'kmaq use a cross design made up of little dots.

2. Make 51 counting sticks by cutting the skewers in half (you will have one extra half skewer).

3. Draw an arrow's point and shaft on one of the craft sticks. On the other three, draw the upper part of the arrow with the feathers, or "fletching."

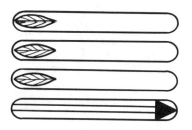

How to Play

1. Sit on the floor across from the other players with a towel under the bowl. Put the dice in the bowl.

2. Pick up the bowl with both hands and hit it on the towel with enough force to flip the dice.

3. If any dice flip out of the bowl, that turn is over. For each dice that lands with the decorated side up, the player gets points. Each player gets three turns in a row.

How to Score

Players get one counting stick for each die that lands decorated side up.

1 decorated die = 1 counting stick (1 point)

2 decorated dice = 2 counting sticks (2 points)

3 decorated dice = 3 counting sticks (3 points)

4 decorated dice = 4 counting sticks (4 points)

5 decorated dice = a stick with arrow fletching
(5 points)

6 decorated dice = the stick with the arrow point
(6 points)

3. If a player wins all four arrow sticks, he or she gets an extra four counting sticks. When there are no more sticks, the game is over. The player with the most points wins.

JOSEPH BRUCHAC, ABENAKI (1942–)

Joseph Bruchac was raised by his storyteller grandparents. Now he is one of the most popular children's book authors in the world. He still lives in his Abenaki grandparents' house on the Vermont–New York border. Bruchac feels it is important to preserve Abenaki culture and language. He has traveled around the world teaching traditional Native skills and performing with the Dawnland Singers. Mr. Bruchac's books share true stories about diverse Indian cultures and his Abenaki heritage. *The Great Ball Game* and *Jim Thorpe's Bright Path* are just two of his many books. He has his grandfather's storytelling talent, and he has been featured at the British Storytelling Festival and the National Storytelling Festival in Jonesborough, Tennessee.

The Pequot

The Pequot (PEE-kwot) have lived in southeastern Connecticut for over 10,000 years. They were among the first nations to encounter English colonists. In 1637 they were involved in the Pequot War, the first major conflict between Native people and English colonists in New England. It had a devastating impact on the tribe. Many of them were killed during the war, and they lost much of their land. The Pequot scattered, but eventually many returned to their homeland.

In the late 1970s the Pequot began a remarkable comeback. They approved a tribal constitution and began a series of projects that would help them provide jobs for their people and income for the Pequot government. They won a court case in 1983 that gave the tribe federal recognition and the right to buy back lands that were sold illegally by the state of Connecticut in 1856. "Federal recognition" means that the United States recognizes the Indian nation's rights to govern itself and make its own decisions. In 1998 the Pequot opened a museum on their reservation. There, visitors get a chance to experience a 16th-century woodland Pequot village.

ELIZABETH GEORGE, PEQUOT (1894–1973)

Elizabeth George stood in the way of bulldozers that threatened to plow up the grounds of the Pequot Indian Reservation in Connecticut. She pulled up surveyors' stakes as non-Indians tried to claim tribal land. Mrs. George was the last remaining resident on the reservation in the early 1970s. She wanted to hold onto the land for future Pequot generations. Younger Pequot had moved to areas where they could find jobs and make a living. The state and greedy developers were eager to take over the land they had moved from. Mrs. George died in 1973 but, instead of the Pequot losing their reservation, they came home.

Mrs. George's descendants tried different businesses, like farming and raising pigs, but none were successful. Times were hard, and the community was rural and isolated. Finally they got a grant to open a bingo hall. Businesspeople from Malaysia lent them money to build a casino. Today, the once-poor nation owns one of the most successful casinos in the world, a shipbuilding company, and many inns and hotels. Elizabeth George's descendants can be proud of the Mashantucket Pequot Museum and Research Center, which features educational programs for kids, exhibits, and a chance to study Pequot culture.

The Wampanoag

For 10,000 years, the Wampanoag (WAMP-ah-nog) have lived on the island of Martha's Vineyard and in southern Massachusetts and eastern Rhode Island. They are well known because of their encounters with the English colonists who arrived on the Mayflower in December 1620. In the first few months after the colonists came to the place they called Plymouth Colony (present-day Massachusetts), many colonists died from scurvy, poor nutrition, and inadequate shelter. As the "starving time" turned to spring, Tisquantum (called Squanto by the English), an English-speaking Wampanoag, and several other Indians met with the colonists at Plymouth Colony. Tisquantum told the English that Massasoit (MASS-ah-so-it), a Wampanoag leader, wanted to hold peace talks with them. Massasoit believed the English and their weapons would be helpful to the Wampanoag. In return, his people could help the English if they were attacked. The colonists agreed to the meeting. Talks were held and resulted in the Treaty of 1621.

By the fall of 1621, the English produced a successful harvest and decided to rejoice together. Massasoit and 90 men joined in the three-day feast. A letter written on December 11, 1621, by Edward Winslow, a founder of Plymouth Colony, is the only account of the feast. Winslow did not call the harvest meal "Thanksgiving." To the religious colonists, a day of thanksgiving meant praying and fasting.

The 1621 treaty kept the peace for 50 years, but the relationship between the Wampanoag and the English went downhill after Massasoit died in 1661. More English had moved to Plymouth Colony, building up the towns. Their cattle, sheep, and goats strayed onto Indian lands, ate Indian crops, and destroyed Indian clam beds. The English often used dishonest ways to acquire Indian lands when the rightful owners refused to sell. They insisted that the Wampanoag observe English laws and customs. They pressured the Indians to become Christians. They demanded that the Wampanoag return the muskets that the Indian people had acquired through trade over the years. From 1675 through 1676, the Wampanoag and their allies tried to resist English theft of their lands. They fought a war against the English. Both sides killed as many people as they could. The Indians were defeated, and their resistance ended.

The Wampanoag Today

Although the Wampanoag population and lands were reduced in size over the past hundred years, the descendants of the surviving Wampanoag still live in New England. Today, the largest Wampanoag communities are located in Massachusetts, in the town of Aquinnah on Martha's Vineyard and in Mashpee on Cape Cod. They remember and honor their Wampanoag language, arts, stories, traditions, and celebrations. Children are taught to conserve the land and not pollute. They are taught to always leave enough fish and clams in the waters to allow for reproduction.

Make a Stewed Cranberry Dish

For hundreds of years, the Wampanoag people have harvested cranberries in the fall. People dry some of the harvest, store the dried berries, and later, in winter, add them to stews or eat them as a healthy snack. Long ago, Wampanoag and other Indians ate the vitamin C-rich wild cranberries and never got illnesses like scurvy, a disease caused by lack of vitamin C. Most Americans only eat cranberries at Thanksgiving dinner, but this tart red fruit can be enjoyed for breakfast, lunch, or dinner. Try this stewed cranberry dish that is tangy, sweet, and healthy.

What You Need

Adult supervision required
1 12-ounce package of cranberries
½ of a 12-ounce can of unsweetened
　　pineapple juice concentrate
1 apple, cored and diced
1 orange, peeled and diced
½ cup of water
Saucepan and cover

What You Do

1. Put all ingredients in the saucepan and bring to boil. Stir.
2. Lower the heat until the mixture is just simmering.
3. Cover and cook, stirring occasionally, for 15 minutes or until the fruit is soft, thickened, and mushy.
4. Serve warm or cold by itself as a side dish, over ice cream for dessert, or over hot cereal for breakfast.

Serves 6

CRANBERRY DAY

On the second Tuesday in October, in the town of Aquinnah on Martha's Vineyard, Wampanoag children are excused from school to take part in an important annual harvest celebration called Cranberry Day. Elders and youngsters go together to the bogs and pick cranberries, mostly with their hands and sometimes with scoops. Afterward, families enjoy a community lunch together. Elders tell of past Cranberry Days, when cranberries were picked for several days, and singing, dancing, and storytelling took place after a long day of cranberry harvesting. In the evening, the non-tribal community is invited to the tribal building for a potluck dinner, games, drumming, and singing. Families prepare dishes with cranberries so everyone can taste some of the harvest.

The Delaware Indians

Delaware Indians originally settled in what is now Delaware, New Jersey, Pennsylvania, and southern New York. The name Delaware comes from the Englishman Lord De La Warr, after whom a bay, river, and U.S. state all later came to be called Delaware. The tribe's own name for itself is Lenni-Lenape, or "true men" in their Algonquian language.

The Delaware Indians lived in small communities of 25 or 30 people. They usually lived near a stream at the edge of a forest. The forest provided saplings (baby trees) and the bark needed to make houses. People used elm and chestnut bark to make wigwams and longhouses, much like to the Iroquois did. Longhouses were made with rounded ends and curved roofs. Some were 60 feet long and 20 feet across. Usually there were only a few Delaware houses in a village. Like the Iroquois, each family had its own "apartment" and its own fireplace, and each longhouse held several families. Some Delaware villages had leaders who helped make decisions for the group. They were called *sachems*, but after the European traders and colonists arrived, they mistakenly called these leaders "chiefs."

In 1682 Tamanend, the Delaware leader, and other tribal representatives signed a treaty of peace and friendship with English Quaker William Penn, the founder of Pennsylvania. Of all the early colonial leaders, William Penn is believed to have been the most fair in his dealings with Indians. Penn promised peace and religious freedom to the Indians who lived in the colony. The Delaware are known for being the first Indian tribe to sign a treaty with the newly formed U.S. government at Fort Pitt (present-day Pittsburgh) in 1778. Although the Delaware seemed to get along with the colonists at first, conflicts later emerged that forced many Delaware to Indian Territory (present-day Oklahoma) and Canada.

Delaware Storytelling

The Delaware people keep tokens to remind them of their stories. They store them in storyteller bags. When people had to grow all of their own food, it was important to work really hard during the spring, summer, and fall so they could preserve enough food to get through the long, cold northeastern winters. Storytelling was usually done in the winter, when everyone stayed indoors to stay warm. Today, the Delaware continue to keep their storytelling tradition alive.

The storyteller opens his bag and picks up an object that sparks a memory. He or she might use horsehair to tell about an exciting adventure that happened while riding a horse or a corn kernel to talk about a special meal. When the storyteller is finished with the stories, he or she replaces the items in the bag and says, "And now I tie it up."

ERNEST W. GILMAN JR., MOHEGAN (1934–2006)

Ernest Gilman whose Native name was Kiwa, served the Mohegan Nation for over 40 years as a tribal council member, tribal elder, and Pipe Carrier. Gilman's duties as Pipe Carrier included blessing important events as well as conducting other tribal ceremonies. One such ceremony marked the return of a succotash bowl of the great Mohegan leader Uncas.

Gilman spent much of his time helping the tribe get federal recognition. After the Native American Graves Protection and Repatriation Act was signed into law in 1990, he helped the tribe recover Mohegan remains and artifacts from museums. He also managed the annual Mohegan Homecoming for 24 years, where everyone looked forward to his famous clam chowder.

CREATE A DELAWARE STORYTELLER BAG

Think about a special time in your life. Write a story about it. Find a few small objects that will help you remember the story, and save them for your storyteller bag.

What You Need

10-inch-square piece of chamois, felt, or
   other fabric that doesn't fray easily
Ruler
Pen
6-inch round object (such as a plate or bowl)
Scissors
Newspaper
Fabric paints or permanent markers

What You Do

1. To make a tie, measure a line ¼ inch from one edge of the fabric. Using the pen, draw a line from edge to edge. To make the body of the bag, put your round object as close to the other edge of the fabric as possible. Trace a circle around it. Cut out both pieces.

2. Put down some newspaper on your work surface. Using the fabric paints or markers, draw designs on the fabric circle. Let it dry completely.

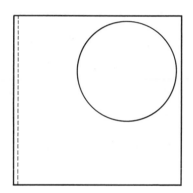

3. Flip over your fabric so the designs are on the bottom. Put your memory objects in the middle of the circle. Pull up sides around objects until you have a pouch. Tie it with the strip of fabric you cut off earlier.

4. When you want to tell a story, open your pouch, pick up a memory object, and begin!

Design a Delaware Gorget

The Delaware fashioned stone into highly polished beautiful pieces of jewelry called gorgets. They could be used as ornaments on hair fasteners, as buttons on winter robes, or as guards to protect wrists from the lash of the bow string when shooting arrows. Make this gorget from clay. You can wear it as a necklace, bracelet, or barrette.

What You Need

Newspaper

Self-hardening clay

Bamboo skewer

Toothpicks or small knitting needle

Imitation leather cord (sinew) or jewelry cording (available at craft stores)

Cup of water

What You Do

1. Cover your work surface with newspaper. Pull and shape a piece of clay into a rectangle about 1 inch by 2 inches and about ¼ of an inch thick. Use a tiny bit of water to smooth and shape it.

2. With the skewer, poke a hole about a half inch from each end. Make sure the holes are large enough to thread the sinew or cord through.

3. Using the toothpicks or knitting needle, gently carve the Delaware designs shown below into the clay. Let dry.

 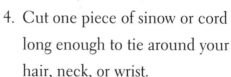

4. Cut one piece of sinow or cord long enough to tie around your hair, neck, or wrist.

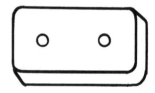

5. Thread the cord through the two holes in the dry gorget so that the ends are on the back side of the gorget. Pull tightly. Tie the ends around your neck, wrist, or hair.

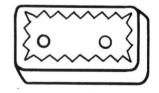

32

The Delaware Indians Today

Most of today's Delaware Indians are located in western Oklahoma and Kansas as well as Canada. Descendants of various Delaware divisions still remain in the east. A community of the Ramapough Tribe can be found in Mahwah and Ring-wood, New Jersey, and Hillburn, New York. The Nanticoke Tribe is located in southern New Jersey and Delaware. Members of the Sand Hill Band of Lenape and Cherokee Indians live throughout New Jersey.

The Mohegan Nation

At one time the Mohegan (Mo-HEE-gan) and Pequot were united as one group and lived in the upper Hudson River Valley of New York State. They moved into present day Connecticut and built towns sometime in the late 1500s. After a few years, the group divided into the two separate tribes that exist today. In the 17th century, the English invaded Mohegan territory, and many Mohegan were killed by both war and European diseases. In spite of the devastation, the great Mohegan leader Uncas believed that cooperation rather than conflict was the way to resolve differences. However, the unity and way of life of the Mohegan were changed forever, and many people were forced out of their homelands. Through their struggles, however, they remained strong, and they were able to reunite. Today, they once again govern their own community on tribal lands in central Connecticut. They also provide jobs and children's programs for both Mohegan and non-Native peoples. Like their famous ancestor Uncas, they collaborate with the surrounding community.

Cook Succotash

The word "succotash" (SUCK-ah-tash) is probably from the Narragansett (nare-ah-GAN-sett) Indian word *msíck-quatash*, which means "boiled whole-kernel corn." It is usually a hearty stew, and each tribe prepares it a different way. One of the artifacts returned to the Mohegan tribe was a wooden succotash bowl that belonged to the great leader Uncas. It is hundreds of years old, and it was used in religious ceremonies. This succotash recipe is inspired by the Mohegan people.

What You Need

Adult supervision required
4 ears of corn on the cob
½ cup of water
1 8-ounce can of tomato sauce
1 12-ounce package of frozen lima beans
2 tablespoons vegetable oil
Salt and pepper, to taste

Medium saucepan
2 red bell peppers, chopped with seeds removed
1 bunch of scallions or green onions, chopped

What You Do

1. Shuck the corn. Have an adult slice each cob into 4 pieces.
2. Put the water, tomato sauce, lima beans, oil, and a little salt and pepper into the saucepan and bring to a boil. Reduce the heat to a simmer and cover. Cook for 6 minutes.
3. Add the corn cobs, peppers, and scallions or onions to the pot. Cover again and cook for 5 minutes. Remove the lid and turn up the heat until most of the liquid has evaporated. It should take about 5 more minutes.

Serves 6

ORIGIN OF THE POTATO CHIP

Potatoes have been cultivated by American Indians for thousands of years. The potato chip, however, is a modern invention. It was created by George Crum, who is believed to have been from the Mohawk Nation. He was a cook who worked at Moon Lake Lodge in Saratoga Springs, New York. In 1853 a customer sent a plate of French fries back to the kitchen because they were too thick and soggy. Crum cut the potatoes into paper-thin slices and fried them. These crisp "Saratoga" chips delighted Crum's customer. Crum never tried to widely distribute his potato chips. But other potato chip makers did, and now the snack is eaten by people all over the world.

The Shinnecock Nation

The Shinnecock (SHIN-eh-cock) Nation, on New York's Eastern Long Island, is one of the oldest reservations in the United States. The ancestors of the Shinnecock were great fisherman and whalers, and for thousands of years they sailed the Atlantic shores in their dugout canoes. Today, the Shinnecock still have a great interest in the ocean, and they operate the Shinnecock Shellfish Hatcheries and Environmental Center. They are attempting to restore the health of the ocean's wildlife by keeping baby clams and other young wildlife safe in the hatchery and then releasing them into the ocean.

Every Labor Day weekend they host one of the largest powwows in the Northeast. Thousands of holiday tourists shop at booths set up by Indian vendors and craftspeople from around the country. The colorful variety of regalia reflects the many different nations represented by the dancers. Not only does the Shinnecock Powwow mark the end of the vacation season in the world-famous Hamptons summer resort area, but it is also an important fund-raiser for the Shinnecock people.

MARGUERITE A. SMITH, SHINNECOCK

(Contemporary)

Marguerite Smith is an attorney and educator from the Shinnecock Indian reservation located on New York's Eastern Long Island. She has devoted her life to standing up for the rights of Indian peoples. She protects the rights of Indian children by advocating for health and family services. Ms. Smith and other Shinnecock work hard to preserve their tribal lands and keep the area from being overdeveloped by the surrounding wealthy non-Indian community. By making sure the land and sea are healthy, the Shinnecock feel the land and sea will take care of them and their descendants. Their shellfish hatchery and organic gardening projects are examples of how to live in harmony with the environment. Ms. Smith is also a board member of the First Nations Development Institute, an organization that helps Native people develop businesses that are good for people and ecosystems.

❖ 3 ❖
Southeast

Spectators stand to honor the color guard, which is poised at the edge of the Chickahominy (CHICK-a-hom-eh-knee) powwow arena with the Chickahominy and American flags held high. Native veterans are in line behind the color guard. The Head Man and Lady Dancers follow, with the rest of the dancers behind them. All are dressed in Native clothing; some wear traditional clothes in the style of their ancestors, others wear colorful, modern "fancy dance" outfits. Moving as one steady beat, the drummers begin to pound out a song on the big powwow drum. Called the Grand Entry, the color guard leads the dancers into the powwow arena, circling around the large area and officially opening the Chickahominy Fall Festival and Powwow, the longest-running powwow in Virginia.

The Chickahominy were some of the first people to meet English colonists centuries ago; their reservation is not far from historic Williamsburg. But guests at the Fall Festival get to experience a bit of Native America that existed long before the tall ships sailed to the Eastern Seaboard. Traditional arts are demonstrated and traditional dances, like the Canoe Dance, are performed.

At one time, the Chickahominy and other closely related Powhatan people led lives that centered around the beautiful rivers in the area. The rivers were full of fish and other wildlife. Chickahominy neighbors, the Pamunkey (pa-MUN-key) and Mattaponi (MAT-ah-po-NI) have been raising shad in fish hatcheries and releasing them into the wild since 1918. For thousands of years, the shad have traveled the waters of the Mid-Atlantic

Map of Selected Native Nations of the Southeast Today

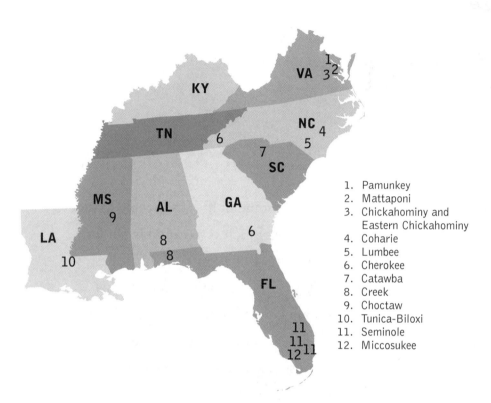

1. Pamunkey
2. Mattaponi
3. Chickahominy and Eastern Chickahominy
4. Coharie
5. Lumbee
6. Cherokee
7. Catawba
8. Creek
9. Choctaw
10. Tunica-Biloxi
11. Seminole
12. Miccosukee

region, providing food and a balanced ecosystem. Pollution, dams, and overfishing threaten the little silvery fish and their spawning grounds, which are important to Virginia's Native communities and the very rivers themselves. Not only does a healthy river provide food for Virginia's Native peoples, but it also provides clay, which the people excavate from the riverbanks to create their famous pottery.

The Powhatan

The Powhatan (Pow-uh-TAN or pow-HAT-un) Chiefdom consisted of the Chickahominy, Pamunkey, Mattaponi, and more than twenty-five other tribes living in some 200 villages located in what is now Virginia. The individual nations paid tribute to Powhatan (also known by his informal name, Wahunsonacock). Powhatan took his formal name when he became the supreme chief, before the English established the colony of Jamestown in Virginia in May 1607. The English terms "king," "emperor," and "ruler" used by the colonists to refer to Powhatan were inappropriate. Unlike royalty in Europe, Powhatan performed everyday tasks like hunting and fishing. Also, he was addressed to his face by his personal name, rather than by a title.

The Jamestown colonists, weakened by sickness and starvation, depended on the Indians for survival. The Indians supplied them with corn, venison, and fish. By 1613, the English began growing the valuable cash crop tobacco, which required more land. The English convinced Indians to sign away huge areas. Tobacco depleted the soil, so new fields were required every few years. Boatloads of colonists moved in to help grow the tobacco crop. They carved the land into plantations, cut down trees, drove away game, and ruined Indian hunting grounds. Still, Powhatan preserved peace with the English until he died. But his brother, who became the next leader, grew tired of struggling with the colonists. He ordered an attack on Jamestown in

1622, which set off warfare for many years, ending the Powhatan tribes' power. Many Native peoples were forced out of Virginia; those who stayed were placed on small reservations in Virginia, where their descendants still live today.

Pamunkey Pottery

Pottery making has been practiced by the Pamunkey of Eastern Virginia, one of the Powhatan tribes, since before the tribe's first contact with Europeans in 1607. The women have dug clay for their pottery from a vein in the Pamunkey River. The opening of the community's clay mine was a great feast day for the Pamunkey. The whole community was present, and each family took home a share of the dull-gray-colored clay. The women made clay bowls, cups, and other objects by hand. They used a rubbing stone, handed down in the family, to polish an object's surface. Potters decorated pieces with texture or carved designs with a stick, thorn, or fingernail.

During the 1800s, Pamunkey potters peddled their old-style gray-and-black-mottled stone-polished ware throughout Virginia. Change came in the early 1930s, when the Pamunkey Pottery Guild was founded by a group of women. The guild set prices for the pieces of pottery and helped market it. Teachers sent by the state introduced molds, which made the potters feel that they were making vessels by hand. Molds also gave potters the ability to quickly reproduce the

LINWOOD CUSTALOW, MATTAPONI (1937–)

As tribal historian, Linwood Custalow teaches children and adults how the Mattaponi still fish the waters in the same way his ancestors taught early European settlers to fish. He educates people on the dangers that threaten the Mattaponi River, like overbuilding and reservoirs. He is a leader in the movement to keep the river clean and healthy. Dr. Custalow was the first Native person to graduate from a Virginia medical college and the first Native person to be licensed as a medical doctor in Virginia. He is also a writer and has written a biography about Pocahontas, *The True Story of Pocahontas: The Other Side of History.*

same vessel hundreds of times. When potters learned that colorful pottery would sell better to tourists, they painted, glazed, and decorated their pieces with picture writing.

Today, potters work in the two distinct Pamunkey styles: one as old as the Pamunkey traditions themselves—blackware—and the other a product of the 1930s, with picture writing designs that tell stories. Potters also still use the ancient method of coiling soft clay to make pottery.

Make a Pamunkey-Type Bowl

Pamunkey pottery can tell a story. Try your hand at making a bowl to tell about something important in your life.

What You Need

Newspapers

1 pound of self-hardening clay

Mussel, clam, or other type
    of shell

Bowl of water

Paper

Pencil

Paintbrush

Tempera or acrylic
    craft paints

What You Do

1. Cover the table with newspapers.
2. Take a small quantity of clay and form a round, flat bottom for the bowl.
3. Roll pieces of clay into slender "snakes" the width of a pencil and about 10 inches long.

4. Take one coil and wind it around the edge of the flat bottom. Join the base and coil by smoothing the clay together with the shell. Dampen the clay with water so it will be easier to smooth out.
5. Place another coil on top of the first and smooth the clay together.
6. Continue adding "snakes" of clay, stacking one over the other, until the bowl is the height you want.
7. Smooth the surface of the bowl with the shell. While smoothing, place one hand inside the bowl to support the wall.
8. Allow the bowl to dry for a few days.
9. Pick a few pictures to tell a story about you and your family. Put the images in order on a piece of paper. Add geometric designs.

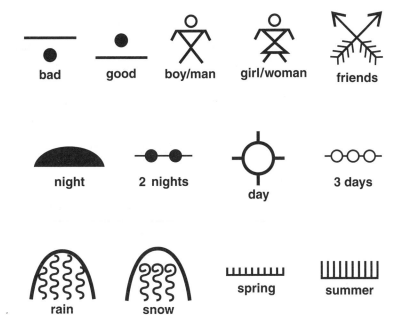

bad   good   boy/man   girl/woman   friends

night   2 nights   day   3 days

rain   snow   spring   summer

10. Using your paper as a guide, paint the pictures and geometric designs that tell your story onto the bowl.

11. Use your bowl to display decorative objects or to hold school supplies. Do not put anything wet in it.

Southeastern Nations

The Catawba (Kaw-TAH-bah), Cherokee (CHAIR-oh-kee), Coharie (Kah-HAR-ee), Chickasaw (CHICK-ah-saw) Creek, and Choctaw (CHOCK-tah) all made their homes in the Southeast. And that's not even all of the tribes beginning with the letter C! At one time, at least 150 to 200 different Native nations lived in the Southeast area of the United States. For the most part, they lived in permanent villages, usually located in river valleys. The southeastern climate has always been excellent for growing crops. Because days are warm and moist most of the year, Native farmers could grow and harvest numerous vegetables and two crops of corn, which was important to their diet. Today, many Natives who live in the Southeast continue to farm.

AMERICAN INDIAN FOOD INVENTIONS

Over 62 percent of all the food the people of the world eat today was originally developed by American Indian scientists! They shared ideas with Native people from all over the western hemisphere. Present-day countries did not exist, and people and ideas traveled across today's borders. Some of the crops developed throughout the Americas are popcorn, tomatoes, potatoes, peanuts, string beans, vanilla, chocolate, and peppers.

NANCY WARD, CHEROKEE

(1738–1822)

The Cherokee, like many other tribes, had a matrilineal society. This means that, although men's and women's roles were equal, the children belonged to the mother's clan. Women were in charge of farming and were leaders. The Ghighua, or Beloved Woman, was chosen for her position because of her brave and wise deeds. She was an ambassador, a peace negotiator, and a judge. Both men and women leaders listened to her. The most noted of the Cherokee Beloved Women was Nancy Ward, or Nan'yehi ("One Who Goes About"). Nan'yehi negotiated treaties and discouraged her people from selling any Cherokee lands. Working for the tribe's welfare until she was very old, she always kept her word. She was saddened that none of the treaties were honored by non- Indian Americans.

☀ Choctaw Traditional Account

Bayous are small, sluggish rivers or creeks in the southern Mississippi Delta region of the United States. "Bayou" is from the Choctaw word *bayuk*, which means small stream. The way it is told, a long time ago the Choctaw could not go into the bayous without getting very sick. A poisonous vine lived in the bayous and caused great harm to the people. But it liked the Choctaw and didn't want to make them ill. The vine asked the other beings to take some of its poison so that the people would not get sick anymore. The bee and wasp took some poison, but promised to only use it to defend themselves and to buzz a warning before stinging. The water moccasin took some too and vowed to only use it for self-protection and to flash a warning first by opening his mouth wide to show the white inside. Finally, the diamondback rattlesnake accepted the poison, promised to only bite if he was stepped on, and vowed to give a warning first by making a rattle sound with his tail. The Choctaw were then able to use the bayous.

The diamondback rattlesnake helped the people even more by keeping the rodents and insects from eating the corn crops. To show appreciation for the snake's help, the Choctaw use diamond shapes to decorate their baskets and on their clothing.

Sew a Diamondback Rattlesnake

Diamondback rattlesnakes, like all snakes, would rather avoid people. They prefer using their poisonous venom to kill their food. You should never pick up any snakes outside. But you can keep this stuffed snake around to remind you of how helpful snakes can be. You can even put him at the bottom of your door to stop cold, wintry drafts from coming inside.

What You Need

Adult supervision required

8 inch-by-41 inch piece of of light-colored, medium-weight flannel or cotton

Straight pins

Scissors

Needle and thread

Black fabric or acrylic paint

Paintbrushes

4-inch square red felt

Newspaper, old socks, or old clothes for the stuffing

Jingle bells

Yardstick

What You Do

1. The brighter side of the fabric is called the "right" side. If your fabric has a right side, fold the fabric the long way with the right side of the fabric inside. Pin it together.

2. Cut off a triangle at one end (as shown below) to form the snake's head.

3. Sew the edges together with tiny stitches. Start at the head and stitch all the way along the body to the tail. Do not sew the end closed. Turn the fabric right side out, making a long tube.

4. Flatten out the tube and paint big black diamonds going down the snake's back. Paint black eyes and a black mouth on the head.

5. Cut out a tongue from the red felt and sew it underneath the mouth.

6. Crumple up newspaper, or shred old clothes or socks to stuff the snake. Use a yardstick to push stuffing into the head and body.

7. When the snake is fully stuffed, sew up the tail.
8. Sew jingle bells onto the tail to create a "rattle." Press your snake snugly along the bottom edge of the door to keep out the drafts.

The Nations' Battles to Keep Their Lands

Southeastern nations were among the first to have contact with European explorers, traders, and soldiers. Their lives were never the same again. By the 1600s, measles, chicken pox, and other European diseases had swept through entire villages and wiped out thousands of Native people, who had no natural immunity to the foreign illnesses. Battles with the French, Spanish, and English also reduced tribal populations.

Soon after, in the late 1820s, great numbers of colonists demanded that prosperous Indian nations with extensive land holdings in the Southeast be cleared out of their way. The five large nations in the Southeast—the Cherokee, Creek, Choctaw, Chickasaw, and Seminole (SEM-eh-nole)—farmed lands coveted by plantation owners. The U.S. government's Indian Office, which was in charge of handling the day-to-day business of keeping the peace with Indian nations, tried to convince tribal leaders to leave voluntarily in exchange for tracts of land hundreds of miles away in a place called Indian Territory (present-day Oklahoma). During the 1820s and 1830s, the state of Georgia tried to remove the Cherokee who held lands within the state's borders. In 1827 the Cherokee told the American government that it was a "sovereign" (independent) nation and could not be removed without its consent. Georgia passed laws that took Cherokee lands and abolished its government, courts, and laws. It distributed Cherokee lands to the state's white citizens. The Cherokee, led by their leader, John Ross, refused to move. They defended their right to remain in their homelands, pointing to treaties they had made with the United States that guaranteed them their lands. Eventually the Cherokee case made its way all the way to the U.S. Supreme Court. In 1832 the Court ruled in *Worcester v. Georgia* that the Cherokee had a right to stay in their homelands. But in spite of the legal victory of the Cherokee Nation, President Andrew Jackson authorized the Indian Removal Act of 1830, which forced Indians living east of the Mississippi River to move to Indian Territory west of the Mississippi River. The president ordered the army to forcibly remove the Cherokee and other Native peoples beginning in the early 1830s.

About 100,000 First Nations citizens from dozens of nations were forced at gunpoint to leave their ancestral homelands. More than 60,000 were people from the Southeast. Accounts tell of how the Cherokee were rounded up like cattle by U.S. soldiers, while Americans stood ready to move onto their farms and homes, taking over their animals, plows, mules, crops, and even their furniture.

Because the government didn't prepare well, the Native people did not have enough wagons, blankets, or food. Under military escort, they suffered from hunger, extreme cold, and diseases like pneumonia on the long trip. It took several months to reach Indian Territory, which is now the state of Oklahoma. Thousands died during the forced marches, which are now called the "Trail of Tears."

Not all the people from southeastern tribes were evicted from their homelands. When the soldiers came, some hid in caves deep in North Carolina's mountains or in the swamps of Florida's Everglades. Descendants of Cherokee, Seminole, and other Native people who were not captured still live in the Southeast in big cities, in small towns, on Indian reservations, and in other Indian communities.

OSCEOLA, SEMINOLE (circa 1804–1838)

Even as a teenager, Osceola had great leadership abilities. He fought for the right of the Seminole people to remain in the Southeast and not be forcibly removed to Indian Territory (present-day Oklahoma). Osceola planned and won successful battles against the U.S. military. His strategies confused U.S. generals sent to capture him and put down the resistance he led. He had great influence over Seminole war actions. U.S. General Thomas S. Jessup offered Osceola a truce, but he did not honor it and Osceola was captured. Because the U.S. government did not keep its word and tricked the Seminole, critics call the action one of the most terrible events in American military history. Osceola was imprisoned at Fort Moultrie on Sullivan's Island, near Charleston, South Carolina, where he died, still a young man. His death and the treatment of the Seminole made headlines around the world. Osceola's influence lived on long after his death.

The Seminole Never Surrendered

In 1842 U.S. president John Tyler ended military action against the Seminole who refused to move away from their Florida homeland. More than 20 million dollars had been spent and 1,500 American soldiers had died. It was the most expensive war the United States had ever fought, yet the outnumbered Seminole could not be defeated and a peace treaty had not been signed. A few years later, Seminole leader Billy Bowlegs led an attack on a U.S. Army survey party trespassing in Seminole territory. The army sent out all of its reserve troops to capture Bowlegs. Although they captured him, they were never able to get the Seminole to sign a peace treaty. By 1859 the United States gave up. It was never able to force, lure, or persuade the Seminole to leave their Everglades homes. The descendants of these resisters make up the Seminole Tribe of Florida, the Miccosukee Tribe of Indians of Florida, and the Independent, or Traditional, Seminoles.

WEAVE A MICCOSUKEE-STYLE KEY CHAIN

The Miccosukee began to finger weave pouches, straps, sashes, and garters from European wool in the 19th century. Their geometric designs often featured white beads. Today, finger woven sashes and bandoliers are part of the regalia of many different Indian nations. Make a mini-weaving to decorate a key ring.

What You Need

2 12-inch long strands of thick yarn or jewelry cording , 1 red and 1 blue (or 2 different colors of your choice)

Metal key ring

Tape

White tile or pony beads (available at craft stores, optional)

What You Do

1. Fold the red cord exactly in half. Fold the looped end over the key ring, and pull the ends through the loop. Pull the strands tightly so the cord is firmly attached to ring. Do the same with the blue strand, pushing the loops together. You will now have 4 strands.

2. Tape the ring to a table edge. The cords should hang straight off the edge of the table. Starting on the left, weave over the strand directly to the right, then under the next strand. Keep going in this pattern until you get to the right. Do the same with the next three strands until you have 3 strands in your right hand—2 red and 1 blue. You will have 1 blue strand in your left hand. Hold them all firmly so the design will be tight.

3. This time, start weaving from right to left. Begin by going *under* the first strand this time. Weave 3 strands to the left, until you have one strand in your right hand—it will be red.

4. Do this over and over, going from one side to the other. Always start weaving *over* the next strand when starting on the left and *under* when starting on the right. After an inch you will begin to see a swirled design.

5. When you think your design is long enough, tie the strands together in a knot.

6. Add as many beads as you want to the separate strands, tying a knot before and after each bead. If you don't add beads, you will have nice fringe instead.

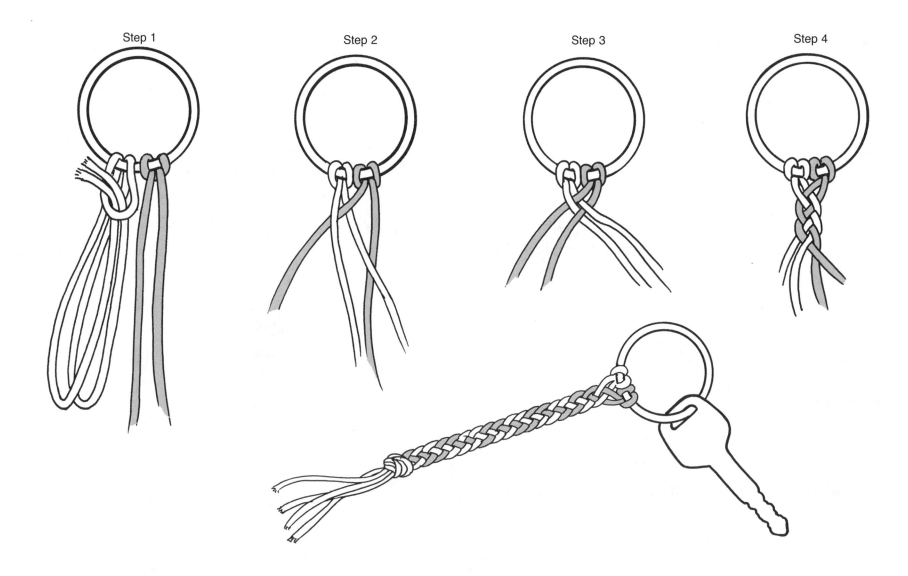

Step 1   Step 2   Step 3   Step 4

Stew Seminole-Inspired Possum Grape Dumplings

This delicious dessert is usually made from wild possum grapes that grow along creeks and in the woods. They are gathered in the fall. You can make a similar dish with grape juice.

What You Need

Adult supervision required

Apron

2 cups flour

2 teaspoons baking powder

¼ teaspoon salt

Medium-sized mixing bowl

1 teaspoon butter, melted

Purple grape juice, divided

Teaspoon

Large pot

What You Do

1. Put on the apron, because grape juice stains.
2. Put the flour, baking powder, and salt in the mixing bowl. Mix well.
3. Add the melted butter and 1 cup of grape juice to the flour mixture, and mix into a dough.
4. Bring the remainder of the grape juice to a boil in large pot.
5. From teaspoonfuls of dough into balls.
6. Drop each dough ball into the boiling grape juice.
7. The dumplings are done when they float to the top of the boiling juice.
8. Remove when done and serve with a little of the boiled grape juice poured over them.

Makes approximately 24 dumplings

Betty Mae Tiger Jumper, Seminole (1923–)

Born in a *chickee*, a dwelling made from palmetto trees that features poles, thatched roofs, raised wooden platforms, and open walls on all four sides, Betty Mae Tiger Jumper grew up speaking the Creek and Miccosukee languages until she attended a boarding school in North Carolina, where she learned English. She graduated in 1949 and was the first Seminole woman to earn a high school diploma. During the 1950s, Jumper, who became a nurse, worked tirelessly to stamp out diseases and improve her people's health. A health clinic in Hollywood, Florida, is named after her. Now a renowned storyteller, Jumper appears regularly at folklore festivals where she tells her people's traditional stories.

Seminole Patchwork

What do the words cross, sacred fire, arrow, zigzag, bird, wave, mountains, and diamondback rattlesnake all have in common? They are names of colorful patchwork designs on Seminole Indian clothing. There are different stories about how this wearable art form came to be. One is that, in the 1800s, when the Seminole fled from white settlers and soldiers into the Everglades swamps, they had very little clothing. They took their worn-out clothing apart and pieced it back together to make new garments. Later, the women re-created these beautiful fashions using hand-cranked sewing machines obtained from traders. Cotton cloth was very expensive, so they never wasted any of the fabric, but instead integrated even the tiniest scrap into their designs. Today Seminole people dress like other Americans, but they still wear the beautiful patchwork outfits on special occasions.

CRAFT A SEMINOLE-PATCHWORK-DESIGN BASEBALL CAP

What You Need

Tape measure

Baseball cap (it's best to use one you already own)

3 ½-inch satin or grosgrain ribbons at least 8 inches long in three different colors

Scissors

Fabric glue

2 ¼-inch satin or grosgrain ribbons at least 8 inches long in the same color but different color from the ribbons above

Ruler

Pencil

2 pieces 12 inches long x 5 inches wide of lightweight, non-stretchy cloth (scrap fabric is fine)

What You Do

1. Use the tape measure to measure around the baseball cap, just above the brim. Don't include the opening in the back of the hat in the measurement.

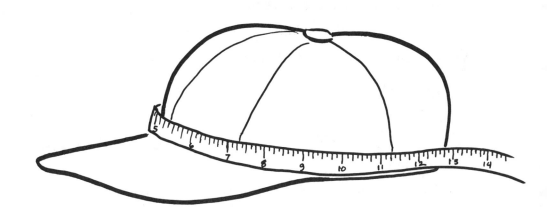

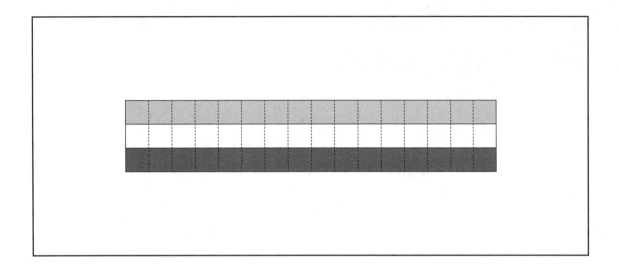

2. Cut each of the three ½-inch-wide ribbons to match the measurement of your baseball cap. Glue these ribbons, side by side, onto one of the pieces of cloth (see illustration above). The ribbons should line up exactly. Cut off any cloth that isn't covered by the ribbons.

3. Using the ruler and pencil, measure and mark off 3 equal sections of the ribbons. You will have three rectangles that are the same size. Cut along your lines.

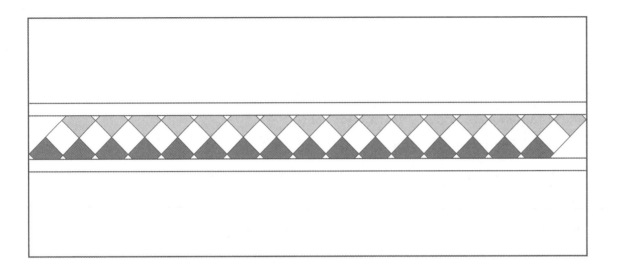

4. Turn the 3 rectangles 45 degrees to the right, with each piece touching its neighbor. Glue them onto the second piece of cloth.

5. Cut each of the two ¼-inch-ribbons to match the measurement of your baseball cap. Glue one ribbon to the top of the patchwork design, and the other to the bottom (see illustration above). The ribbons should line up exactly. Cut off any cloth that isn't covered by the ribbons so that you have a patchwork-design rectangle.

6. Glue the rectangle onto the cap.

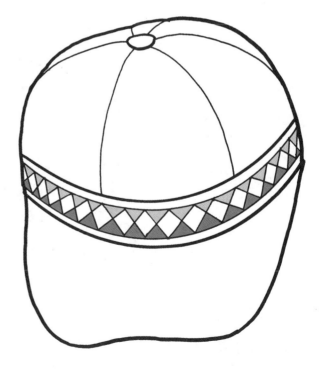

Choctaw Stickball

On the Choctaw Reservation in Philadelphia, Mississippi, children and adults play a team sport called *kabocca*, or stickball. Popular among Choctaw and other Indians in the Southeast for hundreds of years, stickball has been called "the little brother of war," because it was once used to settle disputes within and between tribes. It is a rough-and-tumble game with few rules. Equipment includes handcrafted hickory sticks and a woven ball that is about the size of a golf ball. The traditional ball was a rock wrapped in leather. Each team tries to advance the ball down the field to the other team's goalpost using only their sticks, never touching the ball with their hands. Points are scored when the ball strikes the opponent's goalpost. Indian stickball is now an official part of the State Games of Mississippi.

THE CHEROKEE PHOENIX

The Cherokee government in New Echota, Georgia, published the *Cherokee Phoenix* from 1828 until 1834. It was the first American Indian tribal newspaper and the first paper to publish news in an American Indian language. Since 1834, more than 2,000 newspapers and magazines have been published by Indian tribes, organizations, schools, and urban centers.

Cherokee Language

Tunes sung in Cherokee float over North Carolina's Great Smoky Mountains as children and adults sing from Cherokee-language songbooks. They learn songs, as well as everyday conversation, in Cherokee at the Big Y community Cherokee language class taught on the Qualla Boundary, the Eastern Band of Cherokee reservation in North Carolina. Belting out a melody is a fun way to practice the ancient language and makes it easier to remember the words. Like English, Cherokee has different dialects. But unlike the English alphabet, which has 26 letters, the Cherokee "syllabary" has 85 characters. A syllabary is a set of written symbols that represent syllables, which make up words. The length and pitch of a Cherokee vowel can affect its meaning, a characteristic not found in English. "Use it or lose it" is the attitude of the class members; it is necessary to use the language on a regular basis so it can remain part of Cherokee life. At one time, speaking a Native language like Cherokee was strictly forbidden in government-run boarding schools. Now Cherokee people want to preserve their language for future generations.

Many people speak and write Cherokee today. To translate it into English, the syllabary must first be converted into the English alphabet, then the letters have to be translated into English sounds. Cherokee, like most Native languages, is very complex. For instance, there are two words for brother—one is

LEARN SOME CHEROKEE WORDS

Here are some common phrases and their pronunciation in Cherokee. Try to learn a few!

Hello	*Osiyo* (Oh-see-YOH)
Good-bye	*Do-na-da* (dough-na-DAH)
Yes	*V* (uh)
No	*Tla* (kla)

used by another brother, and a different word is used by those who are not brothers. There are also both formal and informal ways of speaking. The word *ka-ma-ma* is the word for butterfly. But it is also the word for elephant! Can you guess why? Elephants are from Asia or Africa, so there was no Cherokee word for them. It is said that when Cherokee people saw elephants for the first time, they said their ears looked like big butterflies, and the name stuck.

Southeastern Tribes Today

Native people work in a variety of jobs, own businesses, and operate museums and amusement parks. Many are employed by their tribal governments, schools, and hospitals, while others preserve their traditional arts and work in tourism. For almost a hundred years, the Cherokee of North Carolina and the Choctaw of Mississippi have been holding fairs. Visitors are entertained by rappers, cloggers, country and gospel singers, and antique car and truck shows. Feasts of Indian foods, like *banaha* (a type of cornbread) and hominy, are served up along with traditional singing, dancing, and demonstrations by traditional artisans. Games and storytelling are part of the festive occasions, too.

The Catawba Cultural Preservation Project

The Catawba Cultural Preservation Project in Rock Hill, South Carolina, offers tribal members classes in pottery, basket weaving, bead working, drumming, and dancing. Catawba also share their culture with visitors so they can learn about today's Catawba and their history. Catawba children attend a special summer camp to learn more about their culture. At Camp Kic-A-Wah, kids tend an herb garden that features herbs used for medicine and cooking.

CYNTHIA LEITICH SMITH, CREEK (1967–)

Cynthia Leitich Smith's award-winning novels include *Tantalize, Rain Is Not My Indian Name*, and *Jingle Dancer*. Some of her stories are about American Indian kids living in cities and small towns with all kinds of people, and many deal with subjects like death and love. Leitich Smith hosts a Web site (www.cynthialeitichsmith.com) that introduces readers to children's and young adult literature resources. "I love to write," Smith says. "I can pretend all the time and make it my life's work. I write for the child inside of me, for Native Americans and non-Indians, [and] for kids from age four to age one hundred and beyond."

Grow a Corn, Bean, and Squash Garden

Catawba, like Native farmers in many areas of the United States, planted corn, beans, and squash together. These three plants have a "symbiotic" relationship—that means they help each other grow. Corn grows tall and strong and gives the bean plants a secure place to climb. The beans have bacteria on their roots that absorb nitrogen from the air and change it into a form that the corn can use. The large, prickly squash leaves keep the soil from getting too much sun and prevent weed growth. They help keep the soil moist, and small animals, who don't like the prickles, look for food elsewhere.

When eaten together, the three plants provide most of the proteins found in meat. Corn, bean, and squash dishes, like succotash, are not only tasty, but very nutritious, too. The Iroquois people call the plants the Three Sisters. Try growing some indoors (if you can, transplant them to an outdoor garden in the spring). Plant the three together in a container, and plant other seeds separately in different containers. Watch to see if the seeds grow better when planted together or when planted alone.

What You Need

Pesticide free seeds: 3 corn seeds; 3 bean seeds, 2 "mini" pumpkin seeds

3 clean 8-ounce plastic containers, such as yogurt or cottage cheese containers

Water

Newspaper

Gravel

1 large pan, such as an old dishpan, with sides that are 4 to 6 inches high

Small bag of potting soil

What You Do

1. Place the corn seeds in one of the plastic containers. Fill the container with water and let the seeds soak onvernight.
2. Cover your work surface with newspaper.
3. Remove the corn seeds from the plastic container and discard the water. Place a layer of gravel in the bottom of the plastic container and in the bottom of the large pan. (The gravel will allow for drainage.) Fill the plastic container and the pan with potting soil.
4. Plant two of the corn seeds in the pan. Plant the third corn seed in the plastic container. Water both containers

until the soil is moist, but not wet. Place both containers in a place with direct sunlight. Let sit for 1 to 2 weeks, watering whenever the soil feels dry, until the corn plants in the pan are at least 4 inches high.

5. Place the bean seeds in one of the empty plastic containers. Place the pumpkin seeds in the other empty plastic container. Fill the containers with water and let the seeds soak overnight.

6. Cover your work surface with newspaper.

7. Remove the seeds from the plastic containers and discard the water. Place a layer of gravel in the bottom of each plastic container. Fill both containers with potting soil.

8. Plant two of the bean seeds in one of the plastic containers, and plant one of the pumpkin seeds in the other plastic container. Water both containers until the soil is moist, but not wet. Plant the remaining bean and pumpkin seed in the pan with the corn plants.

9. Place all contians in direct sunlight and water the plants whenever the soil feels dry. Keep track of which plants grow best!

The Lumbee Tribe

The Lumbee (LUM-bee) Tribe is the largest tribe in North Carolina and the largest tribe east of the Mississippi River. Most Lumbee live in Robeson County and neighboring counties, which are considered to be their homeland. The

HENRY BERRY LOWRIE, LUMBEE

(circa 1844–disappeared 1872)

Henry Berry Lowrie, a Lumbee born in Robeson County, North Carolina, was "conscripted" (forced) to work for the Confederate army, as were many other free men of color in the South during the Civil War. His father and brother were accused of harboring Union soldiers and executed by the Confederates. Lowrie was angry and sad that his family had been murdered, and he organized a band of men to protect Indian people from discrimination, mistreatment, and violence. He searched for justice and fairness. He was called the "Indian Robin Hood" because he was able to steal thousands of dollars' worth of provisions from general stores and share them with North Carolina's poor Indian, black, and white people. Since 1976, Lowrie's legend has been presented every summer in the outdoor drama *Strike at the Wind!* Lowrie just vanished into thin air in 1872. No one really knows what happened to him.

Indians were not forced to leave their homeland during the removal period in the 1830s and 1840s because they owned their lands privately like other citizens in the state, not together as a tribe.

Under the North Carolina constitution of 1835, Lumbee people, like other American Indians in the state, lost many of their civil rights. They were not allowed to own weapons, vote or hold office, attend public schools, or serve in the military. During the Civil War, around 1863, they were forced to help build Fort Fisher, the largest Confederate fort near Wilmington, North Carolina. Some Lumbee escaped, and others hid to avoid being caught by the local authorities.

Since Lumbee were prevented from attending white schools, they fought for and won the right to attend their own schools and select their own teachers. By the 1920s, the Lumbee had built more than 30 one-room schools in their communities.

One of the most famous examples of Lumbee activism happened in 1958. Several hundred Lumbee of Robeson County defended their community against a hate group. The Ku Klux Klan was planning to hold a rally to scare Indian people. The Lumbee drove the hooded Klan off their land without anyone getting injured. Photos of triumphant Lumbee holding up the abandoned KKK banner were published in newspapers throughout the world. The Klansmen never held another public meeting in Robeson County.

LONGLEAF PINE TREE

The longleaf pine tree is native to the Southeast. This very strong tree is resistant to fires, and it can live for 500 years. Before non-Natives arrived in the western hemisphere, there were vast forests of the longleaf pine in the South. Their strong timber was excellent for shipbuilding, but the U.S. Navy and merchants used so many of the beautiful trees to build boats that the long leaf pine almost became extinct. Today, only 3 percent of the original longleaf pine forests remain.

In the 1800s, Lumbee women began to view the longleaf pinecone in a different way—from the bottom up! As a result, fanciful geometric designs based on the pinecone popped up on rugs and quilts. A hundred years later, two Lumbee tribal members, Hayes Alan Locklear and Kat Littleturtle, used a longleaf pinecone motif in a dress for Miss Lumbee, and a new tradition was born. Every year the tribe chooses a Miss Lumbee from contestants in the Miss Lumbee Pageant. The longleaf pinecone patchwork dress is now a Lumbee symbol, and all the Miss Lumbees wear the design.

Stamp a Lumbee-Inspired Longleaf Pinecone Table Runner

What You Need

Newspaper

3-foot-by1-foot piece of cotton fabric

Fabric glue or needle and thread

Longleaf pinecones (or other type of pinecone)

Paintbrushes

Fabric paint or washable ink (in assorted colors that will show
  up against the color of your fabric)

What You Do

1. Cover your work surface with newspaper.
2. Make a hem all the way around your table runner by
   turning over and gluing or sewing the edges.
3. Spread out your fabric on the work surface.
4. Very lightly apply paint to the surface of a pinecone. Use
   different parts of the pinecone to get different effects—its
   top, bottom, and sides. Use a separate pinecone for each
   paint color.
5. Firmly lay or stamp the pinecones on the fabric. You can
   gently but firmly roll the pinecones completely around
   to get a different effect. Don't press too hard and don't
   move them too quickly.
6. Make any design you like with your color choices. You
   can cover the entire table runner or just do a design
   down the middle or around the edges.
7. When the fabric is dry, place it in the middle of the
   dining table and enjoy a meal.

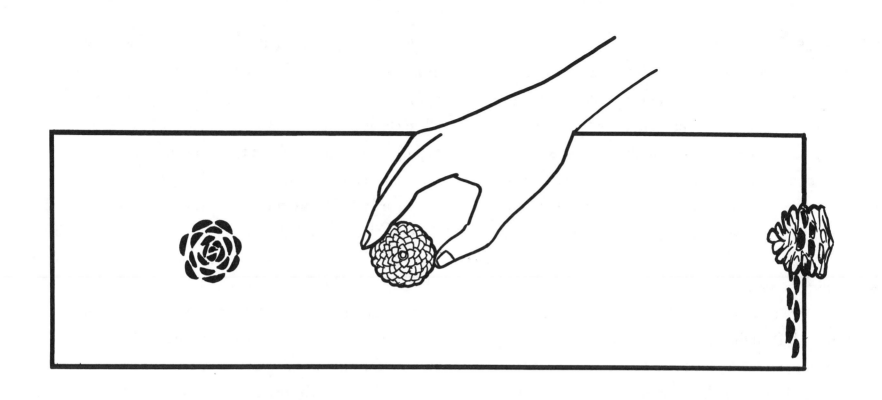

The Tunica-Biloxi Tribe

The Tunica (TYOON-uh-cuh) and Biloxi (Beh-LOX-ee) Indians have lived on their reservation near Marksville, Louisiana, for over two centuries. The tribes speak completely different languages. Tunica speak Tunica and the Biloxi speak a Siouan language. In the late 1600s, the Tunica and Biloxi tribes planted and harvested corn, pumpkins, and beans. After coming into contact with non-Indians, they began to raise peaches and melons. They also hunted deer, turkey, and buffalo and fished the numerous waters.

The Tunica and Biloxi people were excellent traders. They used salt from the many salt domes in Louisiana to trade for goods, primarily from the French. They also traded with the Spanish who claimed lands in the region. After 1803, when the United States bought the Louisiana Territory, the Indians had to deal with a new flood of white traders. These people were not always honest, and the Indian people were often cheated.

Earl J. Barbry Sr., a descendant of chiefs, has guided the tribes since his election as tribal chair in 1978. Under his leadership, a handful of tribal members made many trips to Washington, D.C., where they did research to prove that the Tunica-Biloxi Tribe was indeed a tribe that had a long continuous history. Finally, the Tunica-Biloxi people became federally recognized in 1981. Recognition brought in some funds to provide much-needed health services to tribal members. But recognition also gave them the right to open a tribal casino in 1994. Profits from the casino can be used to benefit the tribe. Thanks to Barbry and other tribal council members, there have been some amazing changes on the reservation. Modern, air-conditioned homes have replaced shacks with no indoor plumbing. Dirt roads have been paved, and the local school bus, which once did not carry Indian children, now stops on the reservation.

In 2005, when Hurricane Katrina devastated New Orleans, Louisiana, with massive flooding, the Tunica-Biloxi people received no more than a little bad weather and rain. The community turned its convention center into a refuge for hundreds of people fleeing the hurricane. Tribal Chairman Earl Barbry was given an award by the National Indian Gaming Association for the generosity extended by the tribe to hurricane victims.

4

Midwest

Jingle dancers make music as they fly across the powwow arena. Their jingle dresses are adorned with hundreds of tin cones that shimmer and tinkle as they keep time to the drum beat. Only girls and women are jingle dancers. Although the dance is performed by many different Indian people across the country, it began with Ojibway (oh-JIB-way) people from the Midwestern region as a healing dance. Today, many girls take a vow to heal the earth with their dancing.

The Midwest Region

The Midwest boasts all five Great Lakes, and countless rivers, streams, marshes, and other lakes. The Ojibway made their homes in the western and northern Great Lakes region, in parts of present-day Wisconsin, Minnesota, and Michigan. Ojibway bands also spread into North Dakota. Other First Nations peoples who built villages in this watery region included the Potawatomi (POT-ah-what-ah-me), Sauk (sack) and Fox, Menominee (meh-NOM-eh-nee), and Winnebago (WIN-eh-bay-go). Their homelands were around the western Great Lakes. South of the lakes were the Kickapoo and Miami tribes in Ohio and Indiana, the Shawnee in southern Ohio, and the Illinois in the state of the same name.

Native peoples in the Midwest also lived amid forests of birch, elm, maple, and oak. They used the forest resources for most of what they needed. Birch bark made excellent material for houses as well as for canoes, which were used to travel on waterways, the

Map of Selected Native Nations of the Midwest Today

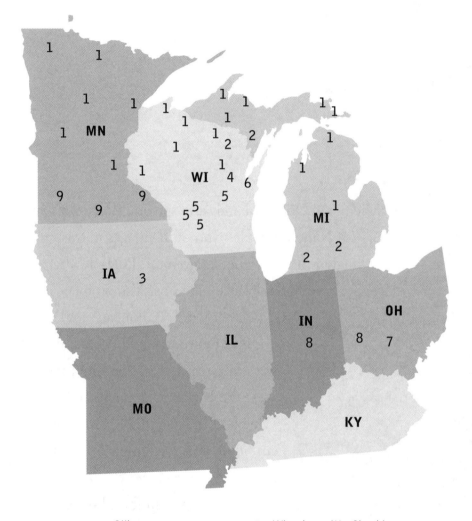

1. Ojibway
2. Potawatomi
3. Sauk and Fox (Meskwaki)
4. Menominee
5. Winnebago (Ho-Chunk)
6. Oneida
7. Shawnee
8. Miami
9. Sioux

"highways" of long ago. Maple trees were a source of sugar. Men and women set up camps where they collected maple sap, boiled it, and produced sugar that was used in seasoning food.

The Ojibway

The Ojibway were one of the largest tribes in North America. People cleared land near water to build their villages. They used birch bark for their houses (called wigwams), canoes, and containers. Most villagers relied on hunting and fishing in the countless lakes, rivers, and ponds in the area, as well as on gathering wild plants. They also grew corn, beans, pumpkins, and squash in small patches. Wild rice was also an important part of the Ojibway diet. To avoid starvation when food was scarce, people preserved and stored as much food as possible.

Today, more than 20 bands of Ojibway live on reservations in Minnesota, Wisconsin, and Michigan, as well as in North Dakota and Montana. There are more than 50 bands in Canada. Ojibway people also live in Minneapolis, St. Paul, and other cities in the United States and Canada.

The Ojibway made treaties in 1833, 1836, and 1842 that protected their fishing rights. But there have been some state legislators, fishermen, and other non-Ojibway who have tried to take these rights away. During the 1980s, anti-treaty protestors tried to stop Ojibway from fishing by firing guns and throwing rocks at them. Ojibway went to court to defend their treaty rights. Today, Ojibway work with environmental organizations and citizen action groups to keep industries from polluting their lakes and killing their wild rice and fish.

Ojibway Language

The Guinness Book of World Records lists the Ojibway language as being the most complex in the world. It has more than 6,000 verb forms. English and Spanish have fewer than fifteen and Japanese has two. Ojibway people have worked hard to keep their language alive. Ojibway language classes take place at tribal schools, colleges, and culture camps.

For almost 200 years, the U.S. government prevented or discouraged Indian people from speaking or learning their own languages. Some languages died out completely. But a number live on, and today the Ojibway and other tribes encourage people to relearn their own tribal languages. Interactive computer programs offer Ojibway youngsters a way to learn the language. Other children attend Ojibway language immersion schools, where they hear and speak their ancestral language all day.

IGNATIA BROKER, OJIBWAY
(1919–1987)

Ignatia Broker is a real-life Wonder Woman. Broker received the Wonder Woman Award in recognition of her dedication to make the world a better place. The Wonder Woman Foundation (now called the Women Officials' Network Foundation) recognizes women over age 40 for heroic accomplishments. Born on the White Earth Reservation in Minnesota, Broker spent many years in Minneapolis. She educated the public about American Indian people and taught Native peoples about their rights. She helped found the Minnesota Historical Society, and her Ojibway lessons are still used in the Minneapolis Public School District. Broker also wrote *Night Flying Woman*, a children's novel based on her family's history.

Make an Ojibway Seasons Apron

Make this apron and decorate it with Ojibway words. You can keep your clothes clean during art and cooking projects and learn some new words at the same time.

What You Need

Adult supervision required

Newspaper

Ruler

7-inch-by-24-inch rectangle of plain heavy fabric, such as heavy cotton, canvas, or denim

Fabric glue

Pencil

Fabric markers

Needle and thread

4 shoelaces

What You Do

1. Measure a ½ inch hem all around the fabric. Turn the ½ inch over and glue it down.

2. Using a ruler and pencil, lightly draw lines dividing the fabric into four equal parts. In each quarter, write the Ojibway word for a season. Then write the English translation. Use the pencil to sketch a picture of something that represents that season. For example, a flower could be used for spring and a snowflake could be used for winter.

3. Use the markers to trace over your words and pictures.

4. Sew one shoelace on each corner of the top of the fabric, so you can tie it around your neck. Sew one shoelace about halfway down the side on each side so you can tie it around your waist.

Ojibway words for seasons:

Ziigwan (ZEEG-wuhn)	Spring
Niibin (NEE-bin)	Summer
Dagwaagin (DUG-wah-gin)	Fall
Biboon (BIH-boon)	Winter

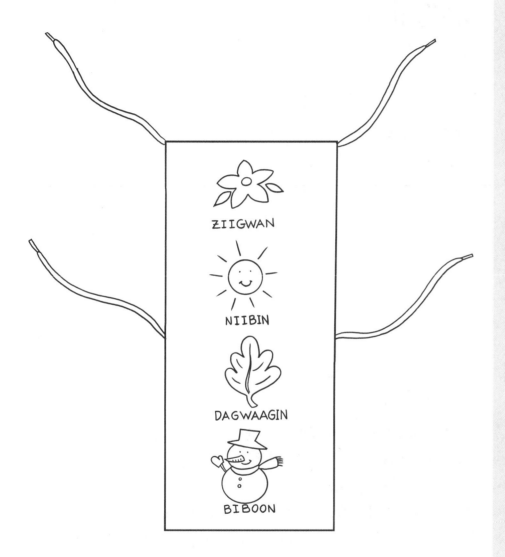

ZIIGWAN

NIIBIN

DAGWAAGIN

BIBOON

Winona LaDuke,
Ojibway/Anishinaabeg (1959–)

When she was 18 years old, Winona LaDuke spoke to the United Nations about Native environmental concerns. She was the youngest person to do so. She presented her research on the problems of mining uranium on the Navajo reservation and the effects on Native miners who were exposed to unhealthy amounts of radiation.

LaDuke was born in Los Angeles and attended Harvard University, where she educated others and wrote articles about all the problems caused by polluting the environment. Today she lives on Minnesota's White Earth Reservation, where she founded the White Earth Land Recovery Project and the Indigenous Women's Network. She began Native Harvest, a store on the White Earth Reservation that sells hand-harvested wild rice and other Ojibway-grown foods, like maple syrup and wild rice pancake mix.

In 1996 and 2000, LaDuke was the Green Party's vice-presidential candidate. LaDuke has also written books, including one for children titled *The Sugarbush*.

Take a Mini-Walk to Your Own Special Place

In traditional times, Ojibway children learned to be helpful community members. They sometimes gave up meals so that they could learn what it felt like to be hungry and to have compassion for those who had no food. They also learned how to be quiet, patient, and observant of their surroundings. These skills were important for survival in the natural world, and they helped children grow up to contribute to their community by being good hunters, good farmers, and caring people. We live in a very noisy, busy world, and we sometimes miss the little everyday occurrences, like ants traveling to their home, birds singing different songs, or plants growing their leaves. Sometimes giving your mind a rest from schoolwork, television, or street sounds is a way to feel more calm and relaxed. Try this exercise to hone your listening and observation skills and to experience the difference between being busy and being peaceful. You will have created a special place inside your head that you can remember when you are upset, angry, or tense.

What You Need

Adult supervision or permission required

Old clothes that you don't mind
  getting dirty

6 feet of string

2 heavy rocks

Magnifying glass

Notebook

Pencil

What You Do

1. Put on your old clothes and find a spot outdoors that catches your interest. A local park or playground would be a good place.
2. Lay out the string in a straight line and secure it with rocks at each end. It might be nice to start your "string path" at the base of a tree.

3. Sit quietly at one end of the string and close your eyes. What do you hear? What do your smell?

4. Open your eyes and very slowly walk along the string to the other end, looking at the ground. Listen, look, feel, and smell everything on your path. Turn around when you reach the end. Walk back along the string, but this time use the magnifying glass. Notice each tiny blade of grass, leaf, flower, stone, or insect. When you reach the end, lie down or sit with your back to a tree. Look at the sky, listen to the sounds, and feel the earth beneath you. Close your eyes for a few moments and remember all you have experienced.

5. Open your eyes and write down in your notebook all that you have seen, heard, felt, and smelled. Make sure you take everything with you when you leave the area.

6. Before you go to sleep, recall the day and all the sights, sounds, smells, and feelings. Think of being very peaceful and comfortable. If you feel worried about homework, sports, or other parts of your life at any time, close your eyes and remember your "mini-walk" as a special place to go to in your imagination.

Construct Snowshoes

Most Indian nations that endured long, snowy winters used snowshoes. The high snow did not keep people from calling on neighbors or hunting for food. Snowshoes distribute weight to a larger area so the snowshoer stays on top of the snow and doesn't sink to the ground below. Although the snowshoe was probably invented by Eastern Native peoples like the Wabanaki and Iroquois, groups from the Midwest, Plains, and Northwest Coast areas also used them, as did Native peoples in Canada and Alaska.

At the Sault St. Marie Culture Camp in Michigan, Ojibway kids have learned to make snowshoes in a traditional way. Heating ash over an outdoor fire makes it flexible. They shape the wood into tennis racket shapes. Then they make spiderweb designs with leather straps to fill in the "tennis racket." It takes a few days and lots of patience, but the results are beautiful and practical.

If you want to walk in deep snow and do not have any snowshoes, you can make these. Walking with snowshoes feels different than regular walking—it's kind of like swimming with flippers. Have fun taking a walk on top of the snow!

What You Need

2 thick limbs or boughs from a fir or
   pine tree, each about 1 foot wide and 2 feet long;
   try to find limbs on the ground so you don't have to hurt
   a tree gathering your wood.
2 2-foot lengths of heavy string
Lace up boots or gym shoes
Lots of snow!

What You Do

1. About 5 to 6 inches from the base of each bough
   tie a tight knot around the stem.

2. Flip each limb over and tie again.

3. The branches point up on one side of the limb and down on the other. Make sure the ends and sides of the limb are pointing up, away from the ground, for the next step.

5. Tie the string around your boot toe. If possible, thread and tie the string through your laces. You should be able to move your heel up and down.

6. Walk on the snow with your feet far enough apart that your "snowshoes" don't touch each other.
7. When walking across a slope, turn your feet slightly uphill so the snowshoe grabs the snow. When walking downhill, bend your knees more and lean back so that you don't fall forward. Your shoe or boot should be able to turn easily in every direction; if it doesn't, you won't be able to move forward.

4. Put a boot on each branch, on top of the tied string.

The Wild Rice People

In the southern part of the Great Lakes area, communities farmed crops of corn, beans, and squash in the rich soil. In the north, where wild rice grows in shallow parts of lakes and streams, this plant, which is really a grass, became a major source of food for the Ojibway, Menominee, some Winnebago, and other Indian groups. Wild rice was so important to the Menominee that they became known as the Wild Rice People to neighboring nations.

Ojibway basket makers have long been known throughout the world for their beautiful birch bark creations. They construct a wide variety of containers such as pots, buckets, and boxes. Containers were often folded and sewn up with roots or the inner bark of cedar. Pitch and gum from pine trees made the containers watertight. Birch bark boxes were used to store clothing and food, and pots were used for cooking and other tasks. Some were used to process wild rice. After loosening the outer covering of the rice kernels by stamping on it, a process called "jigging," the wild rice is put in large baskets and tossed high into the air. The wind removes the outer covering, or husks, so that the cleaned rice can fall back into the basket. This last part of processing the rice is called winnowing.

Cook a Wild Rice Dish with Walnuts and Fruit

Wild rice is not rice at all, but a tall grass with edible, rice-like seeds. Wild rice is low in calories, and it towers over other grains when it comes to amounts of protein, minerals, B vitamins, folic acid, and carbohydrates.

What You Need

Adult supervision required

2 cups of wild rice, rinsed in cold water and drained

1 small onion, chopped

5 cups of water

1 large pot with tight-fitting lid

1 cup chopped walnuts

1 cup chopped dried fruit (apricots, blueberries, mangoes, or cherries)

What You Do

1. Put the rice, onions, and water into the pot and bring to a boil. Lower heat, cover, and simmer for 40 minutes.
2. Add the nuts and dried fruit to the pot. Mix well.
3. Cover and cook for 20 more minutes, stirring occasionally. Serve hot.

Serves 6 to 8

Ojibway and Potawatomi Porcupine Quillwork

Ojibway and Potawatomi people decorated clothing and baskets with lovely designs created from porcupine quills. Porcupine quillwork is one of the oldest kinds of embroidery in the world. Quillwork takes a long time to make. First, one has to find a dead porcupine and remove the quills from the carcass. Then the stiff, pointy quills have to be softened and, if desired, dyed before they can be used. The quills are folded, twisted, wrapped, braided, and sewn. Then it takes weeks and sometimes years to embroider the quills into flowers and geometric designs, usually on leather clothing. Quilled leather is harder to take care of than beaded leather because the quills are very fragile and can be easily broken.

Once Ojibway and Potawatomi people started trading for glass seed beads from European traders after 1675, they used them more often than quills to make their elaborate and beautiful designs. The colorful images were usually based on flowers, as they are today. Beadwork is like a painting done with beads instead of paints.

Quill a Box, Potawatomi Style

Today, some artists still use the ancient art of quillwork to decorate baskets and make earrings, but not many use it on clothing. All the complicated patterns are handwoven onto the baskets and other containers. Use some toothpicks as "quills" to make a Potawatomi-style box for your jewelry or watches.

What You Need

Newspaper

Small wooden box (available at craft store) or cigar box

Acrylic paint, if desired

Paintbrush, if desired

Colored pencils or markers

Wood toothpicks

Scissors

2 to 4 cups (one for each color of dye)

1 to 2 cups of hot water

1 to 2 teaspoons of white vinegar

Food coloring

Tweezers

Glue

Varnish, shellac, or polyurethane, if desired

What You Do

1. Cover your work area with newspaper. If you want to paint the box, do that now. Leave the box open to dry so it won't be painted shut.

2. Draw your design on the box, and color it in with the colored pencils or markers. Potawatomi people use flowers and geometric shapes. You can use any design you want, like a cat, dog, flower, or star, but try to keep your design to just a few colors.

3. Arrange the toothpicks on top of your design to see how many you will need of each color. You may have to cut them so they will fit into each colored area. Add a few extra just in case one breaks or gets lost.

4. Make dyes from the food coloring. Use one cup for each color and add ½ cup hot water to each. Add ½ teaspoon of vinegar and drops of food coloring to get your desired shade.

5. Soak the toothpicks in the dyes until you get desired colors. Use the tweezers to remove the toothpicks from dyes. Let them dry on the newspaper, making sure each color is separate.

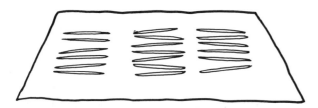

6. When the toothpicks are dry, glue them onto your design. You can use the tweezers to pick them up and place them if you find that easier. Fill in all the colors with corresponding toothpicks: red toothpicks on red areas, blue toothpicks on blue areas, yellow toothpicks on yellow areas, and so on.

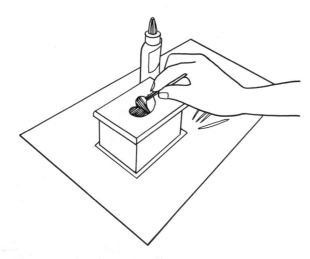

7. If you want to you can coat your "quillwork" with varnish, shellac, or polyurethane to protect it.

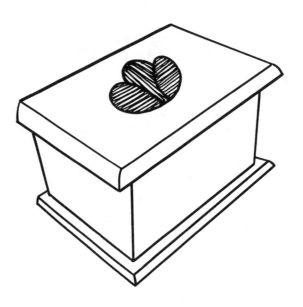

Winnebago Appliqué Ribbonwork

Before contact with Europeans, Winnebago used porcupine quills as well as moose hair, shells, seeds, and clay to decorate clothing. After they began trading with the French, they developed a brand-new fashion that they are famous for today. They cut patterns from birch bark, often handing them down from mother to daughter. The patterns were used as guides to create distinct designs from brightly colored silk ribbons.

Today, as long ago, the rainbow hues of ribbons are laid in straight rows or strips, then sewn onto a dark background. Patterns are used to trace and cut floral or geometric shapes. It takes patience and great skill to sew the many layers. The shapes adorn skirts, shawls, moccasins, shirts, bags, and even doll clothes.

Design a Winnebago Appliqué Ribbonwork-Style Notebook Cover

This cover can be put on the notebook you use to record your observations from your "mini-walk" to your special place. The Winnebago word for applause is *Hââââ!* (hah). Give yourself a big hand for making the cover!

What You Need

Notebook with a cardboard
    cover

Sheets of different colored of
    construction paper, includ-
    ing black

Pencil

Scissors

Glue

Clear contact paper, if desired

Marker (choose a color that
    will stand out on the
    construction paper)

What You Do

1. Lay your notebook on a sheet of black construction paper. Using your pencil, trace around the notebook. Cut out the shape and glue it to the front.

2. Draw 2 maple leaves, each about 3½ inches long and 2 inches wide on a bright color paper. Cut them out. Put one of your leaves on different-colored paper. Using it as a

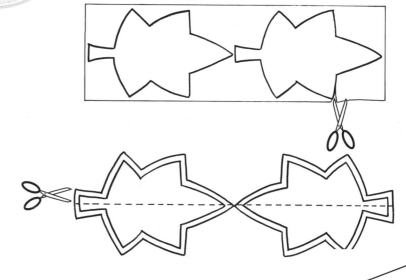

guide, make two more leaves a little larger. Cut them out. Cut each leaf in half the long way.

3. Glue the larger leaves onto the black construction paper as shown. Glue the smaller leaves on top of them.

4. Write the word Hââââ! with the bright marker underneath.

5. Cover the notebook cover with clear contact paper, if you'd like.

6. Every time you use your binder, give yourself a big "Hââââ!"

Tecumseh's Alliance

After the American Revolution, thousands of land-hungry American intruders flooded onto tribal lands in the Midwest. The Menominee, Ojibway, Potawatomi, Winnebago, and other Indian nations joined Shawnee leader Tecumseh's alliance that resisted the American advance into the region. An alliance is an agreement, made between two or more nations, to cooperate.

Born near present-day Springfield, Ohio, Tecumseh (circa 1768–1813) had an extremely difficult childhood. He was only six when his father was killed by white settlers who had squatted illegally on Shawnee lands. His mentor, Cornstalk, was a great Shawnee leader who was also murdered by settlers. Later, two of his brothers were killed in battles against the United States. Tecumseh saw destruction and death all around him. His life and the lives of all he knew had been changed forever, and Tecumseh vowed to defend the rights of Indian peoples.

As a very young teenager, Tecumseh had fought with the British in the Revolutionary War against the American colonists who had been so destructive to the Shawnee. After the war, he continued to protect Shawnee homelands against the Americans greedy for land. Some Native people were tricked into selling lands they did not personally own to Americans. Others were greedy and sold these lands for personal gain. Tecumseh advocated that Native people owned the land together and that no one person or group of individuals could sell it without the consent of the entire community.

He traveled far and wide to organize a confederacy among different tribes as a way to protect Indian lands, peoples, and culture. He and more than 1,000 of his followers joined the British Army in the War of 1812 against the United States. Because of his great military skill, Tecumseh served as a brigadier general, and he helped capture 2,500 American soldiers. He earned a reputation for treating his prisoners with dignity and tolerance.

On November 7, 1811, a U.S. force under the command of future President William Henry Harrison wiped out Prophetstown (also called Tippecanoe), which served as Tecumseh's headquarters. This attack put an end to Tecumseh's hope of a broad Native alliance. He was killed at the Battle of Thames on October 5, 1813. Tecumseh had spent much of his life building his confederacy, but it dissolved after his death.

After the alliance fell apart, the Potawatomi, Ojibway, Winnebago, and other tribes fought with the British against the Americans in the War of 1812. The war was a defeat for the Great Lakes tribes. More and more white farmers, loggers, and merchants moved onto lands once occupied only by Indian people. The U.S. government wanted the tribes to give up some of their lands so these non-Indians could live there. The Menominee nation, however, was able to keep much of its land in the Great Lakes area because the land was swampy. Few white farmers wanted to live there.

The first treaties signed by the Potawatomi following the war made peace and forgave past grievances. Eventually, however, the tribe was persuaded to give up land in exchange for sums of money. The Shawnee in Ohio tried to stay neutral during the war and were able to remain on their lands until 1831. The Winnebago made peace with the Americans in St. Louis in 1816. Their first treaty with the United States did not involve giving up land and called upon both sides to forgive and forget injuries suffered during the War of 1812. In 1819 and 1820, the U.S. government urged some Ojibway groups in Michigan to give up land where they presently lived and move to land nearby. The government promised them silver, farming utensils, and cattle for signing the treaties.

Indian Removal

The growing population of the United States needed more land. The solution was "Indian Removal," a 19th-century policy of the U.S. government that aimed to relocate all Ameri-can Indian tribes living east of the Mississippi River to lands west of the river. Between 1825 and the early 1850s, the U.S. government subjected over two dozen Native groups in the Midwest to the removal policy. Government agents pressured Indian leaders of these groups to make treaties that required them to give up their lands and move west of the Mississippi River. In the northernmost parts of Michigan and Wisconsin, people living in Ojibway, Menominee, and Potawatomi villages refused to budge. These small, independent communities rejected all U.S. government efforts to move them. Their lives were dependent on the streams and lakes where they had built their villages and fished. They lived among trees, plants, and animals that provided all the essentials they needed. The U.S. government did not force Indian groups out of the region, so they continue to live in their homelands today.

To the south, tribes in Illinois, Indiana, and Ohio did not succeed in keeping their lands. The Shawnee, Wyandot, Kickapoo, and Sauk were directly in the path of large numbers of American farmers, merchants, and developers who wanted their rich farmlands. Sometimes there were violent conflicts between Natives and non-Natives over environmental resources. With a few exceptions, most Indian nations in the southern Midwest were powerless. They were forced by the U.S. government to sign treaties, and then they were pushed west.

Sauk and Fox

Outright military force was used to make the Sauk and Fox move. They had lived for generations in southern Wisconsin and northwestern Illinois, growing crops of corn and squash and also hunting. Americans had been inching their way onto Sauk and Fox lands since the early 1800s, which led to conflict. In 1831 Sauk leaders made a treaty "ceding" (giving up) tribal lands. They agreed to move to Iowa. But the government did not supply enough food to make up for the crops the Sauk and Fox would not be able to harvest before moving. Black Hawk, a well-respected Sauk leader, needed food for his people. In 1832 Black Hawk's group returned to its former planting grounds in Illinois. When the people refused to abandon the land, the Illinois governor sent federal and state troops to push Black Hawk back across the Mississippi River, using force. Black Hawk tried to surrender but because there was no interpreter to translate Black Hawk's language, negotiations failed. In a 15-week war that bears his name, U.S. troops killed hundreds of unarmed Sauk people. Black Hawk was captured, and the Sauk nation was forced to give up more land.

In 1989 the Wisconsin State Assembly apologized to descendants of the Sauk and Fox Nation for the war and for the massacre of an estimated 1,250 Sauk and Fox people. The assembly admitted that the campaign against Black Hawk's people was marked by "blunders, violence against noncombatants, and other improper conduct by troops."

RAY A. YOUNG BEAR, MESKWAKI (1950–)

Raised on the Meskwaki (meh-SQUAK-ee), also known as Fox, Tribal Settlement in central Iowa, Young Bear's first language was Meskwaki. He first composed poetry in his Native language and then translated it into English. Although a famous publishing company wanted to print his first book, it took him a long time to get the courage to allow it to be published. Because his poetry is so different from conventional poetry and doesn't follow poetry rules, he was afraid that he would be harshly criticized. However, today he has several published books of poetry, including *The Rock Island Hiking Club* and *The Invisible Musician*. Young Bear follows the wishes of his grandmother, who urged him to "preserve and collect the language of the Meskwaki," and he considers himself to be her messenger. He and his wife are the founders of the world-traveled Black Eagle Child, a performance troupe that presents Meskwaki culture to audiences around the world. Young Bear attended several colleges and is a visiting professor at the University of Iowa.

Compose a Poem in Ray Young Bear's Style

Young Bear's poetry is a mix of tradition, history, and dreams, and it incorporates all five senses (sight, hearing, taste, smell, and touch). Many of his poems have no punctuation or capital letters. They move from the present to long ago in a couple of lines. Here is one of his poems. You might want to read more in one of his many books before you try your hand at this different style.

"Grandmother"

by Ray A. Young Bear

if i were to see
her shape from a mile away
i'd know so quickly
that it would be her.
the purple scarf
and the plastic
shopping bag.
if i felt

hands on my head
i'd know that those
were her hands
warm and damp
with the smell of roots.
if i heard
a voice
coming from
a rock
i'd know
and her words
would flow inside me
like the light
of someone
stirring ashes
from a sleeping fire
at night.

Write down the name of a person in your life who is very important to you or whom you admire. Now remember a dream you've had, and write it down. Recall and write down a recent happening in your life. Now use each of your five senses—sight, sound, smell, touch, and taste—as you write your poem. Include the person you admire, the dream, and the event in your life. Take a deep breath and start writing. Don't worry about spelling, commas, or periods. Just blend the past, present, and your dreams together to create your poem.

Red Wing and the Early Movie Industry

Many Winnebago were forced to leave their homes in Wisconsin and were placed by government troops on South Dakota reservations. However, many fled to Nebraska, which the U.S. government accepted. Although the Winnebago are not originally from the Plains, today there is a Winnebago Reservation in Nebraska. One famous Winnebago born on Nebraska's Winnebago Reservation is Red Wing (1883–1974).

Red Wing graduated from the Carlisle Indian Industrial School in Carlisle, Pennsylvania, in 1902. Sometimes called Princess Red Wing, she was the first Native American actress, and she became one of the most popular silent screen stars of the early 20th century. She and her husband, actor and director James Young Deer, made up the first American Indian "power couple" in Hollywood. In 1909, she starred in *Red Wing's Gratitude*, which was directed by Young Deer. She went on to star in several more films directed by a variety of famous Hollywood directors, including Cecil B. DeMille.

THE MESKWAKI ELEMENTARY SCHOOL

Wikiups are domed, single-room homes used by a number of Native American tribes. The Meskwaki Elementary School is on the Meskwaki Indian Reservation, almost in the middle of Iowa, and is patterned after these ancient Meskwaki (Fox) dwellings. Sunlight streaming in from floor-to-ceiling windows provides natural heat, which makes this building good for the environment. Meskwaki designs are found in the school's carpets and tiles. Children study their traditional Meskwaki culture along with math and English in this beautiful building.

Although the movies portrayed Indian people in a racist and stereotypical way, Red Wing's work was highly acclaimed. Red Wing was in great demand, as she was beautiful, outgoing, and extremely talented. Unlike most actresses of her time, she often performed her own stunts, like riding horses at breakneck speed and getting trapped in fires. Red Wing's acting career ended in the 1920s, and she became an advocate for Native American rights until her death in New York City.

Movies about American Indians often do not portray a realistic view of Native cultures and peoples. Native people are often shown as being mean, stupid, or bloodthirsty. The vast differences among Native tribes are not shown. The "Hollywood Indian" usually has been depicted as a Sioux chief with a feathered headdress. He is always riding a horse and he lives in a tipi. He speaks in broken English, and he is only seen as good if he helps white people. The story lines of most films treat Indians as if they are in the way of "progress" and as if they are foreigners in their own country. Frequently, the actors portraying Indians aren't even Native American.

This unrealistic and unfair view of Native life helped shape the incorrect image that non-Indians have of Indian people. Today, there are many more Indian actors including Graham Greene, Tantoo Cardinal, and Adam Beach. There are Native filmmakers and writers, including Sherman Alexie and Thomas King. You can see some films made about or by Native peoples: *Tales of Wonder*; *Edge of America*; *Letter from an Apache*, *The Hand Drum*, *Good Looking*, and *Children of the Long-Beaked Bird*. These movies can give people a better view of what life is really like for Native people. However, the film industry still makes it hard for Native directors, actors, writers, and stories to make it to the big screen.

Termination

In the 1950s, most of the U.S. Congress wanted to abolish tribal governments and reservations without the consent of Indian groups. The U.S. government wanted to eliminate the financial support of Indian programs guaranteed by treaties. It wanted to shift the financial costs to the states. The government wanted to save the money it spent on Indian education, health care, housing assistance, and other social programs for Indian people. This harsh policy was called "termination." Indian opposition was substantial, but it didn't help.

Between 1954 and 1966, Congress passed laws ending the government's relationship with more than 100 tribes and bands, with little concern for the well-being of the groups or for fulfilling the government's legal obligations to the treaties. The Menominee of Wisconsin was the first tribe to lose its reservation. This tribe and other groups simply stopped existing in the eyes of the government. Termination also involved a federal policy called relocation. The government encouraged Native people to leave reservations and move to cities.

One reason termination caused panic among Indian peoples was that tribes would no longer receive federal funds to finance basic services. Money the government gave to Indian tribes was like the funds that all local and state governments received from the federal government to build roads, schools, and electric and water utility plants. Tribes did not have the necessary money to support these services, and the funding tribes received from state governments after termination was too small to take care of their overwhelming health, housing, and education needs.

Congress saw that termination did not lead to tribes becoming self-sufficient. Terminated tribes could not govern properly because they lacked money to pay for police, judges, road repairs, programs for elders, and other government services. Many of the tribes terminated under the policy were restored to their original status as federally recognized tribes by Congress.

ADA E. DEER, MENOMINEE (1935–)

Ada E. Deer's motto in life is "one person can make a difference." In the 1970s she led her own Menominee Nation in its struggle to regain rights and land. Largely because of her efforts, the government admitted its mistake and reversed termination. A federal law restored the government's special relationship with the tribe. It took many years to undo the damage done by termination, but after a long struggle, the Menominee Reservation was restored in 1975. For making a difference, Deer has been honored by the Girl Scouts of the USA, the White Buffalo District Council, and the University of Wisconsin. Raised on the Menominee Indian Reservation in northeastern Wisconsin, Deer was the first woman to head the U.S. Bureau of Indian Affairs, a federal agency, and she has helped many Indian nations.

☀ Menominee Traditional Account: The Origin of Night and Day

This is the way it is told. One time Rabbit was walking through the forest. He saw Owl perched on a branch, but only glimmers of light were coming through the tree. It was almost dark, and Rabbit could not see very well.

Rabbit asked Owl, "Why do you like it dark? I don't like it to be dark, so I will make the daylight." Owl said, "If you think you are strong enough, then do it. Let's have a contest to see who is strong enough to change it to light or dark, and whoever wins can have it the way that he likes."

Rabbit and Owl called all the animals and birds together. Some wanted Rabbit to win so that there would always be light. Others liked the dark and wanted Owl to win. Rabbit would keep repeating, "Light, light" while Owl would keep repeating, "Night, night," until one of them made a mistake and said the opponent's word.

The contest began. Over and over, Rabbit said, "Light, light," while Owl kept repeating, "Night, night." The birds and animals rooted for their heroes. Finally, Owl accidentally repeated Rabbit's word "light" and lost the contest.

Rabbit decided that it should be light, but he also reasoned that there should be night, too. That way, Owl and the animals and birds he represented would also benefit. Everyone was happy.

JACOBUS FRANCISCUS "JIM" THORPE, SAUK AND FOX NATION/POTAWATOMI/ KICKAPOO (1888–1953)

Jim Thorpe's Indian name, Wa-Tho-Huk, translates to "Bright Path." And his life was indeed a bright path, full of glory that led him far from his Oklahoma birthplace. He was an all-around athlete and excelled in many different sports. After Thorpe won Olympic gold medals in the pentathlon and decathlon in 1912 in Stockholm, Sweden, he played professional football, baseball, and basketball. In 1912 New York City honored him with a ticker tape parade; he went on to play football for the New York Giants. He was named "the greatest athlete of the 20th century" by ESPN in 2000.

Stage a Puppet Show

The Menominee account of the "Origin of Night and Day" can be acted out with finger puppets. You can stage a show all by yourself or with a friend. Each finger of a glove will represent one character in your puppet play. Four fingers will be used to represent the sun (light), the moon (dark), an owl, and a rabbit. Other animals are in the story, too. You can choose whichever animals are your favorites to be the other characters so that you have 10 altogether.

What You Need

Pen

10 small squares of different-colored felt

Scissors

Pair of old gloves

Tacky craft glue

Decorations (such as feathers, squiggly eyes, buttons, fabric markers, and sequins)

What You Do

1. Use the pen to draw each character on the felt. Cut out each one, and make sure the characters fit on the glove fingers.

2. Lay out each glove palm side up and glue one character onto each finger. Decorate them with feathers, squiggly eyes, buttons, fabric markers, or sequins. Let them dry.

3. Turn the gloves over so the palm side is down. Imagine that you are looking at the backs of the owl, rabbit, sun, and other characters. Decorate the backs. Let dry.

5. Put on the gloves. Now you have all the characters in the story on your fingers! Act out the play for your family or friends.

❖ 5 ❖
Plains

Rapid City, South Dakota, has basketball fever! The Lakota (lah-KOE-tah) Nation invites both Indian and non-Indian youth teams from all over to compete in the Lakota Nation Invitational held every year. Thousands of spectators root for their teams, but basketball is not the only game featured in this popular tournament. Hopeful athletes also compete in volleyball, wrestling, boxing, cross-country running, and cheerleading. One of the biggest events is the hand game competition, which is based on a traditional Lakota gambling game. Played with skill, lots of gesturing, and a drum rhythm, one game can last over an hour. Elementary and high school students study all year to vie for prizes in the Language and Knowledge Bowls, too. Teams have to answer history, cur-

rent events, or math questions in the Lakota language. To make the Lakota National Invitational really beautiful, student artwork from different reservations is on display, keeping the Plains tradition of art and beauty alive.

The Great Plains

Many First Nations peoples make their homes in the Great Plains, including the Arapaho (Ah-RAP-ah-hoe), Blackfeet, Cheyenne (shy-ANN), Comanche (ka-MAN-shee), Crow, Kiowa, Omaha, Osage (OH-sage), and Pawnee. It is also home to the Lakota, who are also called Sioux (sue).

The region is huge. It stretches from the Canadian north all the way down to Texas and from the Mississippi River to the Rocky Mountains. Most of this area is a prairie of

Map of Selected Native Nations
of the Plains Today

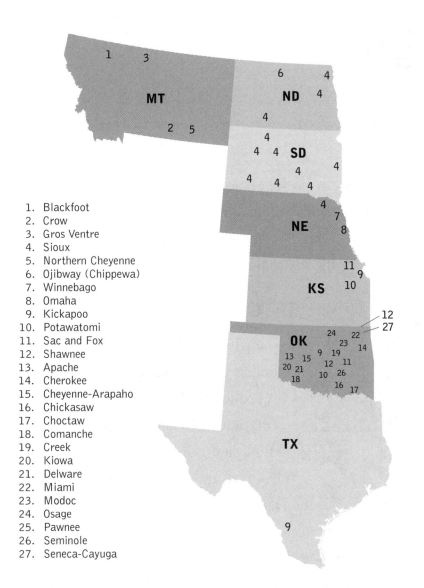

1. Blackfoot
2. Crow
3. Gros Ventre
4. Sioux
5. Northern Cheyenne
6. Ojibway (Chippewa)
7. Winnebago
8. Omaha
9. Kickapoo
10. Potawatomi
11. Sac and Fox
12. Shawnee
13. Apache
14. Cherokee
15. Cheyenne-Arapaho
16. Chickasaw
17. Choctaw
18. Comanche
19. Creek
20. Kiowa
21. Delware
22. Miami
23. Modoc
24. Osage
25. Pawnee
26. Seminole
27. Seneca-Cayuga

rolling hills and tough grasses. It has hot summers and bitterly cold winters. The region includes an extensive grassland spread over parts of North Dakota, South Dakota, Montana, Wyoming, Colorado, Nebraska, Kansas, Oklahoma, New Mexico, and Texas.

Plains Indians

Even though many Native groups are labeled "Plains Indians," they are not all the same. They practiced different religions and they spoke different languages. In order to communicate with one another, Plains people developed a language based on hand signs.

Some people resided in permanent farming communities. Others preferred a mobile lifestyle, and they transported their tipis over vast areas. Depending on its size, as few as 6 or as many as 28 buffalo skins were sewn together to make a tipi covering. Men hunted the animals, and the skins were prepared by the women. They sewed the skins together, set up the tipis, and took them down. The men cut trees into poles for the tipis. The houses were owned by the women, and they decorated and furnished them.

Before acquiring horses, families used dogs to pull "travois" (trah-VOYZ), which held their folded tipis. A travois is a type of cart without wheels. It is shaped like a big A and it is made of poles and leather.

Plains Indians acquired their first horses through trade or by capturing them from other Native people. Horses had returned to North America by way of Spanish ships in the 1500s. They had mysteriously disappeared from North and South America thousands of years before. By the early 1800s, almost every Plains Indian family owned a few horses. These animals transformed buffalo hunting. Instead of hunting them on foot, riders on horseback could easily keep up with fast-paced buffalo. And horses could carry at least four times the load of dogs.

The American Bison

Long ago, the western part of the Plains looked like an enormous field of grass, which was perfect food for huge herds of bison, known as buffalo, that once made their home there. There is no way to know exactly how many buffalo roamed the Plains, but scholars believe that, between 1800 and 1895, the buffalo population fell from an estimated 60 million to fewer than 1,000.

The movement of the huge herds of buffalo molded the American landscape. Their thousands of heavy hooves created permanent trails. The animals had the ability to pick routes that avoided big snowdrifts in the winter and muddy, mucky flatlands in the summer. They had large appetites, and their constant grazing kept forests from springing up and allowed

THE ANIMAL WE CALL A BUFFALO

The animal we call a buffalo is not really a buffalo. It is the American bison, and it is related to the cow, though it is much larger. It's the largest land animal in North America. True buffalo are found in southeastern Asia.

the grassland to flourish and benefit other animals, such as prairie dogs. A long time ago, the buffalo lived in the eastern United States, too, and many eastern Native nations have stories and dances that tell of their relationship with the animals. Today, many of our highways across the country follow the same routes as the great buffalo migrations.

At one time, the Lakota, Comanche, Cheyenne, and other Plains groups followed the migration of the gigantic herds. The buffalo provided almost everything these people needed to live, from food to clothing to tools. Since the buffalo had already blazed the trail, traveling was much easier. The

Natives respected and honored the buffalo. The animal was thanked for giving its life so the people could live. This huge animal was their main source of tasty, nourishing, year-round food. Infants were given choice pieces of meat to suck as were given elders who had no teeth.

Plains women turned bison skin into clothing that was wearable art. They used quillwork to make beautiful designs. Later, when they traded for glass beads, they created some of the world's finest beaded clothing and footwear. They also made bags, boxes, and trunks from buffalo hide. They painted designs on them made from vegetable dyes.

Buffalo provided countless household objects and other necessities of life. Plains communities, like other Native communities, practiced "multiuse conservation." That means that nothing is ever thrown away or discarded unless absolutely necessary. The buffalo grew a heavier, warmer coat in winter, and the people used this thicker hide to make tipi covers, robes, shirts, mittens, caps, moccasins, and bedding. It took a lot of time and effort to prepare the hides for use. The process included scraping off the flesh and sometimes making the hide soft by "tanning" it. Tanning is a method of turning skins into leather by steeping them in a chemical solution. Boats, luggage, snowshoes, saddles, bridles, and baby carriers called cradleboards were made from untanned rawhide. Its waterproof qualities made it the perfect material for "parfleche"

SAY "BUFFALO" IN DIFFERENT LANGUAGES

On the Great Plains, people spoke many different languages. To be able to communicate with people from other nations, they developed a sign language. Below are a few ways of saying *buffalo*.

Arapaho: *heneecee* (he-NAH-chaa)
Blackfoot: *iiníí* (ee-NEE)
Crow: *bishée* (be-SHAH)
Dakota: *tatanka* (tah-TAN-kah)
Pawnee: *táraha'* (tuh-RAH-huh)
Sign: Put one fist on each side of your head with your palms facing your head. Raise your index fingers so they look like horns of the buffalo.

(rawhide) containers people used to store food, clothing, and camp equipment. Bison stomachs were preserved to serve as water buckets or as cooking pots. Contents were cooked by adding heated rocks to water. Bladders carried food and water. Hoofs were cooked to make glue. Horns were turned into cups and spoons. Loose hair was used to stuff dolls and balls for children, and braided hair could be used to make belts. Bones were made into tools, knives, and sleds, and teeth were made into necklaces. Tails made good flyswatters, and buffalo chips (dried dung) were used as fuel.

Whole villages followed buffalo herds over the grassy plains. The journeys of Plains communities were not random or wandering. They plotted their movements based on the sun's path, star constellations, and the migration of the buffalo herds. Religious rituals were also part of this complex plan. The Lakota observed ceremonies in the South Dakota Black Hills, called Paha Sapa by them, which Native people still consider sacred ground. They also believe that humans should only visit the area for ceremonies; the rest of the time, it should only be a place for animals and plants.

Emigrants on Indian Lands

During the mid-1800s, increasing numbers of white explorers, fur traders, emigrants, squatters, homesteaders, and gold miners moved onto Native homelands without the consent of the people. Throngs of emigrants drove off the buffalo and other wild animals. The livestock they brought carried diseases that sickened and killed buffalo. The expansion of the railroads was involved in the slaughter of the buffalo. During the building of the railroads, buffalo were killed for food to feed the workers. After the railroads were built, buffalo were killed because they sometimes pushed the trains off the tracks. During the winter of 1872–73, hide hunters killed 1.5 million buffalo. The hides were sent on trains to the eastern United States to be sold. The bulky robes were popular as a covering during cold weather, and the hides were also made into leather goods. The bones were sold for use in making china and fertilizer. Train companies offered trips to the West, and tourists and professional hunters were told to shoot as many

FRIENDLY ENCOUNTERS

Many Hollywood movies show Native people attacking wagon trains of emigrants moving west. Diaries and other written records kept by some travelers crossing the Great Plains between the 1840s and the 1860s tell a different story. The emigrants described how much they were helped by different Native nations with food and other supplies and how trade between them was friendly. Plains people were hired by the travelers to herd livestock, act as guides, or help them cross rivers.

buffalo as they could from open train windows for sport. The sports hunters left the animals to rot, not even using the meat or skins. Farmers and ranchers who lived on the Plains also had a hand in destroying the herds, as they shot buffalo grazing on land that their livestock needed. All these actions shrank the buffalo herds.

From the 1860s to the 1880s, throughout the southern and northern Plains, the Arapaho, Cheyenne, Comanche, Kiowa, and Lakota fought hard to save their way of life. Without buffalo, Indian people no longer had food, shelter, and other supplies they needed. U.S. soldiers, well equipped with rifles and ammunition, were led by officers who attacked the Natives during the winter, when their food supplies were low and their horses were weak from hunger. It is estimated that, between 1865 and 1890, Indians of the Great Plains defended their homelands against the U.S. government in hundreds of battles.

Ledger Art

There is a long tradition of Plains Indian art. For hundreds of years, Native people throughout the Great Plains drew or painted pictures on rock walls and boulders, hides, tipis, and robes. These images recorded important events for future generations.

During the second half of the 1800s, many Indian men were forced into military prisons. They were given used lined notebooks, called ledger books, from U.S. soldiers, traders, mis-sionaries, and reservation employees. They drew on the pages with colored pencils, crayons, watercolors, and black ink. The artists depicted Plains Indian traditional life—a life that was rapidly dissappearing because of contact with non-Indians. Drawings show tipi villages, gorgeous clothing, buffalo hunts, games, and religious ceremonies. Artists paid lots of attention to horses, drawing them with small heads, arched necks, extended legs, and beautifully detailed horse gear. Numerous drawings show the heroic military accomplishments of individual Indian warriors battling Indian enemies or U.S. soldiers. Many drawings show warriors "counting coup," which was the act of touching their enemies with coup sticks on the head without killing or wounding them. Indian artists also recorded unfamiliar things like trains, sailboats, bridges, lighthouses, churches, and lines of U.S. soldiers in uniform. Often the art reflected the sadness and homesickness the artists felt.

Ledger drawings tell a great deal about historic events impacting Plains people. Today, many of these valuable images from the late 1800s hang in museums and art galleries. Their style has inspired many Indian artists today. They use ledger-like images in their paintings to recall what life was like for Indians living on the Great Plains over 125 years ago. They also use the technique to highlight issues of today's Indian people.

Draw in Ledger Art Style

Ledger art style refers to a style that emphasizes simple images of animals, people, or other objects spaced across the lined pages. The images seem "flattened out," as if someone laid a heavy book on them. Sometimes artists line up images vertically; other artists line them up horizontally. Some artists clump figures together. Sometimes the animals or people look funny or sad.

What You Need

Used lined notebook paper
Colored pencils, crayons, or watercolor paints
Paintbrush (if using paint)
Black ink

What You Do

1. Think of something familiar in your home. It could be a family member, a pet, or a special toy in your room. Draw this person, animal, or another figure in a flat style on the used page. If you draw an animal, show all four legs stretched out.

2. Repeat the image, vertically or horizontally, in rows across the paper.

3. Using colored pencils, crayons, or watercolors, add bright color to the figures.

4. Add details to figures with black ink.

5. You can frame your ledger art or put the paper in a binder, adding more pages of art as you get inspired.

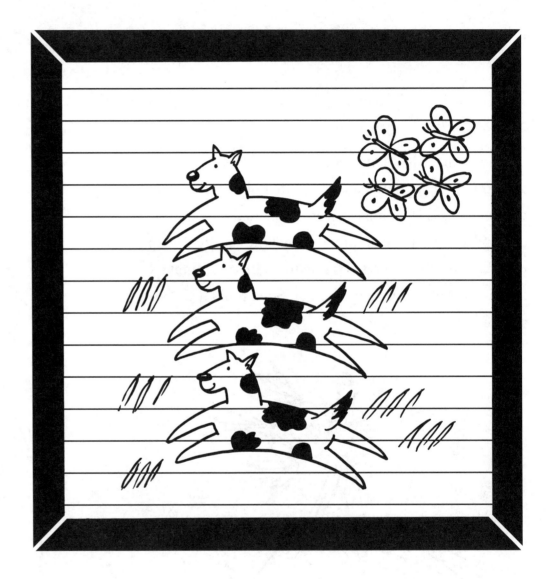

DWAYNE WILCOX, LAKOTA (1957–)

Raised on the Oglala (oh-GLAH-la) Pine Ridge Reservation in South Dakota, Dwayne Wilcox is an award-winning artist. He attended a one-room school house, where his artistic talent was first discovered. Wilcox's teacher and parents encouraged him to do artwork, but supplies were scarce in their poor community. So he did what his ancestors did some 100 years before and began to draw on used paper, his school notes, and homework. Whether he is poking fun at history, presenting great feats of bravery, depicting tragic events, or portraying modern times, Wilcox's ledger art masterpieces feature the funny and serious side of Indian life. He operates the Dog Hat Studio in Rapid City, South Dakota. You can see some of his art at his Web site, www.doghatstudio.com.

Big Foot and the Wounded Knee Massacre

Big Foot (circa 1820–1890), a Minniconjou (Mini-KO-ju) Lakota Sioux, grew up at time when the culture of the Plains people was changing forever. The buffalo herds that had sustained the people had been cruelly reduced in size by white hunters, farmers, and others. The cycles of life that Big Foot's ancestors lived for centuries were destroyed in just a few short years. The Lakota, like most other Indian nations, were forced onto reservations. These tiny pockets of land were all that was left of Big Foot's homelands. The Lakota were not free to conduct their business and lead their lives in their own way.

From his early years, Big Foot was recognized as a skillful negotiator and diplomat. He settled disputes among rival groups, avoiding war whenever possible. Big Foot realized that, to survive, his people must adapt to this form of captivity known as reservation life. He was the first on South Dakota's present-day Cheyenne River Reservation to raise a corn crop, though farming had never been the main way of life for his people. He traveled to Washington, D.C., to lobby for a reservation school. He advised his community to hold on to its culture and religion.

By 1890, conditions on the reservation had deteriorated. People were dying of starvation because their buffalo were almost gone and their crops had failed. The government had ordered that the Sioux could no longer hunt game, but beef rations provided by the government were cut down and unusually late in being delivered. The government also made it against the law for the Lakota to practice their religion or even wear their traditional clothing.

Many of Big Foot's community began to follow Wovoka, a Paiute Indian from Nevada who was a spiritual leader. Wovoka spread the word that if the people observed certain religious practices, the buffalo would return and the white people would disappear, leaving a peaceful world for the Lakota. Many non-Indians were afraid of this message because they thought the Ghost Dance would lead to an uprising against them. National newspapers made the situation worse by making up stories about the Lakota that frightened the non-Indians. These false reports caused panic in the area. U.S. military leaders banned the Ghost Dance in early fall 1890 and threatened to cut off rations to people who continued to participate. In late November the U.S. government moved nearly half its troops to the Pine Ridge Reservation. The government sent Lakota police to bring in Sitting Bull, the famous leader who supported the new religion. He was killed during his arrest.

When Chief Big Foot heard about the killing, he and his followers headed south to the Pine Ridge Reservation to join Chief Red Cloud. Big Foot had no intention of fighting. He wanted to avoid a battle with the soldiers because they outnumbered the Indian people and had better weapons. He was seeking safety for his people. On the journey, in the dead of winter, he fell ill with pneumonia.

In late December 1890, the Seventh Cavalry intercepted Big Foot's band. The starving, frozen group of Lakota, who surrendered peacefully, was forced to a site near Wounded Knee Creek, in present-day South Dakota. A scuffle broke out and, suddenly, the American soldiers fired on the unarmed Lakota. Big Foot and an estimated 300 Indian people, mostly women and children, were murdered. Sixty soldiers were killed and wounded by their own bullets as they fired at the Indians from opposite sides. The bodies of the Indian people who died were buried together in a ditch. Known as the "Wounded Knee Massacre," the horrifying event was one of the worse mass murders in United States history.

Since 1986 the Lakota and other Native people have remembered the tragedy each year by retracing Big Foot's route to Wounded Knee, where there is now a National Historic Landmark.

Maria Tallchief, Osage (1925–)

Maria Tallchief is a world-renowned ballerina and one of the "premiere" (top-ranking) American ballerinas of all time. Maria Tallchief's grandfather helped negotiate a treaty for Osage mineral rights. When oil was discovered on Osage land, the tribe became the wealthiest in the country. The Tallchief family had the funds to give their daughters piano and ballet lessons. They moved to Beverly Hills, California, so their daughters could have more opportunities to learn dance and music. By the age of 12, Tallchief was studying with the famous Russian teacher Madame Nijinska. At 15 she danced a solo performance at the Hollywood Bowl.

After graduating from high school, Tallchief moved to New York City to join the Ballet Russe de Monte Carlo, a highly acclaimed Russian ballet troupe. The company did not give her the credit she deserved and urged her to change her name to one that sounded less Native, but she refused to give up her Osage heritage.

When the world-famous George Balanchine became the troupe's director, he recognized Tallchief's amazing talent. In 1947 she became the first "prima" (lead) ballerina of the newly formed New York City Ballet directed by Balanchine. She was the star dancer until she retired 18 years later. She went on to found the Chicago City Ballet. She served as the artistic director of that company through 1987.

During her exciting career, Maria Tallchief earned many honors and much praise. She was the first American dancer to hold the title of prima ballerina, the first American to perform with the Paris Opera Ballet, and the first to perform in Russia. She was the first to dance the role of the Sugarplum Fairy in Balanchine's version of *The Nutcracker*, and she received Kennedy Center Honors. She was appointed Woman of the Year by President Eisenhower in 1953, inducted into the National Women's Hall of Fame in 1996, and presented with a National Medal of Arts by the National Endowment for the Arts in 1999.

Before Maria Tallchief's success as a ballerina, American dance was considered inferior to European ballet. Maria Tallchief's performances in *Orpheus*, *The Firebird*, *Swan Lake*, and *The Nutcracker* raised ballet to an important art form in the United States, rivaling performances on European stages.

WIND ENERGY

A wind turbine supplies power to the Rosebud Casino on the Rosebud Sioux Reservation in South Dakota. Soon an entire wind farm will be built on the reservation, supplying clean and renewable energy. The winds on the South Dakota plains are some of the strongest in the world.

Plains Reservations Today

During the 1870s, U.S. Army operations forced Plains Indians to move to small portions of their lands, called reservations. Today, these reservations are communities where people live, work, go to school, play, and attend ceremonies and social events. On special occasions, like powwows, festivals, and religious ceremonies, tipis are set up. Community programs sponsor activities for kids to horseback ride, bowl, swim, run, make crafts, and play in midnight basketball tournaments during the summer. Some communities raise buffalo while others are restoring the vanishing prairie ecosystem. Many people live in cities, such as Cheyenne, Wyoming, and Rapid City, South Dakota. Others have traveled far and wide as educators, artists, and dancers.

Tribes, zoos, and Indian stewardship programs have brought back buffalo herds, saving them from extinction. Thanks to the work of the InterTribal Bison Cooperative, an organization of more than 50 tribes that was founded in 1990, the buffalo have grown in numbers and returned to Plains Indian reservations. Supermarkets now carry buffalo meat, which is much healthier than beef.

BILLY MILLS, LAKOTA (1938–)

Billy Mills, born on the Pine Ridge (Lakota) Reservation in South Dakota, won the gold medal in the 10,000-meter race at the 1964 Olympic Games in Tokyo, Japan. To date, no other American has won a gold medal in that event. Mills is the spokesman for the Running Strong for American Indian Youth Foundation.

TRY A GROS VENTRE—INSPIRED HANDS GAME

Games of chance in which an opponent has to guess which hand an object is hidden have always been popular with American Indians. On the Great Plains, people gathered in tipis on bitterly cold winter days to play games that could last for many hours, or even all night. The Gros Ventre people of North Central Montana are fond of playing this particular game. Long ago, they used to play it almost daily.

What You Need

Black marker

2 chicken thigh bones, cleaned and dried

2, 4, 6, 8, or more players (must be an even amount)

Watch or timer

10 sticks

What You Do

1. Use the marker to draw a ring around one of the bones.

2. Divide players into two teams. Sit in two lines so that each person is sitting across from a member of the other team.

3. Agree upon how long the game should last. Then the timekeeper will call start. The first player on one side holds a bone in each hand, moving each one back and forth from one hand to the other, sometimes behind the back. While switching the bones back and forth between hands, sing a song while swaying your body, arms, and hands to confuse the guesser. You can make up your own song or sing one that you already know.

4. When the song ends, the person opposite the player with the bones guesses which hand holds the marked bone. If the guesser is correct, he or she takes a stick and gets control of the bones. If the guesser is incorrect, the bones are passed to a player on the same team.

5. The game ends when all the sticks are gone or the time is up. The side that has the most sticks wins the game.

JANINE PEASE-PRETTY ON TOP, CROW (1949–)

Janine Pease-Pretty on Top, who comes from the Crow Nation in Montana, transformed the tiny Crow tribal college into a fully accredited junior college. Today, many classes there are taught in the Crow language. Ms. Pease-Pretty on Top was the first Crow woman to earn a doctorate degree, and she received a Genius Award from the MacArthur Foundation.

VIRGINIA DRIVING HAWK SNEVE, LAKOTA (1933–)

While growing up on the Rosebud Sioux Reservation in South Dakota, Virginia Sneve always felt there was a special place for Indian people. As a teacher and counselor, she became concerned about the untruths about Indians her own children were learning in books.

The Gros Ventre

In historical times, Gros Ventre (grow VAWNT) were joined with the Arapaho, but they became an independent body in the late 1600s. The women kept gardens of corn, beans, and squash while the men hunted. However, when they acquired horses, the community culture changed. People farmed less and depended more on the buffalo, like other nations in the Great Plains area. Gros Ventre means "big belly" in French. Some say the French called them that because they enjoyed eating; others say that the French did not understand Gros Ventre sign language and misunderstood a gesture made by a Gros Ventre man. However, they call themselves A'ane or A'aninin, which means "white clay people." Today, the Gros Ventre share the Montana Fort Belknap Indian Reservation with the Assiniboine.

She decided to become an author so all children would have the opportunity to learn about real Indian cultures and peoples. Sneve has written more than 20 books, including, "Grandpa Was a Cowboy and an Indian" and Other Stories. In 2000 President Clinton presented her with the National Humanities Medal.

Lakota Giveaways

The Lakota people, like many different Native groups, hold social events called "giveaways." A giveaway honors a special time of life, like a wedding, birth, return home from the military, or graduation. Besides honoring a person's achievements, a giveaway is a way of thanking people for their support and help during times of illness or loss of a loved one.

The family holding the giveaway can spend months making gifts so that each person, from the very young to the very old, receives a thoughtful present. Lakota women often take a year or more to make their famous star quilts to give away. The entire community is invited to the event. Sometimes the family doesn't even know some of the people who come, but they are given presents, too.

Generosity is a traditional Lakota value. To share possessions is more important than holding onto them. A giveaway teaches children about sharing. Generosity shown at a giveaway is not about giving something away in order to get something back. It is about saying thanks for all of one's blessings.

KIM LaFLAMME, BLACKFOOT/ MI'KMAQ (1948–)

As a second grader, Kim LaFlamme took his Indian Dog to school for a report on Indian Dogs and the Native people who developed the breed. His teacher told the class that Indians weren't smart enough to be dog breeders, and his family demanded an apology from the school board for the teacher's harsh words. In seventh grade, he had a kind teacher who encouraged him to contact different reservations to find out if they had any of the famous dogs. He sent out letters and learned that, like his own grandparents, many elders had managed to save some of the animals. Today, LaFlamme has helped save the Indian Dog from extinction and is a recognized breeder. He is very careful to make sure the dogs have good, loving homes, and he also trains them to help handicapped children. LaFlamme's Indian name is "The Dog Man."

Make a Giveaway Book

You can give away "good deeds" by being helpful to neighbors, classmates, family members or other people in your community. Try giving without expecting praise in return.

What You Need

Pencil

Several sheets of construction paper or other colored paper

Ruler, if desired

Scissors

2 6-inch squares of poster board or cardboard

Fine-tip markers in different colors

Hole punch

24-inch piece of yarn or string

What You Do

1. On the scrap paper, write down names of people you would like to honor. Next to each name, write down what you would like to do for that person. You will use this list as a guide when you create your giveaway book pages. Here are some examples:

   neighbor Mrs. Smith: mow her lawn

   brother Jason: make his bed

   teacher Mr. Gomez: clean the blackboard

   Mom: help prepare dinner

   cousin Jennifer: read her a story.

2. Divide a sheet of construction or other colored paper in 4 equal sections. You can use a ruler to do this or you can just fold the paper in half, then fold it in half again and cut the paper on the folder lines. Now you have four pages for your giveaway book. Use more sheets of paper to create more pages for your book.

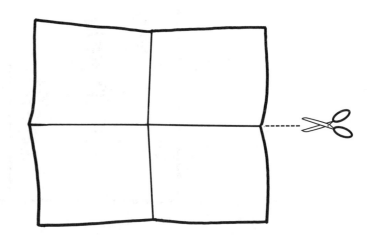

3. On each page, draw a vertical line 2 inches in from the left side of the page. In the section to the left of the line, use the markers to write down the name of one of the people on your list and the good deed that you will do for him or her. In the section to the left of the line, use the markers to write down the name of one of the people on your list and the good deed as if you were speaking to that person. ("I will mow your lawn." "I will help you make dinner." "I will read you a story.") If you want, you can draw a picture there, too.

4. Use the markers to draw pictures or designs, such as a star quilt design, on one of the pieces of poster board or ccardboard. This will be the cover ofyour book. Write "My Giveaway Book" on it

5. Place all of the pages between the two pieces of poster board or cardboard (the "back cover" and the "front cover" of the book). Carefully punch three holes through the covers and the pages, about 1 inch from the left sides. Thread the yarn or string through the holes and tie it to hold your book together.

6. Explain to each person that you are honoring him or her by giving away a good deed and some of your time. Cut or carefully tear the right-hand section of the page that shows the good deed you will do for him or her. Give that section to the person, and keep the left section of the page in your book to remind yourself of the good deed you have done or have promised to do in the future.

American Indian Dogs

At one time, there were hundreds of thousands of dogs in the Great Plains area. Different nations, such as the Lakota, were known throughout North America as excellent dog breeders, and they traded dogs to other communities in many different regions. Indian Dogs were bred to be loyal, intelligent, and sensitive. Not only were they family pets, but they also hunted, herded, guarded, carried packs, and were sometimes babysitters. They hauled tipis and household goods on travois. These medium-sized, hardworking dogs were respected and loved members of the community. But by the 1900s there were hardly any left. Thanks to Kim LaFlamme's efforts, the dogs are making a strong comeback. However, some breeders mate dogs with wolves or coyotes, creating a hybrid that is not a domesticated animal and gives wolves a bad name.

Cook Wojapi Pudding

Wojapi (wo-ZHA-pee) is a traditional Lakota pudding made with huckleberries or chokecherries. You can use blueberries, raspberries, blackberries, and strawberries. It tastes good warm or cool.

What You Need

Adult supervision required

2 pounds of berries (such as blueberries, raspberries, blackberries, or strawberries)

1 tablespoon of honey (or more to taste)

1 cup of water

Saucepan

Spoon

½ cup flour

What You Do

1. Put the berries, honey, and water in the sauccpan. Mash them together with a spoon.
2. Stir in the flour a little at a time.
3. Bring to a boil over medium high heat.
4. Lower the heat and simmer, stirring constantly until pudding becomes thick.
5. Remove the saucepan from the heat and let the pudding cool.
6. Serve as a dessert or for breakfast with granola.

Indian Cowboys

Indian cowboys can be found from the "pampas" (grasslands) of Argentina to the grasslands of Alberta, Canada. Native people have long been considered some of the best horseback riders in the world. The phrase "cowboys and Indians" is incorrect, as many, many Indian people were cowboys in the past and are today. In historical times, Comanche soldiers were famous for being able to stay mounted on their galloping horses while firing arrows. Not only were Plains Indian excellent riders, but they also were famous for breeding hardy, healthy "Indian Ponies," including the Medicine Hat and War Bonnet breeds.

After the U.S. government confined Plains peoples to reservations throughout the western states, many found work on ranches, where their skill with horses was needed. Others traveled with "Wild West" shows, like those owned by Buffalo Bill Cody. They thrilled audiences with their daredevil tricks performed at breakneck speeds. A trick rider could hold on with just one hand and swing his body over the side of a galloping horse or do a handstand on the back of a fast-moving horse. Eventually, some Indians were invited to compete in rodeos because of their remarkable horseback riding abilities.

Today, Indian cowboys and cowgirls participate in rodeos all over North America as well as compete in the Indian Rodeo circuit. Events include bareback riding, saddle bronc riding, calf roping, and barrel racing. Native people decided to form their own rodeo associations to combat the racism they experienced in the regular rodeos. Indian rodeos are sometimes part of Native festivals such as the annual Crow Fair.

TOM REEVES, LAKOTA (1965–)

The horse bucked high trying to throw the rider, but Tom Reeves held on to become the 2001 Professional Rodeo Cowboys Association (PRCA) World Saddle Bronc Champion. The State of South Dakota issued a proclamation in honor of this veteran professional cowboy from the Cheyenne River Sioux community. Inducted into the PRCA Hall of Fame, Reeves was also chosen as captain of Team USA in the 2002 Olympic Command Performance Rodeo. He serves as the rodeo coach at Ranger College in Texas.

HOLD A BIKE RODEO

A bike rodeo is a good way to hold a bicycle safety clinic so that kids can learn bike safety and bicycle safety rules. Organizations like the Kiwanis Clubs, League of American Bicyclists, and Cooperative Extension programs work with communities to sponsor the events. Sometimes bicycle shops are happy to arrange a rodeo. You can organize your friends and some friendly adults into a committee to contact one of the groups mentioned here and invite it to hold a Bike Rodeo in your neighborhood, or you can hold your own.

What You Need

Adult Supervision Required
Bikes
Helmets
Friends
Judges
Whistle

Large area, like an empty parking lot or playground, with no traffic (get permission first)
Chalk
Large objects in use in a barrel racing course

What You Do

1. Safety Check Station: Have an adult check all the rodeo riders for bikes in good repair and proper helmets.
2. Zigzag: Make a zigzag course by drawing two chalk lines about 3 feet apart to make a 30-foot path. Each time a wheel touches the line, one point is deducted.
3. Slowest Race: Lay out a course in a loop that brings riders back to the start. Two riders compete at a time to see who can be the *slowest*.
4. Barrel Racing: Arrange objects, like tires, bricks, and traffic cones, in a crazy pattern and race around the course. Deduct one point each time the rider touches a "barrel."
5. Balance Beam: Draw one center line and two smaller lines on either side, each 6 inches from the center line. Ride the course down and back, trying to stay on the center line. One deduction is made each time a tire touches a side line.
6. Bike Parade: Participants can decorate their bikes and hold a parade. Include tricycle and bikes with training wheels so everyone can participate.

Make Saddle Fenders for Your Bike

Saddle fenders are long vertical pieces of leather that lay underneath a horse rider's legs to protect him or her from the horse's sweat. They come in all sizes and shapes. Some are fancy, and some are plain. Plains people painted designs on their saddle fenders with earth pigments. Sometimes they added beadwork or other decorations to them.

Make sure you use real chamois, not the synthetic "chamois" that is made with microfiber.

What You Need

Pencil

Newspaper

Scissors

Chamois (available at hardware, automotive, and crafts stores)

Paintbrushes

Acrylic paint

Self-stick Velcro

What You Do

1. Using the pencil, make a pattern on the newspaper and cut it out. You can use the shape shown in the illustration or create your own—make it squared or rounded. Make sure it will hang down over either side of your bicycle seat, but don't make it so long that it interferes with your movement, the pedals, or the bike chain.

2. Lay the pattern on top of the chamois and cut out.

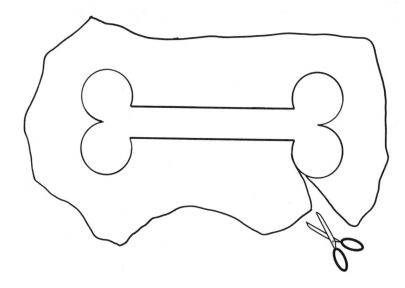

4. Following the directions on the Velcro strip, attach it to the fenders. Make sure the strip is long enough to wrap around the bike seat. Fasten the fenders to the seat.

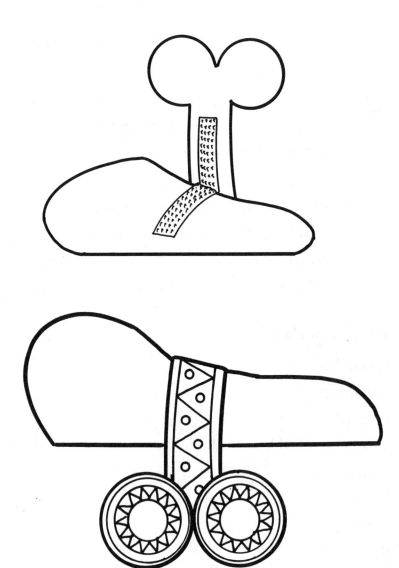

3. Paint on designs of your choice and let dry. Many Plains designs are geometric. You can make squares, circles, rectangles, or triangles.

◈ **6** ◈

Great Basin and Plateau

A dizzying array of colorful spots and striped hooves lets everyone know the Appaloosa horses are on the trail. Every summer, kids in the Nez Perce (NEZ purse) Young Horsemen Project saddle up their beloved Appaloosas and join others on the Nez Perce National Historic Trail, a mountainous stretch of almost 2,000 miles. Not only do they learn to ride and care for the famous breed developed by their Nez Perce ancestors, but they also learn about Nez Perce history. The Nez Perce Historic Trail marks the 1877 site where Chief Joseph and 700 Nez Perce people and their horses tried to escape the advancing U.S. Army.

The Great Basin

Many Native groups have lived in the Great Basin area for thousands of years. Much of the region is made up of moun-tains, canyons, and sandy deserts. The Great Basin is in the shape of a gigantic bowl that is surrounded by jagged moun-tains. The land inside the bowl contains many hot, dry, nar-row valleys divided by high ridges. The region includes present-day Utah and Nevada and parts of the adjoining states of California, Colorado, Idaho, Oregon, and Wyoming. This huge area is very dry and hot in the summer, with temperatures reaching 140°F. It's bit-terly cold in the winter. It rarely rains, so there is not much plant life and growing crops is difficult. For over 10,000 years, Native people figured out how to survive in this challenging environment.

Long ago, Great Basin dwellers broke into smaller groups in the summer and camped by small lakes and ponds, where there was more water. People traveled mostly on foot. If a

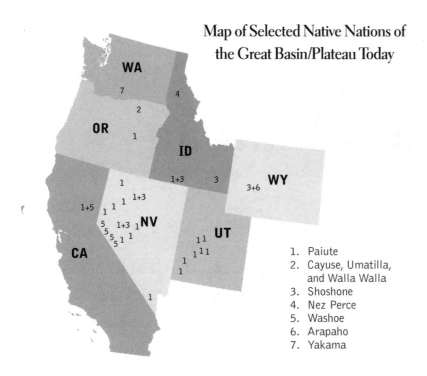

Map of Selected Native Nations of the Great Basin/Plateau Today

1. Paiute
2. Cayuse, Umatilla, and Walla Walla
3. Shoshone
4. Nez Perce
5. Washoe
6. Arapaho
7. Yakama

hunter spotted an antelope, he had to be skillful to catch it. An antelope can run 60 miles an hour. Food often consisted of jackrabbits, antelopes, lizards, sagebrush, reeds, and cactus. In the fall, they gathered in large groups to help each other harvest pine nuts. Pine nut gathering was a time of ceremony, songs, visiting with friends and relatives, and, of course, harvesting the nuts. Today, the best pine nuts still grow on American Indian lands.

The Plateau

North of the Great Basin area, the land grows higher, forming the Plateau region in what are now Washington, parts of Oregon, Idaho, and Montana. The area is bordered on the east by the Rocky Mountains and on the west by the Cascade Mountains. The high-level Plateau lands are a patchwork of trees, mountains, canyons, and steep gorges. Unlike the Great Basin, the hilly region provides reliable sources of food and water. There is a variety of plant foods and deer, elk, and other game. The region's numerous rivers and streams provide fish, especially salmon.

The Washoe Tribe of Nevada

The history of the Washoe (WAH-shoe) Tribe of Nevada extends back 9,000 years. The traditional Washoe people centered their lives around the four seasons. Small groups of extended families gathered at Lake Tahoe in the spring and summer to fish, hunt, and gather plants. In the fall they harvested pine nuts. During the winter, people settled into communities, where they made baskets, repaired tools, and caught up with their friends and relatives. This serene lifestyle was altered by non-Native miners and ranchers who were attracted to the resources of the Washoe's valleys. The intruders fenced the land for cattle and restricted the Washoe's access to Lake Tahoe, pine nut groves, and plant foods. By the 1870s, the Washoe's food sources were depleted. The Washoe were forced to live on the outskirts of the new non-Native towns, where some found employment. Thanks to the emergence of new tribal leadership during the end of the 20th century, the Washoe people have a renewed sense of hope today. Since 1978, the Washoe Hunting and Fishing Commission has managed the conservation of wildlife and other natural resources and regulated hunting and fishing. The Washoe Tribe is developing business opportunities for its members, as well as an alternate energy program involving wind generators, and is marketing arts and crafts. The tribe helps its members by providing computer camps for high school seniors, tutoring students, and offering college scholarships. Elders are helped by nutrition programs.

The Umatilla

The Umatilla (OOM-ah-TIL-la) have lived in the Columbia River region of Oregon for more than 10,000 years. Elk, one of the largest species of deer in the world and one of the largest mammals in North America, were plentiful in this area. Elk have been an important part of Umatilla and other Native cultures for thousands of years. They have helped Indian people survive throughout the centuries by providing a source of meat. Elk also have been used for making clothing and sacred objects like drums. Elk remain part of traditional religious ceremonies, and the Umatilla continue to hunt elk for food.

DAT SO LA LEE, WASHOE (circa 1835–1925)

Dat So La Lee (who was also known as Dabuda and as Louisa Keyser) was born around 1835 in Nevada. She grew up in a traditional way, and, like other Washoe women, she became a skilled "botanist" (a person who has scientific knowledge of plants). She knew when and where to harvest the natural materials needed to make weaving threads. She wove large baskets that stored seeds and nuts, scoop-shaped baskets that separated grain, baskets that held water, baskets that became cradles, and basket nets that caught fish. In 1895 Dabuda met Abe and Amy Cohn, who owned a dry goods store in Carson City, Nevada. The Cohns, impressed by Dabuda's basket-weaving skills, offered her the opportunity to become a full-time artist. The Cohns built Dabuda and her husband a home next to theirs and paid for their food, fuel, clothing, and medical expenses. The arrangement lasted until Dabuda's death. In return, the Cohns owned every basket Dat So La Lee made and controlled most of her life. When customers bought a basket, the Cohns' bill of sale included Dabuda's handprint and information about how she made that basket. When Dat So La Lee died, she was one of the most famous basket weavers in the world. In 1925 her baskets sold for $5,000, which would be almost $60,000 today.

Play Washoe Stone Jacks

Long ago, when Washoe people were not harvesting plants, hunting, or fishing for food, they often played games. Here is one of their favorite games, which is still played today.

What You Need

1- or 2-pound bag of aquarium river rocks or
  aquarium gemstones
4 to 5 players
Open area

What You Do

1. Each player chooses one special stone that he or she likes. That will be each player's "tossing stone." The remaining stones are put in a pile on the ground.

2. The first player tosses his or her tossing stone straight up in the air. While the stone is in the air, he or she tries to pick up one stone from the pile.

3. If the player picks up a stone from the pile and catches the tossed stone before it reaches the ground, the player keeps the one from the pile and takes another turn.

4. If the player drops either the tossing stone or the stone he or she picks up, it becomes the next player's turn.

5. When all the stones are gone, the game is over. The player with the most stones wins.

Construct an Umatilla-Inspired Pouch

The elk became a popular animal figure on Umatilla beaded bags. Umatilla beadworkers were especially skilled at representing the magnificent antlers of elk. Make a pouch with an elk design. It is a handy bag to store keys, money, or a handheld video game.

What You Need

Plain paper

Pencil

4-inch piece of lightweight brown felt

Scissors

Beading needle (available at craft stores)

Beading string (available at craft stores)

#10 beads (available at craft stores)

5-inch by 12-inch medium weight felt,
  any color but brown

Needle and thread

Fabric glue

3 piece of heavy yarn or jewelry cording,
  any color, at least 12 inches long

What You Do

1. Using the pencil and paper, practice drawing an elk head (see illustration). When you are happy with your design, draw the elk head on the felt and cut it out.

2. Thread the beading needle with the beading string and tie a knot. Start at the back of the felt, bring the needle up through the felt so that it comes up through the elk's antlers. String one to three beads onto the needle and let them slide down to the felt. Push the needle back through the felt. Repeat as many times as you want to, following the outline of the elk's antlers and head. When you are finished, tie several knots in the beading string at the back of the felt. Set this aside.

3. Fold the 5-inch by 12-inch heavyweight felt rectangle with shorter sides together. With needle and thread, sew

3 sides together ¼ inch from edge, leaving one long side open for the top of your pouch. You do not have to stitch folded side, but it will look nicer if you do. Turn it inside out so the stitches will not show.

4. Glue on your beaded elk.

5. Braid together 3 lengths of yarn to make a strap and sew the ends to each side of pouch.

The Shoshone

The Shoshone (show-SHOW-nee) lived in the present-day states of California, Idaho, Nevada, Utah, and Wyoming, but most settled in what is now Idaho. Groups of Northern Shoshone lived like people did in the Plains. After they acquired horses, they hunted buffalo for food and hides. Groups in Nevada and Utah moved to particular areas to harvest and gather berries, seeds, watercress, clover, and roots of camas. They matched their movements to the growing seasons. They also hunted bighorn sheep and antelope in the Utah hills. Salmon was a favorite food of groups who set up fishing camps at the mouths of rivers.

Sacajawea and the Lewis and Clark Expedition

Sacajawea, a Shoshone teenager, and her "husband," Toussaint Charbonneau, were hired by the Corps of Discovery, an exploratory team led by Meriwether Lewis and William Clark. President Thomas Jefferson had picked Meriwether Lewis to lead an exploratory expedition of the northern part of the lands gained in the Louisiana Territory, purchased from France in 1803. Sacajawea was the only female on the historic expedition that explored the Louisiana Purchase, which doubled the size of the United States and stretched west to the Pacific Ocean. Besides interpreting languages of other tribes, she acted as a go-between with Indian groups who were suspicious of the crew of men. Lewis and Clark's expedition of over 30 people crossed Indian-owned lands west of the Mississippi River in search of a water pathway the Pacific Ocean. In 1805 and 1806, First Nations peoples living in present-day Montana, Idaho, Washington, and Oregon encountered Lewis and Clark, who were amazed at the kindness and hospitality of the First Nations people. However, that kindness was not returned by the Americans and Europeans. The expedition to the Plateau region set the stage for the stream of people who invaded the homelands of several Native nations.

Sacajawea had been kidnapped by Hidatsa Indians when she was around ten and taken to their upper Missouri village. She was eventually purchased, or won, by the French Canadian fur trader Charbonneau. In 1805 Meriwether Lewis and a small group of men from the expedition encountered Shoshone Indians along the Idaho–Montana border. It was discovered that the Shoshone chief, Cameahwait, who met with Lewis, was Sacagawea's brother. The Shoshone treated the group as guests, sharing what little food they had and providing the group with a tipi for their stay.

Shoshone Parfleche

Lewis saw many rawhide bags, trunks, and boxes of different shapes, called parfleche, piled up inside tipis. These containers held dried meats, dried fruits, or vegetables. Lewis wrote in his journal that the Shoshone stored dried roots in "many parchment hides of buffaloe." Some parfleche held fire-making equipment, while others stored clothes, blankets, or toys. Special bags contained sacred objects used in religious ceremonies. Parfleche was a necessity for people who were constantly on the move. The material was waterproof and unbreakable, even if people were rough with them.

Shoshone and other Indian women became experts, after years of experience handling hides, at making and decorating rawhide containers that stored family possessions. They passed on techniques to their daughters and granddaughters. In some tribes, girls were expected to do good rawhide work by the time they were 14 years old.

Women painted designs on the hide without making any preliminary sketches. They had to be certain about the pattern they wanted to paint. There was no erasing paint once it was put on the hide. They made stunning and complicated designs using ordinary shapes like squares, rectangles, triangles, diamonds, or circles. Shoshone women liked to paint straight lines. Other tribes preferred different designs. Blackfeet women, for example, favored curvy lines and dots. The designs the women used on the outside showed which Indian nation the artist came from and also indicated the contents stored inside. Different nations also added different numbers of holes to tie their containers. These holes, were like tribal autographs. Shoshone women burned in one pair of holes, while Blackfeet women burned in 14 pairs of holes.

Make a Shoshone-Inspired "Parfleche"

What You Need

Parfleche pattern (see next page)

Pencil

10-inch piece of light cream or white imitation
   leather (available at fabric store)

Paintbrush

3 colors of acrylic paints (do not use black)

Black marker

Scissors

Hole puncher

2 5-inch-long pieces of string or yarn

What You Do

1. Use a photocopier to enlarge the pattern on the next
   page to about 10 inches long. Trace it onto the
   imitation leather.

2. Using the paintbrush and paints, paint a design on the
   upper flaps of the parfleche. Use squares, rectangles,
   triangles, diamonds, or circles. Add dots or straight or
   curvy lines. Use the pattern on page 120 for inspiration.

3. Using the marker, in the upper flaps, outline parts of
   the design.

4. Cut out the parfleche.

5. Fold the parfleche along the dotted lines marked A. Then
   fold along the lines marked B.

6. Using the hole puncher, punch 2 holes in each of the
   upper flaps. Lace a piece of string or yarn through each
   set of holes. Tie the flaps together.

7. Put something special in your parfleche.

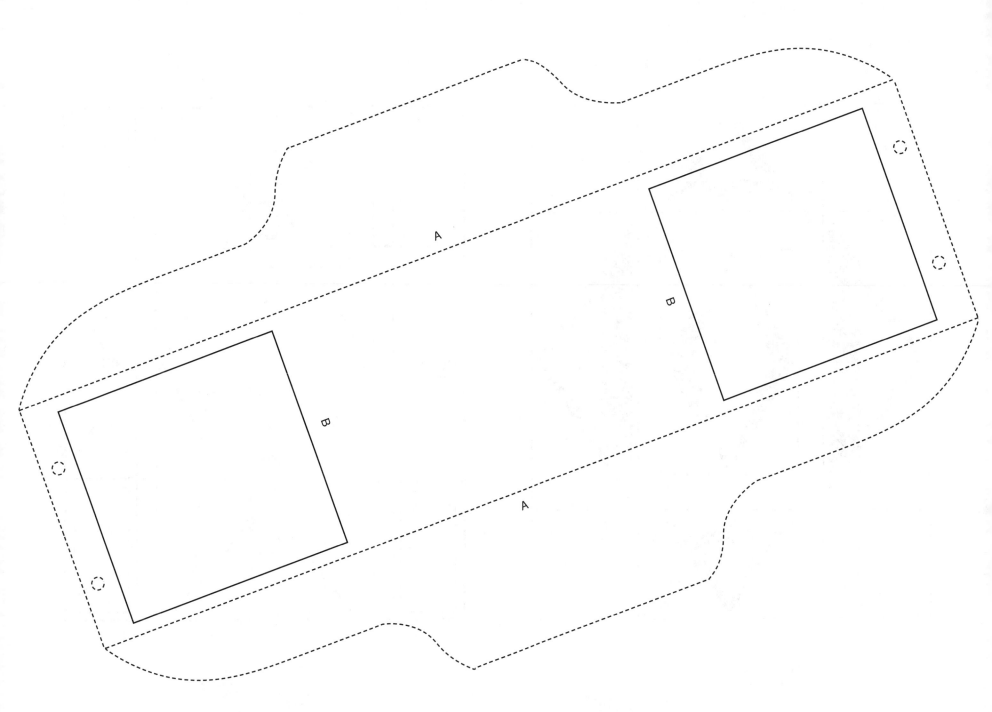

A

B

B

A

119

CORBIN HARNEY, WESTERN SHOSHONE (1920–2007)

A spiritual leader of the Western Shoshone, Harney spent his life teaching about the destruction of Native lands by nuclear bombing and nuclear waste dumping. The Western Shoshone homeland, called Newe Sogobia, in Nevada is considered the most atom-bombed place in the world. Over a thousand atomic bombs have been exploded at the Nevada Test Site by the U.S. military. Harney was not only concerned about First Nations lands and peoples—he fought hard all over the world to protect all people and the environment. Harney's efforts helped convince the Soviet Union to stop nuclear testing, and the Americans followed in 1992. Harney and friends created the Shundahai Network. "Shundahai" is a Western Shoshone word meaning "peace and harmony with all creation." The 2003 Nuclear-Free Future Award Solutions Recipient, Harney was recognized for his lifelong struggle to end the devastation caused by nuclear weapons. Elder Harney died of cancer, which may have been caused by radiation poisoning. Today, the Shundahai Network carries on his work.

Corbin Harney wanted all children to grow up in a healthy world free from environmental pollutants. He wanted the same for all of the earth's waters, lands, plants, animals, birds, and fish. As you eat your meals, think about where the food comes from. Was it grown in healthy soil free of chemicals? Was the water used to nourish it free of radiation and pollutants? If the soil and water are safe, our food will be nutritious and we will be healthy, too.

Create a Shundahai Collage

Human beings are part of nature, too. People often forget that and think that humans do not need the rest of the beings in the world. To keep our planet healthy, we have to live in *shundahai:* "peace and harmony with all creation." Help remember *shundahai* by putting yourself in the middle of a peace and harmony collage. A collage is an art form in which different materials are pasted next to or on top of each other over a surface.

What You Need

8-inch-by-10-inch picture frame with glass or acrylic front

Pencil

2 or more sheets of construction paper

Scissors

Old magazines or newspaper

1 or more photographs of yourself, alone or with friends or family members

Glue

Colored markers

Dried flowers or leaves

What You Do

1. Take apart the picture frame so that the glass or acrylic front and the cardboard insert are separated from the frame. Place the cardboard insert on a piece of construction paper. Using the pencil, trace around the insert. Cut out the shape. Set the parts of the picture frame aside.

2. Think about things in nature that share your world, such as birds and other animals, rivers and lakes, and trees, flowers, and other plants. Find pictures of these in the magazines and newspapers. Cut them out and arrange them on top of the cut construction paper. Play around with your arrangement until you have a design that you like.

3. When you are happy with your design, glue each picture to the construction paper. Glue your photograph or photographs on top of the pictures.

4. Using the markers and another sheet of construction paper, write the work *Shundahai*. Cut it out and glue it onto your collage. If you want to, you can add other words that represent the theme, such as "flowers," "water," "sun," "children," and "stars." Let the glue dry.

5. Glue dried flowers or leaves onto your picture frame. Let the glue dry.

6. Put your collage in the picture frame and put the frame back together.

Honoring Elders

In Native cultures, elders and the wisdom they have are very important. In many Indian communities, the grandparents are responsible for passing on knowledge to the young people. They are often the only tribal members who speak the Native languages or know ancient customs. They are respected and consulted in decisions. Today, American Indian elders are being consulted by environmentalists of all backgrounds on matters of pollution, energy, and sustainable agriculture, which is a method of growing crops that also protects and preserves the environment for the future.

In traditional Indian communities, getting old is seen as just a part of the cycle of life. However, in the general American society, getting old is seen as something bad. People are afraid of growing old, and senior citizens are often mistreated

SARAH WINNEMUCCA, PAIUTE (1844–1891)

In her 1883 autobiography, Sarah Winnemucca, a Paiute (PIE-ute), described how her family was so terrified by the approach of white people that her mother buried her under a sagebrush. Years later, Winnemucca learned English and made friends with white people who supported Indian rights. She served as a translator, and she traveled to Washington, D.C., to argue for the rights of her people. Winnemucca started a school for Indian children in Nevada. There they could learn their own language and heritage. Unable to get government funding, she had to close the school after four years. Winnemucca published a book in English in 1883. It is called *Life Among the Piutes: Their Wrongs and Claims*.

and discriminated against. Even today's Indian kids are not always as respectful to their elders, as Indian ideas have been influenced by American culture.

Many of the people written about in this book are elders and grandparents who have been important citizens of their communities. It is an honor to grow to old age and to have been lucky enough to live that long.

Honor a Grandparent

Compose an "acrostic" poem to honor your grandparent or another elder you admire. In an acrostic poem, the title is usually one word, like *Grandpa* or *Nana*. Each line begins with a letter of the selected word and describes the subject. Your lines can have just one word or several. They don't have to rhyme.

There are four words for grandparents in the Nez Perce language (and over 180 words for relatives!). The word for the grandmother on the mother's side of the family is *Kat'sa*. Here's an acrostic poem about Kat'sa.

K Kind
A Active
T Terrific
S Smart
A Awesome

What You Need

Pencil
Scrap paper
Colored pencils, pens, or fine-point markers
Pretty paper

What You Do

1. Write the word you call your grandparent (for example, Nana, Grandfather, Abuelo, Madea, Opa, or Pop-Pop) in a vertical line down a piece of scrap paper. Write a word for each letter. You can use a dictionary to look up words.
2. Copy the poem onto pretty paper. You can decorate it with drawings if you want to. Give it as a gift to your grandparent.

Indian Lands Invaded

In the 1820s and 1830s, American and British fur trappers and traders moved into Native territories of the Plateau and Great Basin areas. After the Oregon Trail, an overland route from the Missouri River to the Oregon Territory, was established around 1843, thousands of non-Native people traveled the road across Indian lands. Catholic and Protestant missionaries arrived in the 1840s and opened missions among the groups in the Plateau region. After gold was discovered in southern Oregon in the 1850s and in other parts of Oregon and Idaho in the 1860s, miners flooded the region. Ranchers, shopkeepers, farmers, and fortune seekers established settlements that crowded out First Nations' communities and increased pressure on Indians to give up their land. In addition, the newcomers brought diseases like measles, which spread among the Native people, killing many of them.

The Native people were willing to accommodate white settlers so they would not be forced from their homelands, as First Nations in other regions had been. However, an increasing number of forts and military roads began to appear, built to protect the traders, trappers, miners, and squatters who were overrunning Indian lands. More protection led to yet more non-Indians moving in. The newcomers who invaded traditional Indian homelands did not understand the ecosystem. They cut down trees along the trails and riverbanks in Indian territories, paying no heed to who owned the land. Their cattle ate all the grasses, causing animal habitats to disappear. They also wiped out the Indian people's food and medicine plants. Salmon began to vanish from streams that were dammed by mining operations. Soon, news of approaching wagon trains filled Native people with dread.

The Oregon Territory

Between the 1850s and 1860s, westbound wagon trains brought more and more non-Native immigrants from the east, which upset the traditional way of life for Indians in Oregon. In 1843 1,000 immigrants passed through north central Oregon. In 1847 there were 4,000. By 1852, up to 12,000 non-Native people were crossing homelands of the Indian tribes in Oregon each year. They were granted lands throughout the Oregon Territory without permission of the Native people already living there. The most desirable properties, along the rivers, were those most needed by the tribes for survival. In 1855 the superintendent of the Oregon Territory, Joel Palmer, received orders from the government to clear the Indians from their lands. He did this by negotiating a series of treaties with Indians tribes. They were forced to give up large portions of their land and move onto smaller reservations. The largest parcels of Native lands were opened to non-Native settlers.

The Washington Territory

In 1854 and 1855, the new Washington Territory governor, Isaac Stevens, organized several treaty councils with Indian groups. The governor read out the treaty terms in the Chinook jargon, allowed some comment, then invited the tribal representatives to put their names on the treaties. The result was that the Native peoples gave up most of their Washington lands in exchange for small reservations, schools, and livestock.

Stevens promised the Native people a period of two to three years to relocate. Twelve days after the Native leaders agreed to the deal, the governor declared Indian land open to settlement by non-Indians. Yakama (YAH-ka-ma) leader Kamiakin formed an alliance of 14 tribes to protect their lands against American immigrants and government officials. The struggles have been referred to as the Yakama Indian War of 1855. Toward the end of the war, in 1858, 500 Yakama and allied Indians set grass on fire in an attempt to prevent troops from evicting them from their homes. But the troops rode through the smoke, firing on the people until they gave up. Kamiakin, who was defeated in the final battle of the war in September 1858, refused to surrender and escaped to British Columbia, Canada. Eventually he moved back to his father's homeland in Washington, where he lived until his death.

The Nez Perce

The Nez Perce homeland included what is now central Idaho, southeastern Washington state, and northeastern Oregon. The people acquired horses in the early 1700s through trade with other tribes and rapidly became skilled horsemen and horse breeders. They developed the spotted breed of Appaloosa horses that became famous for their speed. They eventually had the largest horse herd in North America.

Meriwether Lewis and William Clark encountered the Nez Perce in the fall of 1805. According to one tradition, Lewis and Clark named the tribe Nez Perce, which means "pierced nose" in French. Only a few tribal members pierced their noses, but the name stuck. They call themselves Nimi'ipuu (nee-me-poo), meaning "the people."

In the journals of the Corps of Discovery, Lewis reported how the tribe provided the crew with shelter and meals of buffalo, dried salmon, and camas bread. In a February 1806 entry, he commented that Nez Perce "horses appear to be of an excellent race: they are lofty, elegantly formed, active, and durable." Lewis and Clark also recorded how peaceful and helpful the Nez Perce people were.

In the years following the Lewis and Clark expedition, fur traders and other French and British Canadians and Americans began arriving in the Nez Perce homeland. In 1863

American officials convinced some Nez Perce bands to sign an agreement giving up their lands. Some bands refused.

Chief Joseph and his followers refused to leave their ancestral homeland in northeastern Oregon and settle on a reservation in Idaho Territory. General Oliver Howard considered the Nez Perce refusal to leave an act of war. However, the Nez Perce stood their ground. The army declared war on them, which led to the Nez Perce War of 1877, one of the most famous stories in military history. Chief Joseph feared for the lives of his people. He fled, leading his small band over 1,700 miles in an effort to escape to Canada. U.S. troops captured them 40 miles from the Canadian border. After Chief Joseph surrendered, he was never permitted to return to his homeland. Government officials sent him to live in Kansas, then Indian Territory (present-day Oklahoma), and finally to a reservation in Washington State.

Today, some descendants of the Nez Perce live in Washington State. Many live and work on the Nez Perce Reservation in Idaho, and others work in cities like Boise and Seattle. Hattie Kaufman, a national news correspondent for *The Early Show*, was born on the Idaho Nez Perce Reservation. The tribe is bringing back the famous Appaloosa horses and reviving interest in the horse culture of the Nez Perce. The Nez Perce Young Horsemen Project helps youth learn the art of good horsemanship and how to manage the horse business.

ROSA YEAROUT, NEZ PERCE (1940–)

As owner of the M-Y Sweetwater Appaloosa Ranch on the Idaho Nez Perce Reservation, Rosa raises the famous Nez Perce Appaloosa horse breed. She is also a storyteller, keeping Nez Perce traditions alive. She always rides on the annual historic Chief Joseph Trail Ride. A few hundred riders, all on Appaloosas, ride part of the same mountainous route that the Nez Perce rode over a hundred years ago when they tried to escape to Canada. Rosa was an advisor for the American Girl Nez Perce doll, Kaya, as well as for the Kaya books. She is also the Whipwoman for the Chief Joseph and Warriors Powwow. A whipman or whipwoman keeps the dancers organized and makes sure that everything is done correctly in the dance arena at a powwow.

Design an Appaloosa Horse

Besides being the famous horse breed of the Nez Perce, the Appaloosa is also the state horse of Idaho. The most prized horses sometimes have spots in the shape of a handprint. See if your Appaloosa horse gives you an opening to tell your friends about the breed and the Nez Perce Nation.

What You Need

18-inch-by-45-inch piece of plain white, gray, brown, or rust-colored cotton fabric

Pencil

Straight pins

Scissors

Black fabric marker

Needle and thread

Black yarn

1 bag of pillow or stuffed-animal filling (available at crafts stores)

Bamboo skewer or knitting needle

What You Do

1. Fold the fabric in half the long way with the good side together.

2. Using the pencil, draw the outline of a horse, filling up as much of the fabric as you can. Draw the legs as if the horse just has two fat ones. Do not draw the mane or the tail.

3. Pin the fabric together and cut out the horse shape from both layers of the fabric.

4. Using the needle and thread, sew around the outside of the horse about ½ inch from the edge. Leave a 2-inch opening at the horse's rear, where the tail would go. Turn it inside out so the stitches are now on the inside of the horse.

5. Place your hand on the rump of the horse and trace around your fingers and palm *very lightly* with marker. If your hand is too big, just draw a smaller hand freestyle. Draw a line to separate the horse's legs. Appaloosas have striped hooves, so draw those lines too. Make a circle where eye should be, and draw on a mouth and ears. You can add more spots, anywhere except over the handprint or eye.

6. Cut 12 6-inch strands of yarn for the mane. Fold each strand in two. Poke your needle through one piece of yarn right at the fold. Then sew the strand between the horse's ears. Continue sewing the separate yarn strands down the back of the horse's neck.

7. Cut 10 12-inch strands of yarn for the horse's tail. Cut one strand that's about 2 inches long. Gather all the long strands together and tie them in the middle with the shorter strand.

8. Stuff the filling into the opening of the horse. Use the bamboo skewer or knitting needle to push the stuffing into nooks and crannies. Sew the opening closed. Poke the needle and thread through the folded part of the tail and sew it onto the rear of the horse. Tie a strong knot.

NATIVE SCIENTISTS TODAY

The American Indian Science and Engineering Society encourages math and science learning for elementary, high school, and college students. There are several Native people contributing to many different areas of science. Here are just a few.

- Dr. Robyn Hannigan (Narragansett) directs a geochemistry research laboratory called Water-Rock-Life at Arkansas State University.
- Dr. Ken Ridgway (Lenni-Lenape) studies the formation, interactions, and evolution of the earth's crust, biosphere, ocean, and atmosphere.
- Dr. Jason Cummings (Lumbee/Coharie) develops and implements new ways of creating computer chips and integrated circuits for advanced technology.
- Dr. Robin Kimmerer (Potawatomi) is a professor at the State University of New York in Syracuse, New York, and works with the Onondaga Nation to restore native plants, especially medicine plants.
- Dr. Robert Megginson (Lakota) is a professor at the University of Michigan and spends summers teaching Native high school students about the relationship between Native cultures and mathematics.
- Dr. Jerry Yakel (Luiseño) studies how the environment impacts health and human conditions at the National Institute of Environmental Health.
- Dr. Marigold Linton (Cahuilla/Cupeño) is a specialist in long-term memory at the University of Kansas and works with Haskell Indian Nations University.
- Dr. Dolly Garza (Haida/Tlingit) uses her university education and traditional ecological knowledge passed down through generations of Alaska Natives to protect her community.
- Dr. Healani Chang (Native Hawaiian) is a professor at the University of Hawaii, where she develops programs for Native Hawaiians to help them use cultural traditions to become healthy nonsmokers.

DEBORAH HARRY, PAIUTE

(Contemporary)

Deborah Harry, a Paiute activist from Nevada, is the executive director of the Indigenous People's Council on Biocolonialism. Some Native people have allowed scientists to study their blood or tissue samples so that cures for diseases can be found. However, sometimes the blood and tissue samples get used in ways that the person did not give permission for and does not believe in, like mixing samples from plants, people, and animals to make different life forms. This is called genetic engineering. Using a person's blood and tissues without his or her permission, especially to make profits, is called biocolonialism. Harry, like Corbin Harney, believes that there has to be balance in the world. Her organization helps Native people protect the original North American plants, animals, and organisms that are too small to be seen with the naked eye. She educates people about the dangers of changing or altering life forms and genetic engineering.

THE TAMÁSTSLIKT CULTURAL INSTITUTE

The Tamástslikt (tuh-MAHST-slicked) Cultural Institute, on the Oregon Trail in Pendleton, Oregon, is owned and operated by people now known as the Cayuse, Umatilla, and Walla Walla tribes. *Tamástslikt* means "to interpret" or "to turn something over and examine it." The three distinctive groups, who have lived together for 150 years, form an alliance called the Confederated Tribes of the Umatilla Indian Reservation. At Tamástslikt, kids get a real glimpse of the peoples' history. Horses rumbling across the grassy plateau, lessons on how to make ancient tools, and films of contemporary events help students realize the influence these Plateau peoples had on the country and the world.

7

Southwest

Golf balls fly into water hazards and fairway bunkers as Cochiti children play a game of golf on the pueblo's demanding 18-hole golf course. Under guidance of skilled golfers, the children learn to drive, chip, and putt. The world-class Pueblo de Cochiti golf course winds through the red-rock canyons of the pueblo, which lies amid the foothills of the Jemez Mountains in New Mexico.

Cochiti youth golf is a vital part of the local athletic program; Cochiti students dominate the high school golf team at Bernalillo High School. Pueblo elders observe that golf has helped nurture a more traditional life by encouraging children to walk in nature for their four-hour rounds. They also practice self-discipline and honesty,

which are key principles of this ancient game from Scotland. Golf has become more popular on reservations, especially among kids, thanks to famous golfers Tiger Woods and Notah Begay. Begay, who is Isleta Pueblo and Navajo, has sponsored countless golf clinics for American Indian junior golfers.

The Southwest has some of the most spectacular landscape in the United States: brightly colored deserts, rugged forested mountain ranges, the immense Grand Canyon, and flat-topped mesas. It covers vast spaces in Arizona and New Mexico, and small parts of southern California, Utah, and Colorado. Rainfall is sparse. Sometimes, rain disappears for several years during times of drought.

Map of Selected Native Nations of the Southwest Today

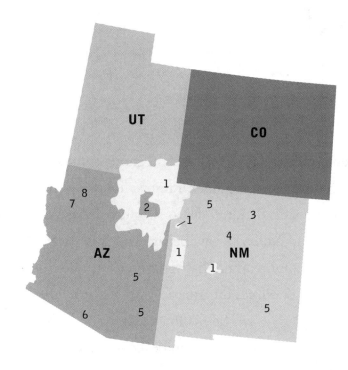

1. Navajo
2. Hopi Pueblo
3. Cochiti Pueblo
4. Isleta Pueblo
5. Apache
6. Tohono O'odham
7. Hualapai
8. Havasupai

The Pueblo Peoples of New Mexico and Arizona

Pueblo peoples made the dry, desert areas of present-day Arizona and New Mexico their homeland. This region contains the oldest continuously occupied settlements in North America. One of the main Hopi villages, Oraibi, in Arizona, is nearly 1,000 years old. Old Acoma, in New Mexico, has been inhabited for at least 800 years. It's also known as "Sky City" because it is built on top of a 365-foot sandstone mesa. A mesa is a high flat area with steep sides; it resembles a large table. In fact, the word "mesa" is Spanish for table.

New Mexico's Chaco Canyon was once the center of the ancient Native culture of the ancestors of today's Pueblo peoples. These ancient peoples farmed the desert lowlands in an area that has long winters with temperatures well below freezing, little rain, and a short growing season. They were master architects, constructing huge towns with large, multi-storied buildings and complex highway systems that connected almost a hundred communities.

Today, descendants of these ancient people live in the same location where the Europeans first saw them: in 19 separate pueblos in New Mexico and in Hopi villages sitting atop three mesas in northern Arizona. Pueblo people mastered irrigation in different forms throughout their history. In early times, farmers used floodwater farming. They planted corn, beans, and squash in the flat or nearly flat land near streams or rivers that flooded. Farmers also diverted excess water from rain or melted snow to the area where they planted crops. Later, Pueblo farmers used canals to bring much-needed water to their crops. They dug networks of ditches that diverted water from a river, bringing it close to their farmlands. Then it flowed through a network of smaller ditches. This allowed farmers to grow their crops without wasting precious water. Pueblo people farmed so successfully that, even in the bone-dry environment, large populations could live successfully in city-like villages.

Early Spanish explorers thought Pueblo people were all the same because they lived in compact villages of box-shaped, flat-roofed houses, often piled two, three, four, or more stories high. They called the earth-colored houses and the people who lived in them "pueblos," the Spanish word for "village." The name "Pueblo" has stuck even though Pueblo people speak several different languages and dialects and have been influenced in different ways by Spanish, Plains, and Apache Indian cultures.

Adobe Bricks

Long before the Spanish arrived in 1540 in what is now New Mexico, Pueblo people who lived in river valleys constructed homes from "adobe," or sun-dried bricks. Some ancient Pueblo sites show evidence that people used stone or wooden frames to make same-sized bricks. The Spanish may have contributed the idea of reinforcing bricks by adding straw to the adobe.

In hot, dry climates around the world (including the Southwest), where stone is not available, adobe is an ideal building material. It does not require wood, which tends to be scarce in desert regions. It does not harm the environment. Adobe bricks are made with readily available material, like tightly compacted earth, clay, and straw. Solar energy hardens the bricks, which become extremely sturdy. Bricks dry quickly under the hot Southwest sun. If a structure is demolished, the adobe can be recycled back into the earth because it's made of natural materials that decompose easily. Thick adobe walls keep the indoors cool in the summer. The thick walls store heat during the day and keep most of the heat from reaching the home's interior. In desert climates, the air temperature drops sharply at night. Then some of the daytime heat stored in the adobe walls helps keep rooms warm. Today Pueblo houses are made from ready-made materials, like concrete covered over with plaster or stucco.

The Pueblo People and Spanish Explorers

For hundreds of years, Pueblo people encountered different nations, not all of them friendly. In the late 1500s, when

Spanish explorers traveled into southwestern lands searching for wealth and slaves, they intruded permanently on Pueblo lands. By the early 1600s the Spanish outlawed Pueblo religion and sent missionaries to convert Native people to Catholicism. The people who resisted were arrested or enslaved. The Spanish used them as examples to others who tried to resist. The Spanish colonial system also allowed the missionaries to take a portion of every farmer's crops to feed themselves and the Spanish soldiers. In years with little rainfall, the Spanish demanded almost all the food the villages were able to grow. Many Pueblo people died from starvation. Still, many Pueblo people secretly held on to their religious beliefs.

In 1680 Pueblo religious leaders rose up against the Spanish government. They drove the Spanish out of Santa Fe, the capital of the Spanish territory (present-day New Mexico). They restored Pueblo traditional religion, which people had been forced to practice in secret. Pueblo warriors destroyed Spanish places of worship and killed 23 priests.

In 1692 the Spanish recaptured New Mexico. Governor Don Diego de Vargas sent soldiers and cannons to persuade Pueblo leaders to surrender. He cut off water and food supplies until the Pueblo people gave up. After the surrender, the king of Spain recognized Pueblo sovereignty and land rights and no longer outlawed Pueblo religion. Some Pueblo resisted the Spanish, but others cooperated with them. The Spanish were able to make an alliance with the Pueblo that lasted until the end of Spanish rule in 1821. Pueblo people were able to hold on to their traditional religious practices, which were combined with Catholic observances. Pueblo soldiers, interpreters, and scouts accompanied Spanish soldiers in military campaigns against neighboring Indian raiders. Due to the Spanish influence on architecture, Pueblo houses now have heavy wooden doors, porches, and enclosed patios.

The Pueblo Peoples and Mexican Independence

In 1821 Mexico declared its independence from Spain and took possession of Spanish lands, which included the Pueblo villages. The Mexican Congress stated that Europeans, Africans, and Indians were all citizens of the country whose property rights would be respected by the government. The Mexican government did not forbid Pueblo people from practicing their traditional life or religion. But corrupt Mexican officials falsified documents and transferred ownership of Pueblo land to Mexicans without their knowledge.

Between 1846 and 1848, the United States and Mexico went to war. By the war's end, Mexico lost nearly half of its territory, the present-day American Southwest from Texas to California. Pueblo lands and people became part of the United States.

CRAFT A PUEBLO-STYLE PENCIL HOLDER

Many artifacts have been discovered in the Southwest. Cylinder jars unique to this area show that the people preferred geometric shapes and designs. Make a Pueblo-style jar that holds pencils.

What You Need

Pencil

Ruler

Tissue paper (at least
   2 colors)

Scissors

Tall, clean clear glass jar

Paintbrush

Clear drying glue

Permanent markers

What You Do

1. Draw and cut out geometric designs of your choice from the tissue paper. Use at least two colors and make sure they will fit on the glass jar.

2. Using the paintbrush, cover the jar with glue. Gently place your designs on the jar.

3. Let the glue dry.

4. Using permanent markers, adorn your design with lines, dots, or more geometric shapes. Let dry.

5. Apply two or more coats of invisible glue so that your designs will protected. Let the glue dry between coats.

The Pueblo Peoples Today

No matter which nation—Spain, Mexico, or the United States—tried to control the Pueblo, they held on to their traditional ways and religious practices. They still live in the land of their ancestors. They speak their languages. They raise corn, which is central to their religious life. Religious societies still conduct sacred ceremonies that have been part of Pueblo culture for thousands of years. But like all cultures, many changes have occurred in Pueblo life. People today use electricity, computers, cell phones, satellite dishes, and automobiles, and they wear western-style clothing.

Storyteller Dolls

In 1964 Helen Cordero (1915–1994) from Cochiti Pueblo began a new tradition by making the first pottery storyteller doll as a tribute to her grandfather. A great storyteller at Cochiti, he always seemed to be surrounded by children. She made an eight-inch-high grandfather figure telling stories to five grandchildren, three perched on his shoulders and two sitting on his lap. Cordero painted open eyes on her grandfather storyteller, but after that she made countless figures with closed eyes and open mouths. She said, "His eyes are closed because he's thinking and his mouth is open because he's telling stories." Today, because of Cordero, hundreds of potters in New Mexico's pueblos create storyteller dolls in all shapes and sizes, including animal storytellers, with dozens of children attached to them.

LEWIS TEWANIMA, HOPI (1888–1969)

Lewis Tewanima, a gifted track star, is a legend to the Hopi Pueblo people. Although he trained as a long-distance runner for less than a year, he competed with the world's best runners in the 1908 Olympics held in London, England. He finished ninth (out of 58) in the 26.2-mile marathon. In 1909 he set the world record for running 10 miles indoors at New York's Madison Square Garden. In the 1912 Olympics held in Stockholm, Sweden, Tewanima received the silver medal in the 10,000-meter run, with a record of 32.06.6 minutes. Afterward, Tewanima returned home to herd sheep on Second Mesa, the Hopi lands of his ancestors in Arizona. Hopis have honored Tewanima's athletic feats by holding an annual race named after him every year on Labor Day.

Sculpt a Pueblo Storyteller Doll

Try making your own storyteller doll to honor someone in your life who tells great tales.

What You Need

Newspapers

12 ounces air-drying,
   self-hardening clay

Container of water

Tools to shape clay, such as pencils, sticks,
   and toothpicks

Paintbrushes

Acrylic paints

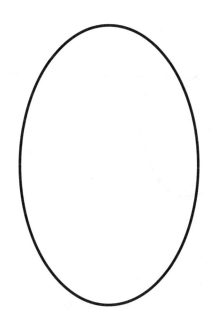

What You Do

1. Cover your work area with newspaper. Use some of the clay to make the body of the storyteller doll by forming a fat oval shape about 5 inches long and 3 inches wide. Pinch and squeeze out two arms and two legs from the body. Bend the legs as if the doll is sitting down.

2. Roll a ball of clay to make the head. Make a hole for the mouth and form a nose by pinching the clay. Firmly attach the head to the body and smooth the clay to make the head and body one piece. The doll does not have a neck.

139

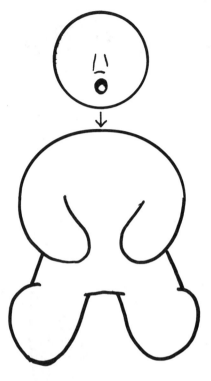

5. While your doll is drying, write a story. Pueblo people, like Christians, Jews, Muslims, and Hindus, have accounts to explain how the world was created or to teach people how to live in a good way. Other stories are just for fun. What do you believe is important for children to learn? Write a story that would teach children about something like safety tips, healthy eating, how not to get in fights, how to be safe, or how to be responsible.

6. Now write a funny story. Imagine your doll telling the stories. Practice on younger children or your brothers and sisters. Maybe you can entertain kids in your school's kindergarten, Brownie or Cub Scout troops, or neighborhood.

3. Form each child by rolling a small bit of clay into a little oval—the body, head, arms, and legs will be formed from one oval. Pull a bit up from the body to make a round head. You can pinch and pull arms and legs from the oval or just paint them on later. Put a toothpick in the bottom of each child and attach it by sticking the other end into the big body.

4. When the clay is completely dry, paint on faces and clothes. You can paint arms and legs on the children, too.

GERONIMO, CHIRICAHUA APACHE (1829–1909)

Apache chief Geronimo fought fiercely for his people's freedom with a handful of warriors. Between 1876 and 1885, he surrendered to U.S. federal agents several times, but he repeatedly escaped to Mexico. Eventually the army committed 5,000 soldiers, along with hundreds of scouts, to hunt for him.

Geronimo could not bear being confined on a reservation. He once said, "I was born on the prairies where the wind blew free. . . . I was born where there were no enclosures." In 1887 Geronimo surrendered for the last time and was sent to a military fort in Florida. Later he was imprisoned at Fort Sill in Oklahoma Territory. Geronimo wanted his story told. While imprisoned, he dictated the story of his life to an Apache interpreter. The interpreter translated his words to English for an Oklahoma schoolteacher, who wrote it down and turned it into a book. *Geronimo's Story of His Life*, was published in 1906. Geronimo provided descriptions of the origins and customs of his people. He remained bitter to the end of his life that he'd surrendered rather than fighting it out in the Mexican mountains.

ROAST A STUFFED PUMPKIN

This recipe combines some traditional Southwestern foods, like pumpkins, beans, and corn, with some other ingredients that are newer to the region.

What You Need

Adult supervision required

2 cups of salted water
Saucepan with lid
1 cup of brown or wild rice, rinsed and drained
4- to 5-pound sugar or baking pumpkin (don't use a jack-o'-lantern pumpkin)
3 tablespoons of vegetable oil
Large frying pan
1 medium onion, chopped
1 red pepper, chopped

1 cup of canned pinto, red, or black beans
1 cup of frozen or canned corn
1 8-ounce can of tomato sauce
1 tablespoon of chili powder
1 tablespoon of salt
1 tablespoon of black pepper
Large baking or roasting pan

What You Do

1. Place the salted water in the saucepan and bring it to a boil. Stir in the rice. Cover, reduce the heat to low, and simmer until the water is absorbed (40 to 50 minutes).
2. Preheat the overn to 350° F.
3. Ask an adult to cut off the top of the pumpkin. Set it aside. Remove the seeds and other "guts" of the pumpkin. (If you want to, you can clean and roast the pumpkin seeds to eat later.) Set the pumpkin aside.
4. Place the oil in the frying pan and heat over medium heat. Add the onion and bell pepper and, stirring occasionally,

cook them until they are soft (about 5 minutes). Add the cooked rice, beans, corn, tomato sauce, chili powder, salt, and pepper. Mix together and heat through.

5. Place about 1 inch of water in the baking or roasting pan. Place the empty pumpkin in the pan and fill it with the bean mixture. Cover it with the pumpkin top and place the pan in the oven.

6. Bake until the shell of the pumpkin is easily pierced with a fork (60 to 90 minutes). Remove the pan from the oven and let the pumkin cool.

7. Slice the pumpkin into wedges. Serve individual wedges topped with the bean mixture stuffing.

Serves 6

The Apache

The Apache arrived in Arizona and New Mexico, as well as in the northern Mexican state of Sonora, in the 1400s. They were divided into two major groupings. The Eastern Apache, which included the Jicarilla (HICK-ah-ree-ya), Mescalero (MES-ka-la-roh), and Chiricahua (CHIR-eh-kah-ah), resembled people of the Plains. They hunted buffalo, and some also farmed. The Western Apache, which included the White Mountain and San Carlos, farmed, like their Navajo and Pueblo neighbors.

When the Spanish arrived during their 1540 expedition, they encountered Apache. One Spanish account described the people as intelligent, tall, friendly, and kind. But the Spanish soon discovered that they could not convert the Apache to Christianity, nor could they make them move into missions. Unlike the Pueblo people who drove off the Spanish in 1680, the Apache did not drive the Spanish away. They preferred to help themselves to Spanish horses, sheep, and cattle. Their swift and daring raids on horseback became famous throughout the region.

In 1848 the Treaty of Guadalupe Hidalgo ended a war between the United States and Mexico. The United States acquired portions of what are now the Southwest and California from Mexico. This huge chunk of land included areas where Apache lived and fought with Mexicans. The United States claimed these lands, and soon American troops began arriving. Apache people considered troops, miners, ranchers, and others to be trespassers on their lands. The Apache, who were skillful fighters, attacked the non-Indians, military forts, and towns, despite the presence of U.S. Army troops.

The various Apache groups, led by Mangas Coloradas (MAHN-gahs KOL-oh-rah-das), Cochise (ko-CHEESE), Victorio (vic-TO-ri-o), and Geronimo (juh-RON-uh-moh), who were famous for their military skills, wanted to hold onto their ways of life. In the mid-1870s, Apaches did not want to be confined to the giant San Carlos (sahn KAR-los) Reservation in Arizona. It had been established in the lowest and hottest parts of the territory. It was filled with people dependent on food handouts from the U.S. government. Many starved, as there was not enough food to go around. In desperation, people left the reservation to hunt and gather plants. The attempts to relieve their misery were called "outbreaks" by the local newspapers. Between 1860 and 1886, Apache bands in Arizona and New Mexico resisted the takeover of their lands and fought against large numbers of U.S. troops and citizens, who were encouraged to kill Apaches. One by one, Apache leaders either were killed or surrendered. Some like Geronimo, became prisoners of war. Others were forced onto reservations.

Apache Today

Today, Apache people live on reservations in Arizona, New Mexico, and Oklahoma. They farm, raise stock, and work in stores, tribal museums, and other tourist facilities. Some make traditional baskets, cradleboards, and beadwork.

☀ APACHE TRADITIONAL ACCOUNT: Why the Bat Hangs Upside Down

Once, long ago, Coyote thought he wanted to get married, but he did not know whom to choose.

His friend Bat told him that maybe he could marry the wife of Hawk Chief, as he had been missing for many days.

MICHAEL LACAPA, APACHE/ HOPI/TEWA (1955–2005)

Famous for his storytelling, Michael Lacapa was an award-winning author and illustrator of several books for young people. He grew up on Arizona's Fort Apache Indian Reservation, where he learned from his elders to share his time and talents with others. And share he did. Lacapa was a teacher, publisher, educational consultant, dad, husband, and artist. He and his wife, Kathleen (Mohawk/Irish/English), authored *Less Than Half, More Than Whole*, a book about children of mixed heritages that is based on their own kids.

But Hawk Chief finally returned and became angry with Bat for suggesting that Coyote could marry his wife. He picked up Bat and flung him into a juniper bush so hard that Bat was stunned.

Bat was stuck upside down in the bush, caught by his long, pointy-toed moccasins. He twisted and he turned, but no matter how hard he struggled, he could not get free.

And from that time on, bats hang upside down—even when they sleep.

Play Concentration with Apache-Style Playing Cards

Indian groups in contact with Spanish explorers and colonists saw printed paper playing cards as early as the 1580s. Apache adopted the colorful, 40-card decks into their social life and made them their own. They made their cards on stiff white rawhide, which were lightweight and easy to carry. The Apache artists imitated Spanish designs–cups, coins, clubs, and swords. They also used the same paint colors: mustard yellow, rust red, royal blue, and black for outlining.

What You Need

Red, yellow, blue, and black colored pencils,
    crayons, or markers
40 unlined white index cards
Any number of players

What You Do

1. Draw matching pairs of designs on two cards, using either designs inspired by the Apache artists or your own designs. Make 20 pairs of matching cards. Decorate the cards on one side only.

2. Mix up the cards and lay them face down on the floor or a table.

3. Each player takes a turn. He or she chooses two cards and turns them face up. If the cards do not match, the cards are turned face down and the next player takes a turn.

4. If a player turns over two matching cards, he or she collects the cards and gets another turn.

5. The game ends when the last pair of cards is picked up. The winner is the person with the most pairs of cards. It is possible for more than one person to win the game.

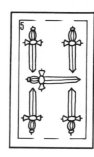

PLAY AN APACHE-LIKE FOOT TOSS GAME

Have you ever played Hacky Sack? The game is contagious. Get a game started and almost everyone joins in. The Apache played a similar game centuries ago.

What You Need

Lightweight stone

At least 2 players

Score keeper

What You Do

1. Decide how points will be scored—by tossing the stone either the highest or the farthest.

2. Balance the stone on the toes of one foot.

3. Throw it as far or as high as you can without touching it with your hands.

4. The player must keep his or her balance in order to score.

5. The best three out of five tosses wins!

The Navajo

The Navajo Reservation, the largest reservation in the United States, is located in New Mexico, Arizona, and Utah. It is larger than the state of West Virginia. Many movies and advertisements have been filmed in Monument Valley on the Navajo Reservation. Movie directors and others love the huge, fantastically shaped red rocks towering 1,000 feet over the desert floor.

Family members usually live near one another. They help each other and cooperate in building houses, farming, and herding sheep. Some people live in houses built to look like their ancestral homes, called hogans. Hogans are six- or eight-sided dwellings made of logs and sod or stone. They traditionally face east, the direction of the morning sunrise.

Navajo Weaving

Besides growing vegetables and melons, a skill they learned from Pueblo people, Navajos became sheepherders and goatherds. These animals provided food, as well as yarn for weaving. At first the Navajos wove clothing, lightweight shoulder blankets, and shawls, or made saddle blankets for horses. After 1880, weavers shifted from making things for their own use to making rugs for the off-reservation market. Today, Navajo rugs, prized for their colors and designs, are purchased by museums and collectors all over the world.

Woven designs can tell a traditional story or show influences from Spanish designs. Some designs record and interpret the world around the weaver by showing scenes and objects from Navajo daily life, including pickup trucks, interiors of trading posts, fair and rodeos, and weavers working at a loom. Some weavers even show cartoon characters and dinosaurs!

Navajo Silversmithing

Over a hundred years ago the Navajo people developed world-famous Navajo concho belts made of silver. "Concho" is from the Spanish word for shells, *concha*, but it has come to mean the round, oval, rectangular, and even butterfly-shaped silver disks that are part of the belts. Traditional concho belts often tell stories about their makers. Each symbol stamped on a concho had special meaning for the silversmith. Some conchos are mounted on leather belts, while others are linked together to form a chain of conchos.

The concho belt is a multicultural art form. The Navajos probably got the idea of conchos from the fancy silver designs on the horse bridles of the Mexican soldiers, and they may have learned silversmithing from the Mexicans. The Mexicans probably learned it from the Spanish. Early Spanish designs were borrowed from the Moors. Early Navajo artists borrowed designs for their conchos from Plains Indian hair ornaments and Spanish and Mexican decorations. Sometimes gemstones, like turquoise, are added. Both men and women wear the beautiful belts.

DESIGN A NAVAJO-STYLE CONCHO BELT

Originally, conchos were formed by hammering designs into silver dollars. Making a belt was not an easy task!

Try your hand at making a concho link belt.

What You Need

Scissors	Hole puncher
Cardboard	Yarn
White glue	Tape
Foil	
Bamboo skewer	
Large turquoise or coral beads	

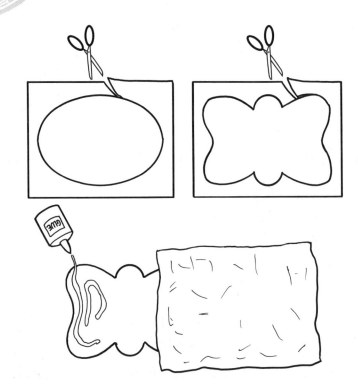

What You Do

1. Using scissors, cut oval and butterfly shapes, like the ones shown, from the cardboard—you can use as many as you like.

2. Put white glue on the shapes, double the foil so it won't tear, and cover each shape with the foil.

3. Using the bamboo skewer, decorate each piece by making indentations (arcs, circles, and squares), being careful to not puncture the foil.

4. Glue on the turquoise or coral beads.

5. Punch a hole in each side of each "concho," ½ inch from the edge.

6. Measure and cut three strands of yarn that each go around your waist twice.

7. Tie the three strands together with a knot at one end and tape them to a tabletop. Braid the yarn.

8. Attach your "conchos" by putting the braid into one hole and out through the other, making sure the yarn is in back of the concho.

9. Adjust the size to your waist and tie a knot to secure the braid. Tie the belt around your waist with the ends in the front or the back.

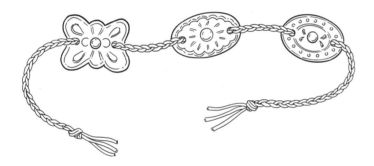

The Navajo Long Walk

Until the 1840s, few Navajo had any contact with the United States government or its citizens. Then, in 1851, U.S. soldiers were stationed in a fort located on valuable grazing land of the Navajo, preventing Indian people from using it. Some bands wanted peaceful relations, but others wanted to drive the soldiers back to the lands they had come from. Navajo leaders Barboncito (bar-bon-SEE-toe), Delgadito (dell-gah-DEE-toe), and Manuelito (mahn-well-EE-toe) resisted so strongly that the army appointed Colonel Kit Carson to subdue them. In 1864 he destroyed Navajo crops and captured or killed their horses, mules, and sheep. Hungry and shocked, Navajos surrendered by the thousands. They were forced to leave their homelands and walk over 300 miles to a New Mexico fort, where they were imprisoned for four years. Thousands died on the "Long Walk." Finally, in 1868, Navajos who survived their imprisonment signed a treaty that permitted them to return to their homelands. The treaty reduced their homelands to an estimated 10 percent of their original size. Many Navajos still live on their reservation today.

LONG WALKS

In 1978 hundreds of American Indians and many supporters walked from San Francisco to Washington, D.C., to call attention to proposed bills in the U.S. Congress that would take away rights of Native peoples. The "Longest Walk" also reminded Americans about the Navajo Long Walk and other forced removals of Native peoples. The 3,600-mile walk successfully halted the passing of the bills. In 2008 there was another "Longest Walk" celebrating this amazing event.

Annie Dodge Wauneka, Navajo

(1910–1997)

The Navajo people suffered much more than losing their lands. At one time, they were a healthy people, but life changed. They were forced to live in areas without enough clean drinking water or adequate health care, and tuberculosis, a highly contagious disease, began to make many people sick. Annie Dodge Wauneka set out to do something about the diseases on the reservation and to help restore the good health of her people. Her father was the first chairman of the Navajo Tribal Council, which he helped create, and Wauneka followed in her father's footsteps to become a leader. In 1951 she became the first woman elected to the Navajo Tribal Council.

Wauneka worked tirelessly to combat tuberculosis and other diseases, which had taken the lives of so many people on her reservation. She believed that good health could be attained by combining both modern medicine and traditional healing practices. She wrote a dictionary to translate English words for medical techniques, such as "vaccination," into Navajo. On her weekly Navajo-language radio broadcasts, she explained how modern medicine could help improve health among the Navajo. Throughout her life, Wauneka fought for better care for pregnant women and new babies, regular eye and ear examinations, and alcoholism treatment. In 1963 she became the first American Indian to receive the Presidential Medal of Freedom. She also served as an advisor to the U.S. Surgeon General and the U.S. Public Health Service. Wauneka not only helped make her people healthier, but she also inspired other Navajos to go into the healing practices.

The Navajo Code Talkers

Navajo is one of the most difficult languages in the world to learn. The Navajo language has over 30 consonants (English has 20) and four vowels (a, e, i, o). There are 48 ways to pronounce the four Navajo vowels. Navajo syllables carry either a high, low, rising, or falling tone. Marks over the vowels indicate whether to make a rising or falling sound. Apostrophes stand for the glottal stop, which is when the speaker pauses for a short second before going to the next syllable.

SAY IT IN NAVAJO

Here are some Navajo words for colors.
Red: *Lichii'* (thlih-chee)
Blue: *Yá Dootl'izh* (yah doe-thl-izh)
Yellow: *Litso* (thlih-tso)

During World War II the Navajo language played a crucial role in the U.S. victory in the Pacific region. The Japanese code breakers figured out American codes as fast as they were written. The U.S. government needed an unbreakable code for relaying messages. The idea for a good code originated with Philip Johnston, a non-Indian engineer raised on the Navajo Reservation. He knew that few people understood the complexity of the Navajo language. John Chee, Carl N. Gorman, Chester Nez, Lloyd Oliver, and 25 other Navajos fluent in Navajo and English, some only 15 years old, constructed and mastered a top secret code. Eventually, over 400 Navajo marines served in the code talker program. They used Navajo words that could be associated with military terms and names of places. The code word for observation plane became *ne-ahs-jah*, or "owl" in Navajo; the code word for submarine became *besh-lo*, or iron fish, in Navajo. The Navajo word for potato meant grenade, and a whale signified a battleship. The Navajo word for America, *Ne-he-mah*, meant "our mother." The code talkers also created an alphabet to spell out words. A stood for *wol-la-chee*, or ant in English. B stood for *shush*, or bear in English. C was for *moasi*, or cat in English. By the end of the war, 411 terms baffled the Japanese cryptographers, who could not decipher one word.

In 2000 Navajo code talker Samuel Billison provided the voice for the G. I. Joe code talker action figure, manufactured by the toy company Hasbro. This was Hasbro's first doll to speak a Native American language. In 2001 the original 29 code talkers were each honored with the Congressional Gold Medal, the nation's highest and most distinguished civilian award. In 2006 the Navajo Nation Council established a Navajo Code Talkers Day. It's a tribal holiday held every August 14.

Indian Boarding Schools

The Navajo people are proud that their language played a valuable role in World War II. At one time, however, Navajo children were forbidden to speak their language in Indian boarding schools. From the late 1880s to the 1940s, many children from Indian nations across the United States were sent to boarding schools located far away from Indian communities. These institutions were designed to separate children, some as young as four or five years old, from their families for most of the school year.

Boarding schools tried to erase the children's memories of home and family. Native clothes and hairstyles were strictly forbidden. So were Native languages. If children were caught speaking their own languages, they were punished. From the moment the boys and girls woke up, they were required to wear uniforms and march in military formations. The children marched to meals, marched to classes, and marched in their free time. Because schools were underfunded, boys cleaned, constructed buildings, planted and harvested food crops, cared for farm animals, dug wells, quarried stone, and made shoes, boots, and wagons. The girls cooked and canned food and mended, sewed, washed, and ironed clothes. Students spent more hours doing chores every day than they spent doing schoolwork. Children who were caught running away were punished and sometimes confined in a dark basement with only a bread-and-water diet. Children were hardly ever allowed to play or just be kids.

Boarding school administrators encouraged students to write to family and friends. They were warned, however, to keep their letters cheerful and to not mention homesickness, sadness, inadequate food and clothing, sickness, overwork, or runaways. Here is a memory from a young Tewa-Hopi child who was sent to Keam's Canyon boarding school in Arizona:

> In 1896, when I was eight years old, I was transferred from the Polacco Day School to the boarding school in Keam's Canyon. . . . When we kids arrived on the first day of school, the first thing they did was to give us baths and cut our Hopi-style hair and make it white man's style. Our families didn't like our hair being cut. Our traditional hairstyle was meaningful. The long hair we boys wore on the sides symbolized rain . . . and it seemed to our parents that the whites were pretty high-handed and insensitive, as well as being ignorant of our ways. (Albert Yava, Tewa-Hopi)

[Permission granted by the Emma Courlander Trust]

Tohono O'odham

The Tohono O'odham [to-ho-no o-ODUM] have lived in the Sonoran Desert in southern Arizona and northern Mexico for thousands of years. Their name means "People of the Desert." Most O'odham lived in two villages. During the spring and summer, the people lived in farming villages in valleys, where they raised beans and other crops. They also hunted small animals. During the winter, they lived in the mountains, where the O'odham gathered food. They used water from mountain springs and hunted mountain sheep and other big game. Some O'odham lived in the dry western desert all year round. They traveled in small groups, hunting, gathering, and trading. They ate a root plant found in the sand dunes and caught shellfish in the Gulf of California. They also harvested seeds, fruits, and leaves of wild plants to use as food or medicine. The Sonoran Desert is filled with the world's largest cactus. People picked the fruit of the giant saguaro and made jam from the red pulp. They also ground the seeds into flour.

O'odham life revolved around available water. Before dawn each morning, young women ran to mountain springs to fill their water jugs with enough water to last their family the entire day. When families lived in valley villages, they trapped water in shallow places and used it for drinking and washing. In years when there was enough summer rain, families planted crops in areas soaked by water.

Arriving in 1519, the Spanish were the first non-Indians in O'odham country. They renamed the people Papago, an insulting Spanish word based on an Indian word for "bean eaters." A food source for the O'odham was the *bav*, a bean grown in the desert. The Spanish introduced their language to the O'odham, but the Indians kept their Native language alive. The Spanish built churches in the Indian villages. They introduced new animals, such as cattle, and new plants, such as wheat. The Spanish built ranches and mines, then forced the O'odham to do the hard work in them. The O'odham rebelled against them in the 1660s and in the 1750s.

The Tohono O'odham Nation's tribal lands were divided by the Treaty of Guadalupe Hidalgo of 1848 and the Gadsden Purchase of 1854, which settled the location of the border between the United States and Mexico. These treaties cut tribal lands in half. The O'odham in the United States became citizens without their knowledge. The United States did not regard the O'odham as former Mexican citizens who owned their land. The United States saw the O'odham as wards of the government, like children, which therefore allowed the government to control their land and lives. Although the U.S. government recognized that the O'odham had been settled on their lands for hundreds of years, it did nothing to stop non-Indians from trespassing on that land. In 1862 the government opened O'odham lands to homesteaders. In 1866 their lands were opened to miners. The government allowed ranchers, railroad companies, and the military to take O'odham lands without their consent.

After years of protest by O'odham against trespassers, in 1916 a Papago Reservation was finally established. It's the second-largest reservation in the United States, roughly the size of Connecticut. Most of the tribe is Catholic, since many of their ancestors were converted during the missionary activities in the late 1600s, but people have also maintained traditional beliefs. In 1984 the tribal council officially changed the tribe's name from Papago back to Tohono O'odham to restore the tribe's identity. Since the 1990s, there has been a cultural revitalization of traditional basket weaving, desert foods, and traditional games. Each February, the annual Arizona Rodeo and Parade is held in Sells, the O'odham capital.

Tohono O'odham Today

Most of the U.S. O'odham live in southern Arizona, but several thousand live in northern Sonora, Mexico. For over 100 years, the Tohono O'odham were able to pass freely over the U.S.–Mexico border. However, in the mid-1980s immigration laws tightened the border to stop illegal immigration and drug trafficking. These same laws also prevent O'odham members from traveling freely between the two countries to collect foods to sustain their culture and to visit family members and traditional sacred sites.

THE HAVASUPAI

The Havasupai (HAVE-ah-soup-eye) and Hualapai (WAH-lah-pie) peoples live in villages along the Colorado River in northwestern Arizona, which provides water for growing beans, corn, melons, and sunflowers. The Havasupai village of Supai, home to people for centuries, is located at the bottom of the Grand Canyon. You can only reach Supai by helicopter, by walking, or by riding a horse down a steep eight-mile trail. The Havasupai are the only people in the United States who get their mail delivered by animals. Computers, televisions, clothes, groceries, and regular mail are strapped onto animals and carried down the trail. Visitors to Supai can send postcards stamped with the "Mule Train Mail—Havasupai Indian Reservation" postmark.

❖ 8 ❖

Pacific States

Pulling together as one, teams of Lummi kids race through the water in their hand-carved canoes at the Stommish War Canoe Races and Water Festival each summer. The annual event for Northwest Coast nations with war canoe traditions is held on the Lummi Indian Reservation near Bellingham, Washington. It features traditional games, music, foods, and many contests of canoe racing. The Stommish festival began after World War II as a way of welcoming Lummi servicemen and servicewomen home from the war.

Pacific States

First Nations peoples of the U.S. Pacific states live in a diverse area of present-day California, Oregon, and Washington. The coastal part of the region has a mild climate; it's not too hot and not too cold. But it rains a lot—sometimes as much as 150 inches a year in places like western Washington. That means the climate is foggy, misty, and damp. The eastern part of Washington gets lots of snow in the winter.

The ocean, freshwater rivers, countless lakes, streams, and bays are home to hundreds of different kinds of fish and sea life, especially salmon, and, until recently, these fish and other creatures were plentiful. The Lummi (LUM-ee), Nisqually (nis-KWAHL-lee), and other peoples netted or trapped salmon. The Makah (ma-KAW), Quileute (KWILL-ee-oot), and others built their villages at the mouths of rivers in order to be close to the open sea, where they hunted whales from their cedar

Map of Selected Nation Nations of the Pacific States Today

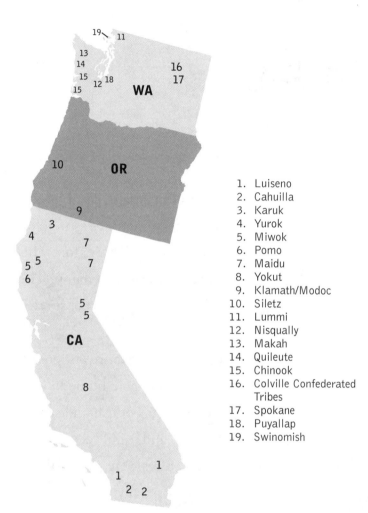

1. Luiseno
2. Cahuilla
3. Karuk
4. Yurok
5. Miwok
6. Pomo
7. Maidu
8. Yokut
9. Klamath/Modoc
10. Siletz
11. Lummi
12. Nisqually
13. Makah
14. Quileute
15. Chinook
16. Colville Confederated Tribes
17. Spokane
18. Puyallap
19. Swinomish

canoes, and to take advantage of river fishing. The Maidu (MY-doo) and Yokut (YO-kut) lived inland, where they feasted on forest animals and managed berry production. They gathered acorns, which can be poisonous to humans, but they knew how to process them into a nutritious food. They pounded the dried nuts into meal, which was cooked into sweet porridge or cakes.

Vast forests of gigantic trees, among the tallest in the world, border the coastal area to the east. These lush evergreen forests of cedar, fir, hemlock, and spruce provided enough wood to make huge longhouses, many kinds of canoes, storage containers, and totem poles. Mountainsides are also covered with lots of plants, shrubs, bushes, nuts, and roots that provided materials for making clothing and baskets.

The red cedar tree is extremely important to people in the Pacific states. They used all parts of the tree: boughs for fuel and medicine; roots for weaving baskets; wood for their houses, masks, bowls, rattles, totem poles, and canoes; and bark for waterproof clothing. Many of these traditions continue today.

The land and sea provided so much food that people lived comfortable lives. They spent half the year using their natural resources to create beautiful and useful works of art. Artists carved animal figures on totem poles, bowls, and other household items, and religious objects. Weavers shredded cedar bark and wove it into waterproof hats, capes, and fine baskets. Some were watertight enough to be used for cooking. They added mountain goat hair to the bark and wove blankets and shirts. Nowadays traditional clothing is worn on special occasions, while baskets, carvings, and other creations are prized by collectors worldwide.

South of Oregon, in northern California, First Nations like the Yurok (YOUR-ock), Klamath (KLAM-uth), and Miwok (MEE-wock), also lived in a rich and mild climate and enjoyed the wealth of food resources. Like nations to the north, some fished and hunted sea and land mammals; others harvested the vast variety of plants. Warfare was rare before non-Indians arrived.

The Miwok

The Miwok people of north-central California were organized in three main groups. The Sierra Miwok (who were the largest of the Miwok groups), the Lake Miwok, and Coastal Miwok all had homelands in north central California. The Lake people ate fish, waterfowl, and other lake foods. The Sierra depended on salmon in the major river valleys. The Coastal people fished and clammed. All of the groups processed acorns as a source of food.

It is believed that, in 1579, Francis Drake, the first Englishman to sail around the world, landed somewhere north of present-day San Francisco. There he met local people, probably the Coastal Miwok, who permitted him to stay while the ship was repaired. After five weeks of friendly interactions, Drake claimed the land for England and returned home. Every year professional performers, Native Americans, volunteers, elementary school children, and musicians reenact the first encounter in northern California between Miwok and Drake.

Today the Sierra Miwok still live on their traditional lands. The Lake Miwok live on small reservations in northwestern California. Some Coastal Miwok live on a reservation north of San Francisco.

Play Tek'me Pu'ku, a Miwok Game

The Miwok people of north-central California played a relay-like game called Tek'me Pu'ku. Try this variation with your friends.

What You Need

5 or more friends (an odd number works best)

Whistle

Chalk

Tape measure

Four cones, bricks, stakes, or anything else that can be used as posts

2 softballs or other similar-size balls

What You Do

1. Find a large open area to play your game. Pick one person to be the judge. Organize the rest of your friends into 2 teams—you can have as many players as you like, as long as there is an equal number of players on each team.

2. Make two tracks at least 6 feet apart. For each track, draw two parallel chalk lines about 40 feet long and 6 inches apart. Put a post at one end of each line. These are the goal posts.

3. When the judge blows the whistle, the starting player from each team kicks the ball down his or her track, trying to score by keeping the ball inside the lines and getting it through the posts.

4. Team members stand on the sidelines. It's their job to keep the ball inside the track. If it goes out, they have to kick it back in and take over the job of trying to score, as in a relay race. The player has to start at the place the ball went out.

5. No one can touch the ball with his or her hands.

6. A team wins by being the first to score by kicking the ball through the team's posts.

The Chinook

The many Native groups who lived in the Pacific states area spoke dozens of different languages. The Columbia River and other rivers served as avenues of travel and trade. The Chinook (Chin-NOOK) people, who lived at the mouth of the lower Columbia River where it opens up into the Pacific Ocean near present-day Astoria, Oregon, became a link between people living in the Plateau region and groups living up the Pacific Coast. The Chinook became famous for their trading business and even developed a special trade language that was used from Alaska to southern California. At first the language combined Chinook and other local languages. Later the Chinook added French and English words into the language after they made contact with European explorers and traders. The Chinook went north in large canoes with dried salmon, sturgeon, fish oil, and seashells from coastal Natives to trade with inland people. They gathered horses, furs, pipestone, and other items from inland tribes to bring back to coastal groups. Anyone who wanted to trade had to understand Chinook jargon, the "trade language."

First Nations Contact with Europeans and Americans

Between 1770 and 1797, Spanish Franciscan missionaries set up six missions in northern California. Miwok, Yokut, Ohlone (Oh-LONE), and other groups went voluntarily at first, drawn by gifts of beads and cloth and the hope of trading. The Native people were polite and accepted baptism out of respect to the missionaries. It did not have the same meaning for them as it did for the Christians, who did not understand or respect Native religions. However, once they accepted the ritual, their freedom ended. If adults refused baptism, their children were baptized and held hostage. People who tried to escape from the missions were whipped and chained as an example to others.

Life was extremely harsh in the missions. Many people fought back: they refused to learn Spanish, disobeyed orders to do backbreaking work, or ran away. Spanish animals (cattle, sheep, and horses) destroyed large numbers of traditional food plants. Thousands of adults and children became ill and died from measles, influenza, and other European diseases. The mission system ended in 1833 when the Mexican government, which won independence from Spain, took over mission lands and buildings. Mexico released the enslaved Native people. Many years had passed, and much of the Indian culture and lands had been destroyed. The surviving Native people no longer had a home or culture to which they could return.

The wealth of natural resources attracted Europeans and Americans. They rushed to acquire the riches found in the Pacific states for themselves in the 18th and 19th centuries. In 1843 the first great overland migration into Oregon doubled the number of people in the region. After that, non-Indian settlers arrived by the hundreds every year. Soon, Native people in the region were squeezed off their own land. They found it difficult to provide food for their communities. This led to conflicts between Native groups and non-Native people. Indians in Oregon and Washington often had no choice but to sign treaties, which required them to move onto reservations against their will.

California Indians Fight to Survive

California Indians also suffered during the gold rush, beginning in 1848, when a flood of gold miners from around the world descended upon the region. New arrivals, who saw Native people as competition (many miners were Indians who had also caught "gold fever"), attacked their villages. Mining destroyed traditional food resources, too. Salmon were killed by the mud and silt stirred up by digging for gold in riverbeds. Logs choked the fishing places. Increasing numbers of non-Indians displaced Native people from their ancestral homelands. Farms took over valuable hunting and gathering grounds where grasses, fruits, and wild plants once grew. The original animals were driven from their territories, while cattle and pigs ate grasses, seeds, and nuts—foods important to Native peoples' survival. In order to keep from starving, some Indians began to steal cattle. This led to violent reactions from non-Indians who did not understand or care about how difficult it was for Native people to survive with no food, clothing, or homes.

By the 1850s, over 100,000 non-Indian fortune seekers had come to California. They traveled into the most remote valleys and mountains searching for gold, timber, and land. Mining camps in the interior were larger than most Indian villages. Across California, groups of white males formed "volunteer armies" that swept down on quiet Native communities and killed men, women, and children. They bought the guns, ammunition, horses, and supplies and were repaid by the California legislature, which passed several acts to pay citizens for "private military" attacks on Indians. The Native population of California's central valley plunged from 150,000 to 50,000. It's a miracle that California Indian groups have survived. Despite the enormous difficulties and losses they faced in the past, surviving tribes all over the state have organized to fight to protect their sacred sites and to fish and hunt and gather plants in ancient places. Some communities have revived their languages, ceremonies, traditional arts, and other cultural activities.

Traditional Native Calendars

People around the world invented calendars as a way of organizing and measuring time. Native American groups in the United States measured their year in "moons." These moons came at almost the same time as the months in calendars used today. Each Indian nation had its own name (in its own language) for each moon. The names of each month differed from region to region because the moons reflected an area's climate; the budding, blooming, leafing, and fruiting of vegetation; the growth and activities of animals, birds, and fish; and seasonal activities. Sometimes several groups within the larger Native nation used different names for the moon. Occasionally names changed from year to year. Here are some names for moons from various California, Oregon, and Washington State groups.

January	Buckeyes Ripe	Pomo of California
February	Big Moon	Nisenan of California
March	Sucker Fishing	Klamath of Oregon
April	Black Oaks Tassel	Foothill Maidu of California
May	Seeds Ripen	Pomo of California
June	Time for Getting Elderberries	Quileute of Washington State
July	Month of Wild Currants and Gooseberries	Makah of Washington State
August	Red Berries Gathered	Yurok of California
September	Acorns Gathered	Valley Maidu of California
October	Small Tree Freeze	Mountain Maidu of California
November	Season of Winds and Screaming Birds	Makah of Washington State
December	Heavy Snow	Klamath of Oregon

Illustrate a Moon Calendar

Today, many tribes print calendars that use their traditional names for months of the year. Try your hand at creating a Moon Calendar for your family or friends. You can make many copies of the calendar by photocopying the pages.

What You Need

Ruler

Pencil

24 sheets of unlined
   8½-by-11-inch paper

12 sheets of 18-by-24-inch
   construction paper

Colored pencils, crayons,
   or markers

Glue or tape

Hole puncher

48 notebook hole reinforcers

4-inch-long piece of yarn

What You Do

1. Draw a calendar grid on one sheet of unlined paper. To do this, lay the paper so that the long side is from right to left and the short side is from top to bottom. Using the ruler and pencil, divide the sheet into 7 equal-sized columns, each about 1½ inches wide. Then divide the columns into 5 equal-sized rows, each about 2 inches tall. Repeat until grids have been drawn on 12 sheets of unlined paper.

2. Think up a descriptive name for each of the 12 months. Try to use names that tell something about your region's climate or about a major holiday, event, or other activity that occurs during that month. Using colored pencils, crayons, or markers, write your descriptive name of a month on one of the blank sheets of unlined paper. Below it, draw an image that represents your month's "name." Repeat until all 12 blank unlined sheets each contain the name and an image of each month.

3. Glue or tape one drawing to the top of each piece of construction paper. Glue or tape one calendar grid to the bottom of each piece of construction paper. Fill in the dates of each month on the calendar grids.

4. Put the pieces of construction paper in order by month, with January on the top and December on the bottom.

5. Punch 2 holes, about 2 inches apart from each other, at the center top of each piece of construction paper. Make sure the holes are in the same place on each piece of

construction paper. Stick a notebook hole reinforcer onto each hole.

6. Fold the yarn in half and thread to loop of yarn through the holes so that the ends are at the back of the last piece of construction paper. Loosely tie the yarn and hang it on a nail in a wall. As each month begins, flip the calendar to the correct month and hang it up again.

The Salish

The Salish (SAY-lish) were once the most numerous people living along the coast and the interior of northern California, Oregon, and Washington. They spoke at least 45 different languages. The Siletz (sil-ETZ) and Tillamook (TILL-a-mook), in coastal Oregon, and the Lummi and others groups of coastal Washington State lived in villages of longhouses made of red cedar trees. Forty or more people from related families lived in them. Larger houses were partitioned into apartments. Houses in a village were sometimes stretched for several miles along a river. Groups in eastern Oregon and Washington lived like their Plateau neighbors. Coastal Salish people caught huge numbers of salmon. Salmon are so important to the Native peoples that they are honored in prayer and religious ceremonies.

Salish and other Native groups did metalwork before European contact. They worked with copper, which is especially soft and easy to work with. Metalworkers hammered copper flat and etched it or twisted it into bracelets, anklets,

MOURNING DOVE, SALISH
(circa 1888–1936)

Credited with being the first American Indian woman to publish a novel, *Cogewea, the Half-Blood*, in 1927, Mourning Dove was the literary name chosen by Christine Quintasket, who lived on the Colville Reservation in eastern Washington. (Humishuma was her name in the Salish language.) Mourning Dove, who was constantly punished in school for speaking Salish, worked as a migrant field laborer and lost many family members to disease. As an adult, although she was worn out from hard work and illness, Mourning Dove promoted the welfare of the Indian people of her region. She became one of the first women elected to her tribal council. For years her last book, *Mourning Dove, A Salishan Autobiography*, was passed from editor to editor. It was her life story, but it was not published until 1990, decades after her death.

pendants, earrings, and rings. Copper was also fashioned into copper beads. Today, Northwest artists like Don Yeomans, Haida, combine ancient and modern designs to create beautiful jewelry.

DESIGN A SALISH-STYLE COPPER BRACELET

Create this bracelet and wear your art!

What You Need

Newspaper

Roll of ¼-inch-wide or wider magnetic strip
(available at craft stores)

Scissors

Copper- or gold-colored acrylic paint

Paintbrush

Copper jewelry cording (available at craft stores)

Wite glue

What You Do

1. Cover a work surface with newspaper.

2. Wrap the magnetic strip around your wrist. Cut the
   strip so that it's 1 inch longer than your wrist
   measurement. Lay it out flat on the newspaper.

3. Paint the strip. Let it dry.

4. Use the jewelry cording to make 3-dimensional shapes on
   your bracelet. You can copy the designs shown here or make
   up your own. Try to create swirls, triangles, or circles. When
   you have a piece of cording shaped the way you want it, glue
   it to the bracelet. Press the cording and the magnetic strip
   together with your fingers as you add designs to make sure
   the cording sticks to the bracelet as the glue dries.

5. When the glue is completely dry, wrap the bracelet around
   your wrist and press the ends together. It's a magnetic strip,
   so it will stay put!

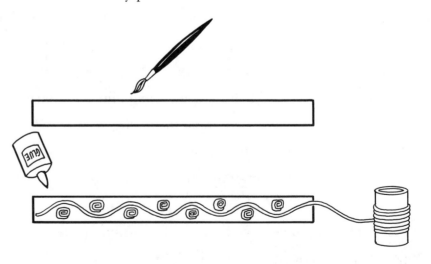

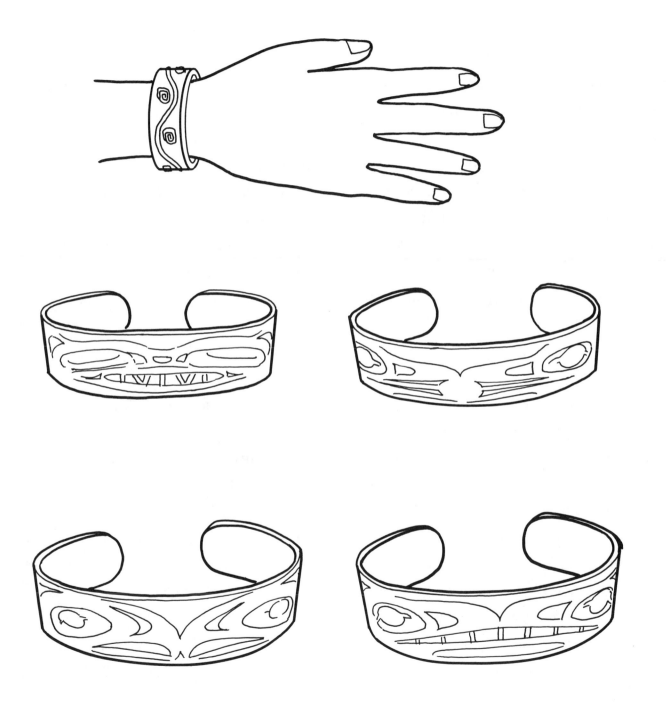

The Klamath

The Klamath (KLAM-uth) ancestral lands included present-day south-central Oregon, north-central California, and parts of Nevada and Idaho. Because of their isolated location, the Klamath were able to avoid contact with Europeans longer than other tribes in the region. They escaped the great epidemics that swept through Indian villages after contact with the British, French, and other Europeans. Their first contact came in 1826, with Peter Skene Ogden, a Hudson Bay Company fur trader. By 1829 trade was established between the Klamath and the Hudson Bay Company. Non-Indian explorers, missionaries, settlers, and ranchers followed.

The Modoc War

After decades of conflicts between Klamath and non-Indian invaders on their land, the U.S. government made a treaty with the tribe in 1864 that forced the people to give up their claim to 12 million acres in return for 800,000 acres in south central Oregon. The Klamath were forced to share the much smaller land base with their rivals, the Modoc Tribe. In 1864 the Modoc people were living on their ancestral tribal lands near the present day Oregon–California border region. But white settlers wanted the rich fertile area for themselves, so the U.S. government forced the Modoc onto the Klamath Indian Reservation in Oregon. It was if they were picked up and dropped into another country's borders without sharing the same customs or language. The Modoc were in the minority on the reservation and endured constant conflicts with the Klamath, who saw them as intruders.

Captain Jack, or Kintpuash, was outraged and saddened by the way his people had been treated. He led his people back to their homelands. In 1870 about 200 men, women, and children traveled south to the land formerly occupied by generations of Modoc, which had become dotted with ranches and white homesteaders.

The U.S. soldiers rounded up the Modoc and pushed them back to the Klamath Reservation in 1869, but conditions had not improved. Again Captain Jack led his people back to their territory. Once more the army soldiers set out to capture the Modoc and force them back to the Klamath Reservation, but a fight broke out between a Modoc warrior and an army soldier, causing what is called the Battle of Lost River.

Captain Jack led his band into a natural maze of caves and trenches caused by lava from an ancient volcano. They defended their stronghold and killed several soldiers and a general, thinking this would be the end to their being dragged away from their homelands. But the U.S. government sent 1,000 soldiers—far more than the number of Modoc—to capture them. In 1873 Captain Jack and his much-reduced force of an estimated 30 warriors were captured. Although it was a

COMPETE IN A KLAMATH FOUR STICKS GUESSING GAME

For over 50 years, the Annual All-Indian Peak-to-Peak World Championship Men's and Women's Basketball Tourney has been hosted by the Klamath Tribe in Chiloquin, Oregon. Sixteen teams from around the country as well as Canada take part in the friendly competition. Klamath kids play basketball, but they also learn Klamath traditional games, like this Four Sticks Guessing Game. This resembles the modern game Master Mind.

What You Need

2 popsicle sticks

2 different-colored magic markers

2 chopsticks

At least one opponent

Towel

What You Do

1. Decorate each popsicle stick with a different colored marker. Make them very different from each other. Leave the chopsticks plain. Study them with the person you will be playing against.

2. Hide all four sticks in a row under the towel without your opponent seeing the order you hid them in.

3. The opponent has a chance to guess the order of the sticks. One point is earned for each correct guess.

4. Take turns. After five turns, the player with the highest score wins.

war, the men were tried like murderers and condemned to death. Captain Jack and five other leaders were hanged. Modoc lives were never the same. Most of the tribe was removed to a reservation in Indian Territory (Oklahoma). Some still live on the Klamath Reservation in Oregon.

Native California Today

The 2000 census reported that California had the largest American Indian population in the United States. The state has over 100 Indian reservations, some of which are the smallest in the country. These small homelands are called *rancherias*. California Natives also live in urban areas of the state. The 2000 census reported that Los Angeles County had the largest Native population of any county in the United States.

Across the state—on reservations and in cities—there has been a revival of Native languages, religious ceremonies, music, and dance, as well as traditional arts such as food preparation, pottery, basket weaving, and hand games. From northern to southern California, powwows, storytelling and bird song festivals, concerts, rodeos, and other celebrations take place. Native Californians participate in all areas of American life, from science to sports.

NAOMI LANG, ICE DANCING CHAMPION (1978–)

Naomi Lang, a member of the Karuk tribe of California, and her partner, Peter Tchernyshev, captured the U.S. National Ice Dance title five times: in 1999, 2000, 2001, 2002, and 2003. They fulfilled their lifelong dream when they competed in the 2002 Winter Olympics in Salt Lake City. Drawing inspiration from her background in ballet, Naomi started ice dancing at the age of 12. Lang is the first American Indian woman to compete in the Winter Olympics.

California Indian Basketweavers Association

In the late 20th century, the art of basket weaving, perfected over centuries by California Indians, appeared to be dying out. Few younger people were learning to weave, and the mostly older women who wove baskets had to deal with the destruction of plant habitats and pesticide contamination of gathering areas. Because some of the gathering sites are on private property, it was difficult to gather the plants used for medicine, ceremonies, and food.

In 1992 some basket weavers formed the California Indian Basketweavers Association (CIBA). The organization helps Native weavers, mostly women, who make baskets, traditional clothing, and other products from native plants gathered from the forests and wildlands of California. CIBA educates the public about the dangers of pesticide use, coordinates with public agencies so that natural materials can be gathered from their sites, and advertises specific basketmakers from California tribes like Karuk, Pomo, and Yurok.

Native women and men who produce and sell baskets and other handcrafted items earn money while preserving their cultural heritage. CIBA members also strengthen the role of California Indian women in overcoming public ignorance about California Native cultures by attending conferences, teaching classes and workshops, and distributing a newsletter.

JULIA PARKER, KASHIA POMO (1929–)

In 2007 Julia Parker, a Kashia Pomo basketmaker from California, was awarded an NEA National Heritage Award, which honors American folk artists for their contributions to national culture. Parker goes out into the fields to gather natural plants and prepare them as her elders once did. She then makes baskets of all shapes and designs for all kinds of purposes. Parker helped organize the California Indian Basketweavers Association, which tries to protect plants from extinction and the harmful effects of pesticides.

Northwest Coast Fishing Rights

In the 1850s the U.S. government, the Lummi, the Makah, and many other tribes in Washington State negotiated treaties. Indians gave up much of their lands in return for promises of cash payments and the right to catch salmon and other fish "at all usual and accustomed grounds and stations." Sometimes these spots were located off the reservation. Tribes had to share these off-reservation fishing grounds with commercial and sports fishermen, who sometimes blocked Indian access. In the 1930s and 1940s, some 300 dams built by the U.S. Army Corps of Engineers and public utility companies flooded ancient fishing grounds. Indians fought back and asserted their fishing rights through court cases and "fish-ins." At fish-ins, people protested state laws that contradicted the federal treaties by fishing in areas the state laws didn't allow. According to federal law spelled out in treaties, they had every right to fish in those places. In the 1960s and 1970s, several court decisions established in law the tribes' rights to fish at their usual fishing grounds.

Today, tribes in the Pacific Northwest have been working to protect fish and shellfish in rivers, bays, and other waters from oil spills, raw sewage from cruise ships, pollution from septic systems, and loss of tree shade that keeps water temperature cooler. Water above 70° F can kill salmon. The Northwest Indian Fisheries Commission, an organization of 20 tribes in Washington, helps to protect the habitat of salmon and other fish.

Importance of Salmon

Many California, Oregon, and Washington State Native peoples live near the ocean and rivers because fish are a big part of their diet. The Yurok of California as well as other Native nations led the movement to protect salmon spawning grounds from commercial fisherman. At fish camps, the entire community joins in the catching, cleaning, and preserving of the salmon. Traditional stories are told, and everyone joins in the singing.

BERNIE WHITEBEAR, COLVILLE CONFEDERATED TRIBES (1937–2000)

Bernie Whitebear actively fought for Indian fishing rights on rivers in the Northwest. The government limits the number of fish that can be caught each year so that enough fish will survive to produce young. Whitebear fought many years of court battles, and a law was passed in 1974 allowing tribes 50 percent of the annual fish catch. Whitebear is also known for his activism on behalf of urban Indian peoples. A resident of Seattle, Washington, he advocated for Indian land rights to an abandoned fort located in the city. He founded the United Indians of All Tribes Foundation, which oversees the Washington Daybreak Star Cultural Center, an urban center for Seattle's Native Americans. The center operates a Head Start program for preschoolers, job training, cultural events like powwows and art shows, and other services that help the American Indian community. Until his death, Whitebear served as director of the center and continued to fight for the rights of Indian people.

DR. RAMONA BENNETT, PUYALLUP (1938–)

A prominent leader from the Puyallup (pyoo-AL-up) Reservation in Washington State, Ramona Bennett was a pioneer for Indian fishing rights. She cofounded the Survival of American Indians Association in 1964, an organization that brought local fish-ins to the attention of the national news media. She served as tribal chairperson from 1971 until 1978.

Bennett participated in the many areas of Indian rights, from health to treatment of women and children. Concerned about the large number of Indian children forced into foster care and then adopted by white families, she founded the local Indian Child Welfare Act Committee and made changes to childhood and family services in Washington State. In 1978 Bennett coauthored the national Indian Child Welfare Act, which protects the rights of Indian children and prevents them from being taken away from tribes. Bennett helped found Rainbow Youth and Family Services, which protects abused children and helps Indian people become foster and adoptive parents. She still serves the Tacoma, Washington, agency as a social worker.

Make Salmon Fritters

Salmon is an extremely important food to Natives in the Northwestern part of the United States. There are as many ways to prepare it as there are people to cook it. Try this salmon fritter recipe.

What You Need

Adult supervision required

16-ounce can salmon

Medium-sized mixing bowl

Fork

1 small onion, grated fine

1 tablespoon of dried parsley

About ½ teaspoon of black pepper

Small bowl

1 cup of fresh, frozen, or canned corn kernels

2 large eggs

3 tablespoons butter, divided

Large heavy skillet

What You Do

1. Empty the contents of the can of salmon (fish plus liquid) into the mixing bowl. Using a fork, break up the salmon and mash the bones (you can eat them!).
2. Stir in the onion, parsley, and pepper.
3. In the small bowl, mix together the eggs and the corn. Add this mixture to the salmon.
4. Using your hands, shape the mixture in to 12 equal-sized balls. Flatten each ball into a small patty and set it aside.
5. Melt 2 tablespoons of the butter in the skillet over low heat. Add the patties and cook over low heat until the patties are browned on the bottom.
6. Add the remaining tablespoon of butter to the skillet. Flip over the patties and cook over low heat until the patties are browned on both sides.

Serves 6

☀ Salish Traditional Account: Coyote Leads the Salmon Up the River

There are many traditional accounts about salmon because they are so important to the Native peoples on the Northwest Coast. This story is based on the Salish-speaking people's account from Washington State.

A very long time ago, the salmon had been trapped for days behind a dam. Five Swallow Sisters had created it and would not let the salmon leave. The people who lived upriver were starving, as salmon was the main source of their food. Coyote felt sorry for the people's plight and wanted to help them.

Coyote disguised himself as a helpless abandoned baby and tricked the Swallow Sisters into taking care of him. For five days, while the Swallow Sisters were busy doing their chores, Coyote worked at tearing down the dam. When the sisters finally discovered that Coyote had made a big hole in their dam, it was too late. The salmon had found the hole and were swimming upstream.

As Coyote led the salmon upriver, he rewarded the villages that had been kind to him. He created rapids and narrow places along the river for people to fish. He promised the people that, if they honored the salmon and never took more than they needed so the fish could spawn, the salmon would return every year.

MARCH POINT

Swinomish (swi-NOH-mish) Indian community high school students Nick Clark, Cody Cayou, and Travis Tom thought about making a gangster movie or rap video with their funds from Native Lens, a special film program for Native youth. Instead, the teens followed their noses to the putrid smell of an oil refinery and chose it as their subject. Their documentary, *March Point*, shows how the refineries threaten not only the environment, but also the economy of the Native people who depend on the natural resources for their livelihood.

Besides filming on their Washington State reservations, they traveled to Washington, D.C., to find politicians who could help. Their filmmaking was so impressive that they ended up getting more funding from PBS and National Geographic so they could produce an hour-long documentary. They interviewed elders, fishermen, and fishing activists. The teens have made a real difference. Their film has brought the illegal taking and polluting of Swinomish lands back into the public eye.

SAY IT IN KARUK

Karuk students at Happy Camp High School in Northern California developed a language Web site so people could learn some words and phrases in Karuk. Try speaking some Karuk with your friends.

Hello	*Ayukîi*	(i-YOU-kee)
Wow!	*EE*	(EYE)
Let's go	*Chôora*	(CHORE-ah)
How are you?	*Hukich?*	(HOOT-kitch)
See you later	*Súva nik*	(TWO-wa nick)
Goodbye	*Ch mi*	(CHIM nee)

9

Alaska

"Noosers" have to be quick, strong, and quiet as they sneak up on an unsuspecting fur seal. Aleut kids lasso a sea mammal and drag it away so the other animals don't become alarmed. Then they save its life by removing fish nets and other ocean trash that has gotten tangled around the animal's neck, cutting off circulation or preventing it from eating. The seal gets mad, but when the noosers are finished, he humps happily back to the sea. The youth are part of the Pribilof Islands Stewardship Program, an Aleut project in which kids participate in field research and learn about the geography, geology, ecology, and biodiversity of their westernmost Alaskan island home. They learn how to gather data and count wildlife populations. No matter how far the fur seals travel, they always come back to the Aleutian Islands to have their babies. Seventy percent of the world's fur seals come from here, and many Aleutian people feel a responsibility to keep the whiskered sea mammals and the rest of the ocean wildlife safe and healthy.

Alaska is the largest state in the United States. It is almost 600,000 square miles— over twice the size of Texas and larger than many countries. Part of the Arctic tundra is in Alaska. The tundra has mosses and bushes, but no trees grow in the region where the ground stays frozen all year round. Around 5,000 glaciers cover large areas of the state. There are 14 mountain ranges, 3 million lakes, and more than 3,000 rivers. Some

1. Iñupiat
2. Yup'ik
3. Aleut (Unangan)
4. Athabascan Indians
5. Tlingit
6. Tsimshian
7. Haida

On March 24, 1989, the *Exxon Valdez* tanker ran aground on Bligh Reef in Prince William Sound, spilling nearly 11 million gallons of crude oil. The oil polluted roughly 1,500 miles of rocky beaches, killing fish, birds, and marine mammals and poisoning deer who fed on kelp. The spill devastated the lives of Native people who have fished, hunted, and harvested plants in the region for hundreds of years.

islands have heavy forests. There are long, narrow, deep inlets of the sea between steep slopes, called fjords. Broad valleys stretch between ice-topped hills.

Iñupiat and Yup'ik

In this diverse and huge landscape, people known as Iñupiat (eh-NEW-pee-ot)—those living along the Arctic coast of Alaska, Canada, and Greenland—and Yup'ik (YOU-pick)—those living in southwestern Alaska along the state's Pacific coast—have lived for centuries in hundreds of small and widely separated villages. The Yup'ik hunted seals, whales, and walruses from their kayaks. A kayak is a boat with a light wooden frame that is covered with animal skins. It usually had two openings in the center—one for the paddler and one for the harpooner. The Iñupiat hunted seals by waiting for them at their breathing holes in the ice.

Contrary to popular belief, Iñupiat and Yup'ik people did not usually live in snow igloos. Like camping tents, snow igloos were usually used for temporary shelters. During the winter, some groups of Iñupiat and Yup'ik people lived in domed driftwood and sod houses. Other groups covered wooden structures with skins or bark.

☀ Iñupiat Traditional Account:
Raven and the Whale

As the Iñupiat say, at the very beginning of time Raven made the world and all that was on it. He decided to stay, as he loved the people and animals and was quite curious about them. Although he had made everything, he did not know everything.

One day, while paddling his kayak out to sea, Raven saw a large whale. When the whale yawned, he rowed right into it. The whale's mouth closed behind him and it grew dark. Raven heard a sound like a drum. He continued to row until he came to the belly of the whale. The white bones of the whale's ribs rose up around him like ivory columns.

A beautiful girl was dancing right in the middle of the whale's belly. Strings were attached to her feet and hands. The strings were also attached to the whale's heart. Raven fell in love right away. He wanted to take her out of the whale and marry her.

Raven expressed his love to her and told her he had made the world. He asked her to marry him and leave the whale. The young girl answered that she could not, as she was the whale's heart and soul. But she invited Raven to stay there with her. Raven showed her his human face by throwing back his beak. He relaxed his wings and settled down to watch the girl dance.

When her steps were fast and lively, the whale swam fast. The whale floated calmly when her steps slowed. Finally she stopped moving and closed her eyes. Raven felt a cool breeze blow from the whale's spout. He forgot the girl's words because he wanted to take her into the world.

Suddenly Raven grabbed her! The strings snapped as he flew with her into the sky. The whale thrashed below in the ocean. The whale's dead body was tossed onto the shore by the waves. And the girl grew smaller and smaller in his arms until she disappeared.

Raven was overcome with sorrow and regret for what he had done. He learned that all things alive have a heart and a soul. Whatever is born also dies. He landed next to the dead whale and cried for a long time. Then Raven began to dance, and he kept dancing for weeks. He began to sing, and he sang for weeks, until his grieving was over. Finally he flew back up into the sky.

Iñupiat Snow Goggles

When Iñupiat men went hunting, they protected their eyes from the Arctic sun with snow goggles. Sunlight bouncing off snow is bright and makes it hard to see. It can even cause eyes to become sunburned. If eyes become burned, it can lead to temporary snow blindness. If this happens to someone while hunting, the person may not be able to survive in frigid weather, especially if he or she is alone.

Make Iñupiat-Style Snow Goggles

Before sunglasses were invented in 1929, Iñupiat people made snow goggles from caribou antlers, bone, wood, bark, and cloth. The goggles had narrow slits that allowed the wearer to see out, but allowed only a small amount of light to come in. A small slit is best because it limits the amount of ultraviolet light that reaches the eye. One can see through a surprisingly narrow hole.

Try making these snow goggles inspired by Iñupiat hunters.

What You Need

Cardboard paper towel or
   toilet tissue roll

Ruler

Pencil

Scissors

Hole puncher

2 8-inch-long pieces of string or yarn

What You Do

1. Flatten the cardboard roll with your hands.

2. Make a pencil dot on the exact center of the cardboard. Then ask a grown-up to measure the distance between the pupils of your eyes. Divide that measurement by two. Put half of the measurement on each side of the dot marked on the cardboard.

3. Cut out a small slit, about ½ inch long and ¼ inch high, for each eye.

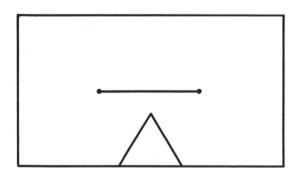

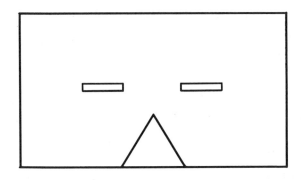

4. Put it in front of your eyes and have a grown-up make a pencil mark where your nose is. Draw a triangle shape for your nose. Cut it out so the goggles can fit on your face.

5. Punch a hole at each end of your goggles.

6. Thread a piece of string or yarn through each hole and tie a knot.

7. Put on your goggles by tying the two cords together behind the back of your head. Go out on a bright sunny day with your goggles on. You will be able to see out, but very little sunlight can get through the slits.

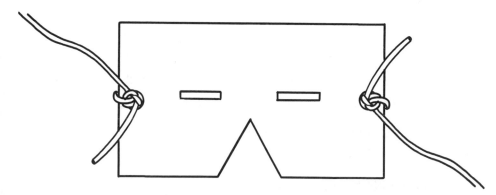

Barrow, Alaska, has the largest Iñupiat community in the world. It also is the largest municipality in the world in terms of land area. Since it is also the northernmost city in the United States, Barrow is often called the "Top of the World." The city is so close to the North Pole that there are 24 hours of daylight each day between May and August. Between November and January, however, the sun doesn't rise, so it's dark most of the time.

The Barrow Whalers is the only Arctic high school football team in America. Games are played on a dirt field surrounded by icebergs. Barrow has streets, but they do not lead into or out of town. The only way to leave Barrow is by airplane or ship.

Aleut

Aleut people live on some of the islands in Alaska's 1,400-mile-long chain of Aleutian Islands (numbering more than 300) that stretch into the Pacific Ocean southwest of the Alaskan mainland. They also live on two of the five Pribilof Islands, which sit in the middle of the Bering Sea, north of the Aleutian chain. The winds have created a treeless landscape with tall, windswept grasses. While summers are short and winters are long, there is a lot of fog and wind, and the weather is always unpredictable.

More people lived on the island chain than anywhere else in the Alaskan area. It is estimated that over 25,000 people made their homes on the islands. Their diet consisted of wild plants, berries, eggs, and a variety of sea life. They ate clams, fish, and octopuses, as well as seals and whales, which they also used to make housing and clothing. They made the frames of their houses with whalebones or driftwood and covered them with grass mats and sod. The thick covering protected the inside of the house from the howling winds. Today environmental architects have devised methods to grow grass on roofs in urban areas. Like traditional Aleutian homes, the grass keeps the buildings warm in the winter and cool in the summer.

The Unangan (oo-NUNG-an), called Aleut by the Russians, possessed special skills for hunting marine mammals from skin-covered kayaks. In the 1740s the Aleut were invaded by the Russians, who quickly recognized the value of sea otters' and other animals' pelts. More and more Russian fur traders came to the islands, and many of them were criminals. At first the Aleut welcomed them, but the Russians were greedy for furs and forced the Aleut to hunt for them. They held Aleut wives and children hostage to ensure the hunters would bring in enough furs. The Russians also broke up Aleutian towns, isolating people on tiny islands so they could control them. The Aleut had no weapons that could match the huge cannons on the ships that were aimed right at their houses. The Aleut did try to defend themselves, but the situation just worsened, and more families were taken and people were killed. The Russians had enslaved the Aleutian people. The overhunting of seals and sea otters, which supplied the Aleut with food, clothing, and even shelter, almost made the animals extinct and destroyed Aleut food and clothing sources. The once densely populated Aleutian homelands had changed forever. Thousands had died from European diseases or been killed for fighting the invaders.

The Aleut managed to survive despite the warfare and diseases that reduced their population. They still get much of their food from the ocean, and they have programs to preserve their islands and ensure that the habitat survives. However, commercial fishing threatens the environment, just as seal hunting did in the past.

No one really knows exactly why early Russian explorers renamed the Unangan people Aleut. Although the Unangan are most often called Aleut, many people today prefer to return to their original name. Their language, Unangam Tunuu, is considered endangered, but there are programs for children to make sure the language continues. Sometimes ideas, feelings, or beliefs cannot be translated into another language because other cultures have no words that correspond to Native vocabulary. Some words are just not able to be translated, and the ideas die. That is why it is important for any group of people to keep its language alive.

Fashion an Unangan-Inspired Wind Chime

The Unangan have over seven words for wind. Sometimes for weeks on end, the winds seem to push around the tiny Aleutian Islands sitting in the middle of the vast sea.

Create this wind chime so you can "hear" the wind. You can use any objects that make a sound when clinked together and that can be strung. Maybe the objects will make your wind chime sing!

What You Need

Adult supervision required

Paintbrush

Acrylic paints in different colors

4 or more unwanted CDs or DVDs

Permanent marker

Hook-and-eye screws

12-inch-long piece of diftwood, dowel, or twig

Fishing line or dental floss

Small objects, each with at least one hole (such as bells or pre-drilled seashells)

What You Do

1. Using the list of Unangam Tunuu words for wind found on the next page as a reference, paint pictures of different types of winds onto the CDs or DVDs. Using the marker, write the Unangam Tunuu word for that type of wind below the picture.

2. Have an adult help you inset the hook-and-eye screws into the driftwood, dowel, or twig. Use as many screws as you want, but space them at least ½ inch apart, and make sure that the number on one side equals the number on the other side so that the wind chime stays balanced.

3. String each CD or DVD onto a length of fishing line or dental floss. Make each string a different length so that the discs won't hang together in an even row. Position each disc so that it's in the middle of its string, and tie the string above the top of the disc so that it doesn't move around. Tie a loop at the end of each string and loop the string over a hook.

4. String other objects, such as bells or pre-drilled seashells, onto other lengths of fishing line or dental floss. Make each string a different length. Tie a knot above and below each object to keep it in place on the string, making sure that, when the wind blows, the objects will bump into the discs and each other and make music. Loop each string over a hook.

5. Tie a length of fishing line or dental floss around each end of the driftwood, dowel, or twig. Use it to hang your wind chime outside.

Wind Words in Unangam Tunuu:

Slachxidaasaadagx̂	A very strong storm
Kachigikûx	It's windy
Slam kakiigux̂taa	A contrary wind
Alaĝulix	To blow into the sea
Asxi – lix	To go against the wind
Qutaxt	Blowing up from the land
Qag	East wind
Agaagalix̂	West wind
Chax̂atax̂	An offshore wind

Aquilina (Debbie) Lestenkof, Aleut (1960–)

Aquilina (Debbie) Lestenkof, of the St. Paul Tribal Government Ecosystem Conservation Office, was awarded the 2005 Wings Women of Discovery Earth Award by Wings WorldQuest. She was recognized for her efforts in merging Native Alaskan knowledge with science to help Bering Sea wildlife. Born on Alaska's Pribilof Islands, Lestenkof's father inspired her to listen to her Aleut people's stories, wishes, and dreams and to preserve the culture. Lestenkof of teaches Unangan youth to care for all the plants and creatures that live near their Alaskan island homes.

After the U.S. government purchased the Alaska Territory in 1867, it licensed outsiders to hunt, to near extinction, the sea otters and fur seals on which the Aleut had long depended. The United States took over management of the Pribolofs and their fur seals when it purchased Alaska.

In an attempt to repair the damage done to Aleut culture, the United States claimed 95 percent of the Aleutian Islands chain as a refuge or military site. The government only permitted Aleut to hunt on the islands. In the early 1900s, codfish and herring industries provided a way for Aleut people to make a living. Decades later, the city of Unalaska, on Unalaska Island in the middle of the Aleutian chain, became the number-one fishing port in the United States. During the fishing season, jobs are plentiful for the Aleut people, who drive water taxis and work at other jobs during the rest of the year.

Aleut Relocation

In 1942, during World War II, Japan invaded Attu and Kiska, at the western end of the Aleutian Islands. Japan made no further moves toward the U.S. mainland. However, the U.S. military forced most Aleut residents out of their homes and away from the islands. Most left with few possessions. They were transported to southeast Alaska to live in abandoned factories, where there was not enough food, medicine, clothing, or heat. Many people died. When the Unangan were allowed to return to their islands, they discovered that most of their homes and property had been destroyed and that their churches and community buildings had been looted by American soldiers who were supposed to protect their property. The Aleutian people tried to get the United States to pay for the damages. It was not until over 40 years later, in 1988, that a U.S. law authorized compensation for the loss of property.

Athabascan Indians

Numerous Athabascan-speaking Indian groups have lived in small traditional villages in vast areas of Alaska's interior. The temperatures in those areas range from 100° F in summer to 60° F below zero in winter. They got most of their food by hunting caribou and mountain sheep, fishing for salmon in rivers, or gathering berries and plants. They also trapped beaver and muskrat. The cold climate and rocky soil could not support farming. The people governed themselves through customs and traditions developed over generations.

The Gwich'in (GWUCH-en) are the northernmost Native nation in North America. They live in 15 small villages scattered across vast areas spanning northeast Alaska to the northern Yukon and Northwest Territories in Canada. Gwich'in means "people of the land." They have lived in the Arctic for at least 20,000 years. For thousands of years, Gwich'in have relied on the caribou herd to meet their needs. The animals provide food, clothing, and tools.

Today, the Gwich'in live near the migration route of the Porcupine caribou herd. In the past few decades, gas and oil corporations have laid over 500 miles of roads and pipelines and built thousands of oil and gas wells, power plants, and gravel mines. These activities have harmed caribou, bear, and other wildlife, as well as the tundra. This damage threatens the Gwich'in way of life. Hunters worry they won't be able to provide food for their families. They also worry that the food is contaminated. Smog and haze from oil and gas industries near villages have increased asthma in the Gwich'in people.

Today, the Gwich'in people are fighting to protect the health and existence of the Porcupine River caribou herd. The Gwich'in have formed an organization of village chiefs from the United States and Canada to speak with one voice against oil and gas development in the grounds of the caribou herd. They work to educate the public and decision-makers about how and why the herd must be protected.

Athabascan women are known for their incredible appliqué beadwork. Some of their large pieces look like paintings. Other pieces look like embroidery on leather. Usually, the design is first drawn right onto the leather. Sometimes they create a pattern on felt which is then sewn onto the leather. They start from the outside of their pattern and bead to the middle. The beads are tight and precise. The beautiful beaded pictures feature flowers, birds, fish, and animals. Clothing, bags, barrettes, gloves, and jackets can be adorned with the world-famous art.

Bead an Athabascan-Inspired "Painting"

It is not hard to learn the basics of beading, but it takes time, practice, and patience to be really good at it. In this activity, the beads are glued onto the design, but if you have the time, try your hand at using beading needles, beading thread, and fabric.

What You Need

5-by-7 inch clear acrylic box picture frame

Scissors

Stiff paper or lightweight cardboard

Pencil

Scrap paper

Markers or colored pencils

Glue gun

Toothpicks

#10 beads in different colors (available at craft stores)

What You Do

1. Remove the cover from the picture frame and set it aside.
2. Cut the stiff paper or cardboard to the size of the box.
3. Sketch a flower, fish, bird, or other design on the cardboard. You might want to write your name, too. You may want to practice on the scrap paper first.
4. Color in your design with the markers or colored pencils. Make sure the colors match the colors of the beads, as that will be your guide for gluing on the beads.
5. Use the glue gun to spread glue over the entire design. Use the toothpicks to pick up beads. Add beads to the corresponding colors of the design until it is completely beaded over. Let dry.

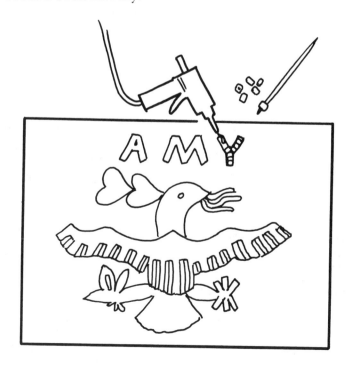

6. Put your beaded painting on top of the box. Replace the cover.

Haida, Tlingit, and Tsimshian Indians

Tlingit (KLIN-kit) Indians have considered the forested areas of southeast Alaska their territory for thousands of years. They were numerous, powerful traders who possessed knowledge of secret routes along the sea as far south as California and north through the mountains into Alaska's interior. The Tsimshian (SIM-shee-an) Indians, who originally lived in Canada, moved to the Annette Island Reserve, in southeastern Alaska, in 1884. In the

early 1900s, Haida (HI-dah) Indians came to live in the area as well. The lands occupied by the three groups were rich in natural resources. There were at least a dozen kinds of saltwater fish, in addition to shellfish, sea mammals, and many land plants. The forests of cedar and hemlock provided an endless supply of building materials that made it possible for the groups to live in large villages. Tlingit people encountered Russians in the 1740s, and the Tsimshian and Haida met the British in the late 1700s. Like other Native peoples across North America, many of these Indians died from new diseases, like smallpox, brought by the outsiders.

Native Art from Alaska

The Native nations in southeast Alaska are famous for their large dugout canoes, elaborately carved totem poles, and other everyday objects, like bowls and storage boxes. David Boxley, Tsimshian, grew up in Metlakatla on Annette Island, Alaska's only Indian reservation. He is one of many carvers who have dedicated their art to both the study and creation of traditional pieces like totem poles, drums, masks, bentwood boxes, rattles, and silkscreen prints. Collectors worldwide, including royalty, seek Boxley's art. He shares his skills, teaching others how to make the beautiful carvings. He believes that artists are the bearers of his nation's culture and has helped bring the totem pole tradition back to Metlakatla. The majestic poles are carved from mature cedar trees. They are like a family's history book, representing the family's clan, accomplishments, adventures, histories, and relatives. The symbols carved on some totem poles show an entire family's past.

Tlingit Indians also erected Ridicule or Shame totem poles to force some person of high standing to meet or recognize an obligation. Many non-Native men are carved on these poles. Another form of shaming a person was to carve him upside down. Sometimes the ears and mouth were painted red as a sign of that person's stinginess.

Haida, Tsimshian, Tlingit, and other Alaska Natives peoples have been using button blankets for over a hundred years. After contact with European fur traders, Native people began to trade furs for wool blankets. Women turned the dull blue or black blankets into beautiful robes by appliquéing family crests and other designs on them, usually in red. At first the design was outlined with shells, giving it an attractive shimmer when light hit it. Later, white mother-of-pearl buttons replaced the shells on most of the blankets. The robes are often part of the regalia worn during special ceremonial times. Today, button blankets are often outlined with shells, buttons, beads, and sometimes metal decorations. Some are made just to sell, while others are only worn at potlatches, totem pole raisings, weddings, and other ceremonies.

WILLIAM LEWIS PAUL, TLINGIT
(1885–1977)

Born in southeast Alaska, William Paul was sent far from home to Carlisle Indian Industrial School in Pennsylvania. The school taught Native children from all over the United States. He went on to complete a law degree, which prepared him to fight for labor rights and Native land rights. He was a leader in the Alaska Native Brotherhood, an organization that sued the U.S. government for taking Indian lands away. For over 30 years, Mr. Paul devoted most of his time to the case. He helped the Native people win their claim.

A button blanket is an important part of tribal traditions. Most Native people prefer to keep their sacred objects private. Because the button blanket is worn in rituals, it would be disrespectful to copy the Tsimshian, Haida, or Tlingit designs. The designs have special meanings.

Design a Button Art Scrapbook Cover

You can create a button cover for your scrapbook. You can use a traditional design to inspire your art, but make sure not to copy any designs of the Haida, Tsimshian, and Tlingit. Be creative and come up with your own special picture.

What You Need

Pencil

Scrap paper

Scissors

2 8½-by-11-inch pieces of felt

Felt glue or craft glue (available from craft stores)

Plain notebook binder (not white, and not a color that matches the felt)

Flat buttons (as many as needed to outline the notebook binder and to use in your designs)

What You Do

1. Draw a design of your choosing on the scrap paper. This will be the front cover of your scrapbook. Do another drawing for the back cover (or you can use the same design on the front and back). Make it something that is important to you, like your pet, favorite game, or favorite flower.

2. Cut out your designs and lay each one on a piece of felt. Trace them each with the pencil and cut them out. Glue each felt design onto the front or back of the binder cover.

3. Glue the buttons onto the felt design. You can make a border all the way around if you have enough buttons, or just add them to your design. You can spell out your name or your initials with the buttons, too.

ROSITA WORL, TLINGIT

(Contemporary)

Rosita Worl grew up being involved in Indian rights. Her mother organized Native workers into unions so that they would have better working conditions in Alaska's salmon canneries. Worl was an anthropology student who did fieldwork with the Iñupiat people in northern Alaska. The only woman on whale hunting crews, she never complained about the cold, as she felt she had to be stronger than the men. Today Worl teaches anthropology and studies the impact that logging and mining industries have on Native communities. She is also the president of the Sealaska Heritage Institute, an organization that preserves and teaches the cultures and languages of the Tsimshian, Haida, and Tlingit peoples.

Non-Indian Settlers Come to Alaska

The first contact of Alaskan peoples with Europeans was with the Russians Vitus Bering and Aleksei Chirikov on July 15, 1741. The Russian ruler Tsar Peter the Great had ordered them to find the passage from the Arctic Ocean to the Pacific Ocean. The Russians established a post on the Tlingit homelands (present-day Baranov Island) in 1799. In 1802 the Tlingit people resisted the invasion into their homeland. There were two historic battles between Tlingit and Russians in 1802 and 1804. In 1802 Katlian, a war hero of the Sitka group of Tlingit, led an attack on the Russian post, capturing it and recovering pelts of sea mammals hunted on Tlingit lands. Katlian's men held the post for two years until the Russians returned with an armada of ships, which bombarded the Tlingits with cannon fire. Katlian and his men were forced to retreat, but he is still considered a hero today.

Once Russian colonists arrived, their goal was to convert the Native population to Christianity and Russian culture. Conversion was encouraged by the Russian tsar as head of the Russian Orthodox Church. Alaska Natives were not allowed to practice their religions, speak their languages, or conduct their traditional forms of government. Orthodox missionaries were generally successful, more so among the Aleuts, Yup'ik, and Iñupiat than the Tlingit. After the purchase of Alaska by the United States in 1867, Catholic and Protestant missionaries arrived and competed for converts.

The Purchase of Alaska

On March 30, 1867, Secretary of State William H. Seward agreed to purchase Alaska from Russia for the bargain price of $7.2 million. At that time, the Alaska Native population was about 30,000, many more than any non-Native population there. No one asked the Native people about the purchase of Alaska. When Alaska Natives learned about the sale, they argued that the land had belonged to them long before the Russians or Americans came. They argued that Russia had no right to sell their land and the United States had no right to buy it, but it was sold anyway.

After 1867 the United States occupied Alaska militarily, using both the army and navy to rule the state. The U.S. military rule ended in 1884. A 1912 act made Alaska a territory of the United States. Its rule over the Alaska Native people was a mixture of neglecting them and forcing them to adopt non-Indian American culture. Around 1900 the schools became segregated in Alaska. White children, along with children who were mixed (Native and white) went to school together. Children who were Native only went to separate schools.

Alaska became the 49th state in 1959. After statehood was established, the territory's population doubled. The increase in population put a demand on Alaska's land and water resources. In 1966 Native villages and organizations formed a statewide organization called the Alaska Federation of Natives. Alaska Native people filed land claims covering the entire state of Alaska in an effort to stop the state from taking land and water the people had never given up. This led to the 1971 law called the Alaska Native Claims Settlement Act, which settled the question of Native land rights. The act gave Alaska's Native people title to 44 million acres of the ancient homelands.

In the early 1900s, 16-year-old George Johnston was concerned that his Tlingit traditions were disappearing. He traveled hundreds of miles west from his Tlingit community in Canada's Yukon Territory to Alaska's coast to study the history of his people. Johnston met with elders, learning as much as he could about the Tlingit religion as well as about the songs and dances. Just a few years later, he ordered a camera through a mail-order catalog and taught himself how to use it and even how to develop and print photographs. From 1920 until 1945 he recorded the lives and culture of the Tlingit people, creating a permanent memory of that time. Johnston's shots were filled with sensitivity, love, humor, and great attention to detail.

One time Johnston purchased a new car, the only one in his remote village of Teslin where there were no roads. He had to build his own street for the car. The four-mile road later became part of the Alaska Highway. Shipped by a small

CREATE A SCRAPBOOK OF YOUR TIME IN HISTORY

Like George Johnston's Tlingit heritage, there are unique parts of your culture that will change or disappear. For instance, the clothes that are popular today will not be fashionable when you are an adult. Your neighborhood may change; you and your friends will get bigger; and the rooms in your house may be decorated differently. But you can remember things exactly the way they are now by capturing their images in photographs, writing down memories, and saving mementoes and souvenirs. Try keeping a personal scrapbook of your life for one month or even a year.

What You Need

Any kind of camera

Notebook

Scrapbook

Glue

Markers or colored pencils

What You Do

1. Think about some things in your life that you would like to record and take pictures of them. Use your notebook to keep a list of your shots, the date they were taken, and who is in them. Keep your camera with you and take pictures of whatever interests you, remembering that you want to record the items and events that you think will be different in a few years. Be sure to ask people for permission to take their photos.

2. Develop the film or upload pictures to a computer. If you are using a computer, you can add captions to your photos.

3. Arrange your images in your scrapbook and add captions. Refer to your notebook for help remembering details. You can include drawings, mementos (like movie ticket stubs), songs, or even writings from you, your family, and friends. On the first page, add a title like "A Month in the Life of (your name)."

paddle boat, Johnston's famous car traveled hundreds of miles up the Yukon River. Not only did the car help his photography project, but it also became the local taxi. He even drove it onto the frozen lake, where he used it as an ice-fishing house. George Johnston's photographs, which can still be seen today, captured forever a piece of a world that was never the same again. You might say he kept a scrapbook of a particular time in history. His community boasts the George Johnston Museum, located right on the Alaska Highway.

A Teenager Designed the Alaska State Flag

A teenager designed the Alaska state flag. John Ben "Benny" Benson Jr. (1913–1972) was only 13 years old when he won a flag design contest for the Territory of Alaska. He was from the Iñupiat village of Chignik.

Native Alaska Today

Despite the impact of non-Native society, cultural traditions and languages of Alaska Native people are strong today alongside snowmobiles, computers, satellite dishes, and cell phones. Technology used for preserving history and sharing community news has grown since George Johnston first picked up a camera almost a hundred years ago. *Heartbeat Alaska*, a television news program, is the first Native-owned, produced, and staffed news program ever offered nationwide in the history of American television. Jeanie Greene, Iñupiaq, is the host, reporter, and producer. Born and raised in the logging and fishing town of Sitka, Alaska, she has won several media awards. Greene receives homemade videos from viewers, although the program has its own production staff of videographers and editors. Her fans send gifts like herring eggs and dried seal meat, which she samples while on camera. People in China, Japan, and England love the popular show as much as Alaska Native villagers. *Heartbeat Alaska* feature stories include Native mushers in the Iditarod race, the breaking up of ice floes in the Yukon, and the World Eskimo-Indian Olympics.

PLAY GAMES FROM THE WORLD ESKIMO-INDIAN OLYMPICS

Practice the following events and then stage your own version of World Eskimo-Indian World Olympics with food, posters, and some of the other activities featured in this chapter. Take turns being the time keeper.

What You Need

Friends

Large open area

Stopwatch or kitchen timer

Sturdy dowel or stick at least 1 yard long

What You Do

1. Seal, or Knuckle Hop: Assume a push-up position at the starting line, but balance on your knuckles and toes. Hop forward, as far and as fast as possible, maintaining this position. The contestant who hops the farthest while keeping his or her back straight and elbows bent wins. This game challenges your strength and endurance of pain.

2. Kneel Jump: Kneel on the floor at the starting line, insteps flat on floor, soles facing upward. Jump forward as far as possible and land on your feet, swinging your arms to gather momentum. The first person to jump farthest in the agreed-upon time limit wins. This event tests a person's quickness and balance—important skills to keep from falling into the frigid Arctic Sea while the ice is moving and breaking.

3. Stick Pull: Two players face each other, sitting on the ground with their feet pressed together and knees bent slightly. The dowel or stick is placed between them, side to side and right over where their feet meet. Each player grabs the stick so that one person's hands are on the inside and the other's hands are on the outside. All hands must be touching. At the start signal, the contestants hold on tightly and try to pull the stick away from each other. The winner is the person who is either able to pull the opponent over to his or her side or the one who can pull the stick out of the opponent's hands. The best two out of three tries wins. This event showed that a person was strong enough to pull a seal up from a hole in the ice.

The World Eskimo-Indian Olympics

To live in the harsh Alaskan climate, Native peoples need to be strong and have many different skills. Ancient games taught children how to be tough and well-rounded to survive. The games left no part of the body untested.

Families and entire villages gathered to feast, dance, and play. Sometimes the gatherings were held to celebrate a successful seal or whale hunt. The temperature outside the warm work house, which was built of driftwood, whale bone, and stone, could be −60° F. But inside the people were comfortable. Young men practiced amazing athletic feats while the whaling captains watched. The captains looked for those who would be helpful to whaling and hunting teams. To be on the team, one had to be strong, fast, and have great balance and agility. The captains also needed their crews to be able to deal with pain and hardship. Like coaches today who scout athletes, captains observed the young men to see who had the best qualities.

Today, these same games are played during holidays and at the annual World Eskimo-Indian Olympics. Native athletes compete in challenging sports like the Four Man Carry, Ear Pull, One Arm Reach, Toe Kick, Seal or Knuckle Hop, Kneel Jump, and Stick Pull.

10 Hawaii

How would you like to learn math by building a traditional voyaging canoe or study science by swimming out in the ocean to monitor the health of a coral reef? At the Halau Ku Mana Charter School in Honolulu, Hawaii, Native Hawaiian kids learn most of their subjects by "doing." School is never boring as the kids zip through the day analyzing all they have learned while sailing, hiking, cooking, and speaking the Hawaiian language. At the core of all their studies are Native Hawaiian values like *Aloha*— love, compassion for all; *Malama*—mutual respect and caring for the land and all its inhabitants; and *Kupono*—striving to always be in a state of *pono* (balance, harmony, and fairness).

Since long before Hawaii became a state and centuries before the United States was a country, the islands have been the homelands of South Sea peoples of Polynesian and Tahitian descent. Volcanic activity formed the Hawaiian homelands, which include eight large islands and over a hundred smaller ones. Kilauea, located on the island of Hawaii, is still one of the most active volcanoes in the world. High forested mountains, lagoons, and rivers were home to many one-of-a-kind animals and plants, like the naupaka flowering shrub.

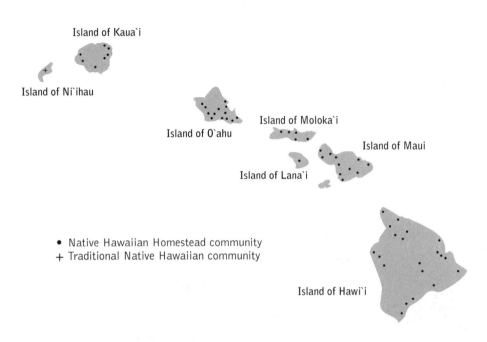

Map of Hawaii Today

Island of Kaua`i

Island of Ni`ihau

Island of O`ahu

Island of Moloka`i

Island of Lana`i

Island of Maui

• Native Hawaiian Homestead community
+ Traditional Native Hawaiian community

Island of Hawi`i

☀ Hawaiian Traditional Account: The Story of Naupaka

One of Hawaii's most famous stories is based on the beautiful flower, the naupaka. The naupaka found in the mountains only grow petals on the top half of the flower. The Naupaka found near the beach have petals on the bottom half only. It looks as if the two types of Naupaka would be a complete flower if they were squeezed together. There are different stories of how these plants came to be this way.

As it is told, in ancient times a handsome young man and a beautiful young woman were very much in love. They wanted to be together forever.

One day when the young man was working alone, the Goddess Pele noticed him. She told him that she was in love with him and wanted him for her sweetheart. The young man told her that he already had a sweetheart to whom he was devoted. Pele grew angry and chased the young man into the mountains, throwing molten lava at him. Pele's sisters heard his screams and saved his life by turning him into a naupaka flower found only in the mountains.

Pele was so angry that she went looking for the young man's sweetheart. She chased the young woman into the sea. To save the young woman from drowning, Pele's sisters turned her into the type of naupaka that only grows near the beach.

It is said that if the mountain and beach naupaka are reunited, the flowers will become whole and the two young sweethearts will be together again.

Native Hawaiian Navigators

Early Hawaiians were seafaring people who had none of the computers and technology used on modern ships. However, they systematically sailed through 16 million square miles of the dangerous Pacific Ocean long before Spanish and Portuguese sailors could even sail beyond the sight of land. By studying the sun, stars, wave patterns, bird flight paths, and cloud formations, they were able to locate islands and navigate ocean currents. They created highly detailed and accurate maps of wave patterns. Entire villages sailed in the huge double-hulled canoes, bringing along their livestock, clothing, and tools in their search for new lands. A double-hulled canoe was built by lashing two very large canoes together with a crossbeam. The two hulls made the craft stable and able to carry migrating families and all their supplies and equipment. The gigantic sails, made of matting, provided enough wind speed to move swiftly through the churning sea. The craft resembled today's catamaran. A medium-size voyaging canoe was 60 feet long and outfitted with working, living, and storage spaces.

The *Hokule'a*

The *Hokule'a* is a huge outrigger canoe crafted just like the canoes of Hawaiian ancestors. Built in 1976 by the Polynesian Voyaging Society, the ship travels to different communities to teach about Hawaiian traditions and to show how ancient Hawaiians were able to navigate the seas using sophisticated methods. The *Hokule'a* has sailed around the South Seas and as far away as New Zealand.

Hawaiian Farming

Polynesian seafarers introduced over 25 food plants to the Hawaiian Islands when they first arrived over 2,300 years ago. The people farmed tropical fruits, sweet potatoes, breadfruit, yams, greens, taro, and other crops. Taro, also called *kalo*, is still an important part of everyday meals as well as special feasts. Every part of the taro can be eaten, and the corm (underground stem) is cooked and made into a porridge-like dish called poi. In Hawaiian traditions, a bowl of poi at the table means the ancestor of the Hawaiian people is present and it would be disrespectful to argue. All conflict is put aside.

There are different varieties of taro. The planters of wetland taro were engineers who built great walls of earth reinforced with stone that enclosed the *lo'i* (pond field). *Lo'i* banks were planted with *mai'a* (banana), *ko* (sugarcane), and *wauke* (mulberry), which was pounded into *tapa* cloth. In the pond field, several varieties of fish were raised, such as *'awa*, *o'opu*, and *aholehole*. An acre of wet *lo'i* could produce three to five tons of food per year. Dryland taro was grown in the rich soil of the forests. The stone borders of these gardens can still be found today.

Polynesians from different places brought a variety of foods like bananas, coconuts, and sugarcane. Pineapples started out in Brazil and Paraguay, but Native people as far north as the West Indies and Mexico soon began to cultivate them. In 1813 pineapple was first brought to Honolulu by Don Francisco de Paula Marin, a Spanish botanist and advisor to Hawaiian King Kamehameha. Today, people usually associate the pineapple with Hawaii, although the plant was developed thousands of miles from the South Seas. It is a big part of the Hawaiian economy.

Make a Hawaiian Fruit Boat

What You Need

Adult supervision required

1 pineapple

1 banana

Juice of ½ lemon

½ cup macadamia nuts

½ cup unsweetened
    shredded coconut

What You Do

1. Have an adult cut the pineapple in half the long way, keeping the top intact. Removes the tough inner core, then carve out the remaining fruit and cut it into bite-sized chunks.

2. Put the chunks in a bowl. Slice the banana and add it to the bowl.

3. Pour the lemon juice over the fruit and mix it up. This will keep the fruit from browning.

4. Add the macadamia nuts. Spoon the mixture back into the pineapple boats (shells).

5. Sprinkle coconut over both halves and serve immediately.

Serves 6

The Kingdom of Hawaii

In 1778 the English captain James Cook landed on the Island of Kauai. He opened the doors to the west, and Hawaiian culture was changed forever. Native Hawaiians went through years of troubled times and, in order to survive the newcomers, they organized themselves into a European-style government called a monarchy. They became the Kingdom of Hawaii and were recognized internationally as a sovereign and independent country. The kingdom made treaties with every major nation, including several with the United States.

Businesspeople from around the world started sugar and pineapple plantations in the fertile Hawaiian homelands. Plantation owners encouraged workers from many countries to come to Hawaii to labor on the large plantations. They often had to live in terrible conditions and were not paid well for their backbreaking work. The plantations thrived and the owners made more and more money, but Native Hawaiians lost more and more of their territory.

The reigning Hawaiian monarch, Queen Liliuokalani, made attempts to restore the rightful power of the Hawaiian people. She proposed a new constitution that would lessen the power of the American and European merchants and plantation owners. It was a peaceful attempt to create a fair balance for the Hawaiians. But, in 1893, the Americans called on the U.S. Marines to protect them, although they were in no danger. The marines came ashore heavily armed and overthrew the constitutional monarch of Hawaii, although no shots were fired. The Hawaiian people were surrounded by a major military force and Queen Liliuokalani was arrested and confined to the `Iolani Palace. All of her powers and the government of the Kingdom of Hawaii were brought to an end. Although the actions violated international law and U.S. treaties, Hawaii was made a territory of the United States and was never again a sovereign nation.

On November 23, 1993, U.S. President Bill Clinton signed United States Public Law 103-150, also known as the Apology Resolution. The resolution "apologizes to Native Hawaiians on behalf of the people of the United States for the overthrow of the Kingdom of Hawaii."

Native Hawaii Today

Today, many Native Hawaiians struggle to be a sovereign nation once again. A sovereign nation has the right to govern itself. Native Hawaiian efforts center on land and water rights, which are sacred to the Hawaiian people as the caretakers of the islands. Native Hawaiian children have special school programs in which they learn the Native language as well as culture and history. Communities are striving to preserve the Hawaiian ecosystem so that Native Hawaiians of the future will be able to appreciate the special culture of living in the middle of the sea.

TAPA CLOTH

Native Hawaiians have a centuries-old tradition of fabric making. They made cloth from the inner bark of mulberry trees by pounding it into beautiful designs. Bed coverings were made in several layers connected at the bottom so sleepers could take off or add on as many covers as they needed. In the 1800s Hawaiian quilt makers began to use cotton cloth to make their bedding, fashioning it into beautiful pieced and appliqué quilts. Many of the designs were inspired by local plants and flowers. They often cut out designs in the same way as a paper snowflake. Quilt making is still an art form among Hawaiians. Some quilts are made to honor a special occasion like a birth or a wedding.

Hawaiian plants, animals, and fish are some of the most rare and unique in the world because of the isolation of the islands. They often had no natural predators until Europeans brought foreign insects, plants, and animals, which invaded and destroyed the natural inhabitants. Today Hawaii is considered to be the "endangered species capital of the world."

There is a swirling mass of plastic garbage in the Pacific Ocean halfway between Hawaii and the U.S. mainland. Called the "plastic ocean," the floating trash heap is twice the size of Texas! Scientists say the toxins released by this debris are entering our food chain and causing obesity, cancer, and other illnesses. The area, known as the "North Pacific Gyre," is really dangerous for marine wildlife. Sea turtles, fish, birds, and other sea life mistake the plastics for food and get very ill after eating bags and other materials. You can help save the oceans and our own health by not using so much plastic. Be careful to dispose of it properly, especially by finding places to recycle it.

DUKE PAOA KAHANAMOKU, NATIVE HAWAIIAN (1890–1968)

Not only did the Native Hawaiians invent methods to sail the oceans, but they also developed surfing. Called the Father of Surfing, Kahanamoku introduced the ancient sport to the world. He was a master surfer, using a 16-foot Koa wood surfboard that weighed 114 pounds. Today's fiberglass boards are extremely lightweight in comparison. Kahanamoku competed in four Olympics, and he won medals in swimming events and water polo. He was inducted into the Swimming Hall of Fame and the Surfing Hall of Fame, and he became one of the 26 all-time sports champions in 1967. Once considered the greatest freestyle swimmer in the world, Kahanamoku developed the flutter kick, which replaced the scissors kick. He was so good at his sport that he once rescued a crew of capsized fishermen on his surfboard.

Quilt a Ma'o hau hele Tote Bag

One way you can help protect the oceans is by using reusable fabric tote bags instead of plastic bags. Hawaii's state flower is the *ma'o hau hele,* or yellow hibiscus in English. It will look beautiful on your tote bag.

Hibiscus, Hawaiian State Flower

What You Need

Adult supervision required

8-inch square of construction paper

Pencil

Scissors

Fusible webbing (available at craft stores)

Iron and ironing board

8-inch square of plain yellow cotton fabric

Canvas tote bag

What You Do

1. Fold the construction paper in two. Draw one half of the *ma'o hau hele* design on it. Cut it out. Open the paper up to have the full design.

2. Following directions for fusible webbing, iron it on the yellow fabric.

3. Trace the design on the back of the webbing. Cut out the design.

4. Lay the fabric on the tote bag so that the yellow flower is facing you. Iron it on.

5. Keep the bag handy so you can shop without having to use plastic bags. Use a cloth tote and save a sea turtle!

Hawaiian Extreme Sports

Native Hawaiians had hundreds of games, including wrestling, swimming, surfing, canoe racing, and fencing. Many of the games men played were often extremely competitive and dangerous and can be compared to today's Extreme Sports events.

PUALANI KANAKA'OLE KANAHELE, NATIVE HAWAIIAN (1937–)

Born on the island of Hawaii, Pualani Kanaka'ole Kanahele teaches the Hawaiian language and culture. She instructs young Hawaiians in the ancient art of the hula to connect them to their roots. The hula is a way to preserve the past through stories, songs, and dance. Pualani not only teaches this ancient tradition to young Hawaiians, but she also travels the world teaching others about Hawaiian culture, too. She believes that her Hawaiian people will become healthier and more balanced if they honor the values and lifestyle of their ancestors. To do this, it is important to learn the Hawaiian language, as many ideas do not translate into English.

But events were not held just for fun; they were often part of a serious religious ceremony. Participating in the contests kept people strong, fit, smart, and coordinated. U'lu maika, a type of bowling, is still played today. On the island of Molokai there are the remains of a seven-mile-long course. Stone disks made from lava, coral, limestone, and other materials were rolled between two stakes about six inches apart. One version of the game was to see who could bowl the greatest distance. Another was to see who had the most skill to bowl the *u-lu* between two stakes. A third was to see how strong the *u-lu* was as each player rolled it against his opponent's. The owner of the *u-lu* that did not break was the winner.

Hawaiian Language

'Aha Pûnana Leo, which means "nest of voices" or "language nest" in Hawaiian, is an organization that has helped save the Hawaiian language from extinction. It was founded in 1983, at a time when there were only a few fluent speakers left among the elderly. As with other Native peoples, the U.S. government had laws that prevented Native Hawaiians from speaking their own language.

Lawmakers felt that, by taking away the languages, Native peoples would be forced to be like other Americans and not be able to hold onto their own cultures and customs. Many things do not translate from one language into another, and those ideas, stories, songs, customs, and history could have been lost forever. On the tiny isolated island of Ni'ihau, there were fewer than 50 children who could speak the language. Schools were started where children learn in Hawaiian. Parents who run the schools often teach and learn along with their children. Kids learn Japanese and Chinese as well as their native language. They also learn about key aspects of Hawaiian culture, such as the practice of *ho'okipa* (hospitality).

SAY IT IN HAWAIIAN

Nearly 70 percent of Hawaii's native species have disappeared. The plants, animals, birds, fish, and insects are even more endangered than the Hawaiian language. Learn the names for some of the endangered species.

Pueo	POO-ay-oh	Short-Eared Owl
Nēnē	NAY-nay	Hawaiian Goose
Noio	NO-e-o	Black Noddy Bird
Honu'ea	HO-new eh-ah	Hawksbill Turtle
'Ulae	OO-la-aye	Lizardfish

PLAY A GAME OF U'LU MAIKA (HAWAIIAN BOWLING)

You can make a game of U'lu maika to play in a much smaller area than the traditional game was played in.

What You Need

Large open area

2 ½-gallon clear juice bottles, clean, dry and with labels removed

Colored sand (green, black, tan, and white) to represent the Hawaiian beaches

Ruler

Chalk or stick

Tennis or other rubber ball

Friends

What You Do

1. Fill the bottles with colored sand, making a nice design. Place them 6 inches apart.

2. Count off 30 steps, walking away from bottles. Mark a line with the chalk or a stick. This will be the spot you stand on to play.

3. Take turns bowling the ball between the bottles. Deduct a point if the ball hits the bottles. Two points are given for every ball that goes through without touching the bottles. The first player to reach 10 points wins.

◈ Resources ◈

Glossary

Abenaki (or Abnaki): nation of Native American and First Nations people, some of whom still live in what is now New England, Quebec, and the Canadian Maritimes; Abenaki are one of the five members of the Wabanaki Confederacy

adobe: a sun-dried brick made of natural materials, like clay, sand, and straw, mixed with water

advocate: a person who speaks in favor of some idea, policy, or person

after contact: a term that refers to the time after Native peoples had encounters with Europeans and Americans, a time in which they experienced cultural changes

Aleut: seafaring peoples, some of whom live in coastal and inland villages on Alaska's Aleutian and Pribilof islands; Aleut people now prefer to be called Unangan, their original name for themselves

Algonquian: a language family of Native Americans in North America, with many regional variations

ancestor: a person from whom one is descended, especially if the person is more remote than a grandparent

Anishinaabe: original name of North American people who are called Ojibwe, Ojibway, or Chippewa

anthropology: the study of humankind

Apache: a group of Native people, some of whom live on reservations in present-day Arizona and New Mexico; there are also Apache tribes in Oklahoma and Mexico

Appaloosa: a horse with a dark-spotted coat pattern on a light background; raised by the Nez Perce people of Idaho

appliqué: needlework technique to decorate clothing in which pieces of fabric are cut out and sewn onto another piece of fabric to create a design

Arapaho: nation of Native people, some of whom live on a reservation in Oklahoma and others of whom live on a reservation in Wyoming

arctic: the north polar regions; very cold weather

artifact: an object made by humans, such as a tool, basket, pottery piece, or weapon, usually from an earlier era

Athabascan: Indian people, some of whom live in small, traditional villages in vast areas of Alaska's interior and neighboring parts of Canada; also the name of a language group

atoll: a ring-shaped coral reef enclosing a lagoon

band: a subdivision of an Indian tribe, often composed of several related families

beadwork: decorative work of beads stitched on clothing, horse gear, and other objects; beadwork replaced quillwork after Indians acquired glass beads from European traders

before contact: a term that refers to the thousands of years of Native history before the arrival of Europeans; preferred to "prehistoric" or "pre-Columbian," terms that suggests no history existed for Native people until the arrival of Europeans or Columbus

Beloved Woman: in traditional Cherokee society, a woman of great influence who became known as *Ghigau*, meaning Beloved Woman, the highest role to which a Cherokee woman could aspire

Blackfeet: a nation of Native people, some of whom live on a reservation in northwestern Montana; they are closely related to three First Nations in the Canadian province of Alberta; sometimes collectively referred to as the Blackfoot or the Blackfoot Confederacy

buffalo: properly called bison, this mammal with a shaggy coat and short, curved horns is a kind of cattle, like a cow; millions of buffalo lived on the grassy plains of North America

caribou: a large reindeer that lives in herds; found in the Arctic tundra of Alaska and Canada

Catawba: nation of Native people who lived in present-day North and South Carolina; many forced to move west of the Mississippi River in 1830s; some members now live on a reservation in South Carolina

Cherokee: a nation of Native people who lived in present-day western North Carolina and Virginia, eastern Tennessee, and parts of South Carolina, Georgia, and Alabama; part of the group was forced to move west of the Mississippi in the 1830s to Indian Territory, present-day Oklahoma; those who escaped the forced march live on a reservation in North Carolina and other areas in the South

Cheyenne: a nation of Native people with two branches—Southern Cheyenne people, some of whom live on a reservation in Oklahoma, and the Northern Cheyenne, some of whom live on a reservation in Montana

Chickasaw: a nation of Native people who lived in northern Mississippi, western Tennessee and Kentucky, and eastern Arkansas; forced to move west of the Mississippi River in the 1830s; today some members live in a community in Oklahoma

chickee: a house of the Miccosukee and Seminole Indians; made from palmetto trees, poles, thatched roofs, and raised wooden platforms, it has open walls on all four sides

Chinook: a nation of Native people in Washington State and Oregon; famous traders who developed a trade language that was a mixture of local languages, English, and French; today some members live on the Quinault and Shoalwater Bay reservations in Washington State

Chippewa: a nation of Native people, also called Anishinaabe (their original name), Ojibway, and Ojibwe, some of whom live on reservations in Michigan, Minnesota, North Dakota, Wisconsin, and Canada

Choctaw: a nation of Native people who lived in southern and central Mississippi as well as Alabama, Georgia, and Louisiana; part of tribe forced to move west of the Mississippi River in the 1830s; today, some members live on Choctaw reservations in Louisiana and Mississippi and some live in a community in Oklahoma

code: a system of words, letters, and symbols used to represent other words or letters to ensure secrecy, especially in transmitting messages

coiling: a technique to make pottery; snake-like coils of clay are built up from the bottom of the pot and smoothed over

Comanche: a nation of Native people who lived across the southern plains; today, some members live in a tribal area in Oklahoma

concho belt: concho comes from the Spanish word for shell, *concha*; concho has come to mean round, oval, rectangular, and even butterfly-shaped silver disks that are added to belts made by Navajo artists

confederacy: a political alliance of Indian nations; there have been (and still are) many confederacies of North American Indians

cradleboard: a board or frame on which an infant is carried; usually made of wood and leather; used by many Native peoples as a portable cradle and for carrying an infant on the back

Creek: a nation of Native Americans who had towns throughout the Southeast, united under a loose organization called the Creek Confederation; forced to move west of the Mississippi River in the 1830s; some members now live in a tribal area in Oklahoma and on a reservation in Alabama.

Crow: a nation of Native people, some of whom live on a reservation in Montana

Dakota: a nation of Native people with numerous bands, some of whose members live today on reservations in South and North Dakota

emigrant: a person who leaves one's country to live in another country

federal recognition: in the United States, the term refers to the process of a tribe being recognized by the U. S. federal government, or to a person being granted membership in a federally recognized tribe. The over 500 federally recognized tribal governments in the United States possess the right to establish the legal requirements for membership as well as form their own government, to enforce laws (both civil and criminal), to tax, to license and regulate activities, to zone, and to exclude persons from tribal territories. Federally recognized tribes cannot make war, engage in foreign relations, or coin money.

giveaway: Native families that give things away (handmade shawls, quilts, blankets, tablecloths, dishes, silverware, foods, and horses) in honor of someone, usually a member of their family, for a variety of reasons including the naming of a relative, college graduation, honorable discharge from the military, and memorial for a deceased relative; giveaways, which show generosity, take place at powwows and on other occasions

Great Basin: an area in the United States that includes Nevada and Utah and parts of Idaho, Oregon, Wyoming, Colorado, and California

Great Lakes: Lakes Superior, Michigan, Huron, Erie, and Ontario; an area in the United States that includes part or all of Minnesota, Wisconsin, Illinois, Indiana, Michigan, Ohio, Pennsylvania, and New York and the Canadian province of Ontario; sometimes this area is included in the Northeast area

Great Plains: an extensive grassland that extends from present-day Canadian provinces of Manitoba, Saskatchewan, and Alberta all the way south to Texas, from the Mississippi River Valley west to the Rocky Mountains; the Great Plains include parts of North Dakota, South Dakota, Montana, Wyoming, Colorado, Nebraska, Kansas, Oklahoma, New Mexico, and Texas

Gros Ventre: a nation of Native people, some of whom live on a reservation in Montana

Haida: a nation of Native people, some of whom live on Prince of Wales Island in Alaska and in villages in Canada

Haudenosaunee: the name of the people often called the Iroquois, Five Nations, or, after 1722, Six Nations; the word means "people of the longhouse," a reference to the long, multifamily houses in which they lived

Havasupai: a nation of Native people, some of whom live on a reservation 3,000 feet below the rim of the Grand Canyon in Supai, Arizona

Hidatsa: a nation of Native people, some of whom live on a reservation in North Dakota

Ho-Chunk: a nation of Native people, some of whom live on a reservation in Wisconsin; its name was Winnebago until 1993, when the Ho-Chunk reclaimed their original name

hogan: a six- or eight-sided dwelling of Navajo people; made from logs and sod or stone; traditionally faces east

homesteader: a person who holds an area of land, usually 160 acres, granted by the U.S. government

Hopi Pueblo: a nation of Native people, some of whom live in villages located on three mesas in Arizona

Hualapai: a nation of Native people, some of whom live on a reservation near the Grand Canyon in Arizona

igloo: a snow house used in the winter by the Inuit in Canada; igloos are used as temporary shelters during the winters in Alaska

Illinois (Illiniwek) Confederacy: an alliance of nations who lived in the present states of Illinois and parts of Missouri, Arkansas, Iowa, and Wisconsin; some of the best-known tribes are Cahokia (Illinois), Kaskaskia (Arkansas), and Peoria (Iowa and Illinois); some members of the Peoria Tribe live in Oklahoma; the French called the tribes Illinois

immigrant: a person who leaves one country to settle permanently in another country

Indian Removal: U.S. government policy, beginning in the 1830s and lasting through the 1850s, which forcibly moved eastern Indian tribes to Indian Territory located west of the Mississippi River; removal made room for U.S. takeover of the lands in the east

Indian Territory: land west of the Mississippi River, primarily present-day Oklahoma; area the United States planned as a permanent homeland for all of the eastern Indians forcibly moved west of the Mississippi River in 1830s and 1840s

Iñupiat: the name indigenous people call themselves in northwest Alaska; formerly called Eskimo

Iroquois Confederacy: an alliance of Indian nations formed before European colonization, includes Mohawk, Cayuga, Onondaga, Oneida, and Seneca nations of present-day New York State; joined by the Tuscarora in the early 1700s; also called the Five Nations (before Tuscaroras joined the confederacy) and Six Nations

kayak: An Iñupiat or Aleut boat made of a light wooden frame covered with watertight animal skins, usually with two openings in the center, one for the paddler and one for the harpooner

Kickapoo: a nation of Native people, some of whom live on reservations in Oklahoma, Kansas, and Texas, and in Mexico

Kiowa: a nation of Native people, some of whom live on a reservation in Oklahoma

Klamath: three nations of Native peoples (Klamath, Modoc, and Yahooskin Band of Snake River), some of whose members today live on the reservation in south central Oregon

lacrosse: a game with origins in a tribal game played by eastern Indians in what is now the United States and Canada; its modern form is played on a field by two teams of ten players each; participants use a long-handled stick with a webbed pouch on one end to aim a small ball into the opposing team's goal; now played worldwide

ledger art: art that dates back to the mid-1870s, when Plains Indians used lined notebooks (called ledgers) to draw and paint pictures representing important cultural events; the art tends to feature flat, elongated images; ledger art has made a comeback today among Native artists

Long Walk of the Navajo: the forced march, beginning in 1864, by the U.S. Army, of more than 8,000 Navajos from their homeland in what is now Arizona to a desolate area in eastern New Mexico called Bosque Redondo, or *Hwééldi* by the Navajo

longhouse: a long dwelling, made with a pole frame and covered with bark, in which several related families live; the Haudenosaunee, or Iroquois, and Delaware lived in longhouses, as did Native families of the Northwest Coast area

Lumbee: a nation of Native people, some of whom live in North Carolina

Lummi: a nation of Native people, some of whom live on a reservation in Washington State

Makah: a nation of Native people, some of whom live on a reservation at Neah Bay, Washington

Mandan: a nation of Native people, some of whom live on a reservation in North Dakota

Menominee: a nation of Native people, some of whom live on a reservation in Wisconsin

Meskwaki: a nation of Native people, some of whom live on a reservation in Iowa

Miami: a nation, once located in the Great Lakes region, pushed west of the Mississippi River; today some members of the Miami Nation live on a tribal area in Oklahoma and in areas of Indiana.

Miccosukee: a nation of Native people, some of whom live on a reservation in southern Florida

Midwest: a region around the Great Lakes and the upper Mississippi Valley; includes Ohio, Indiana, Illinois, Michigan, Wisconsin, Minnesota, and Iowa

Miwok: a nation of Native people composed of three groups: Coast, Lake, and Sierra Miwok; today some members of these groups live on small reservations (*rancherias*) in north central California

Modoc: a nation of Native people whose original homeland was along what is now the California-Oregon border; the tribe is now located in Oklahoma, where many members live today

Navajo: a nation whose reservation extends into the states of Utah, Arizona, and New Mexico; *Diné Bikéyah*, or Navajoland is larger than 10 of the 50 states in America

Nez Perce: a nation of Native people, some of whom live on a reservation in north central Idaho

Nisqually: a nation of Native people, some of whom live on the reservation near Olympia, Washington

Northeast: a region that covers Maine, New Hampshire, Vermont, Massachusetts, Rhode Island, Connecticut, New York, New Jersey, and Pennsylvania

Ohlone: Native people who live in the San Francisco Bay area where their ancestors lived for many generations; people impacted by the Spanish mission system

Ojibwe: a nation of people, also called Anishinaabe (their original name), Chippewa, and Ojibway, some of whom live on reservations in Minnesota, Michigan, Wisconsin, North Dakota, and Canada

Ojibway: see Ojibwe above

Omaha: a nation of Native people, some of whom live on a reservation in Nebraska

Osage: a nation of Native people, some of whom live on a reservation in Oklahoma

Ottawa: a nation of Native people, some of whom live on reservations in Michigan, tribal land in Oklahoma, and southern Ontario, Canada; also called Odawa

Paiute: a nation of Native people, some of whom live on reservations in Arizona, Nevada, Utah, Oregon, and California

parfleche: a storage container that holds clothing, food, tools, and other objects; made from rawhide and often decorated with geometric designs

patchwork: needlework in which various colored patches of material are sewn together, as in a quilt

Pawnee: a nation of Native people, some of whom live on a reservation in Oklahoma

Pequot: a nation of Native people, some of whom live on a reservation in Connecticut

Pima: a nation of Native people, some of whom live on reservations in Arizona

Plateau: a region of the United States that includes land in eastern Washington, northeast and central Oregon, northern Idaho, western Montana, and a small part of northern California

poi: a Hawaiian food made from the thick part of the roots of taro, a tropical plant, that is cooked, pounded to a paste, and fermented

Potawatomi: a nation of Native people, some of whom live on reservations in Kansas, Oklahoma, Michigan, Wisconsin, and Ontario, Canada

potlatch: a lavish ceremony of gift-giving by a host to demonstrate wealth and generosity with the expectation of attending one in return, held by the Indian tribes of the Pacific Northwest and Alaska, especially the Haida, Tlingit, and Tsimpshian

Powhatan Chiefdom: over 30 Algonquian-speaking Indian nations in the eastern United States who paid tribute to Powhatan; one of the most complex Indian societies in 1607, with a population of approximately 15,000 and encompassing over 6,000 square miles

powwow: a traditional festival or competitive event among American Indians across the country which includes socializing, dancing, feasting, selling of arts and crafts, and other events

Pueblos: name for Native peoples who live in pueblos in northern and western New Mexico and northeast Arizona

pueblo: a Spanish word that means "town" or "village" as well as "people" or "nation"; has been applied to the architecture of Indian villages of the Southwest, multi-level houses, interconnected with ladders, made from adobe or stone bricks; the term also came to be applied to the inhabitants as well as to the villages

quillwork: decorative work on clothing, horsegear, bags, and other items made from porcupine quills dyed with vegetable colors; beadwork replaced quillwork once Indians acquired glass beads from European traders

rancheria: a reservation located in California

Removal Policy: a term that describes the 19th-century policy of the U.S. government in which nations east of the Mississippi River were removed from ancestral homelands and forced to move west of the river to Indian Territory, present-day Oklahoma

reservation: land set aside from original Native lands by the U.S. or state governments for use by American Indians; at first Indians were not permitted to leave reservations; today reservations are tribally held lands, protected by the government, where Native people are free to come and go. Some Native people were forced onto reservations far from their traditional territories.

Sac and Fox: two nations, which merged during the 18th century, today known as the Meskwaki, their original name, which means "red earth people"; some people live on the group's Iowa reservation; Sac is also spelled Sauk

Seminole: a nation of Native people, some of whom live on five reservations in southern Florida; other Seminoles live in Oklahoma; closely related to the Miccosukee Tribe of Florida

Shawnee: a nation of Native people, some of whom live on tribal lands in Oklahoma

sinew: tough fibrous tissue connecting muscle to bone; used as thread by Native people, especially with beadwork, before the use of cotton, silk, or polyester thread

Shoshone: a nation of Native people, some of whom live on reservations in Idaho, Nevada, Utah, and Wyoming

Sioux: a nation with branches called the Teton (who name themselves Lakota), Santee Sioux (who name themselves Dakota), and Yankton and Yankonai (who both name themselves Nakota); each branch has different bands; members of different bands live on reservations in South and North Dakota, Minnesota, Nebraska, and Montana; there are also Sioux bands in Canada

Six Nations: six nations, who call themselves the Haudenosaunee, located in upstate New York and Canada; originally the six nations were five: the Mohawks, Oneidas, Onondagas, Cayugas, and Senecas; the sixth nation, the Tuscaroras, joined the five in the early 1700s; together these six peoples comprise the oldest living participatory democracy on earth; also known by the French term Iroquois Confederacy

Skokomish: a nation of Native people, some of whom live on the reservation in Skokomish, Washington; Skokomish means "big river people"

Southeast: a region that includes Alabama, Arkansas, Florida, Georgia, Kentucky, Louisiana, Mississippi, North Carolina, South Carolina, Tennessee, Virginia, and West Virginia; there is no standard definition of the Southeast region of the United States— Georgia is almost always included, Texas is almost never included, and inclusion of other states varies

Southwest: a region that includes New Mexico, Arizona, and southern California; sometimes Texas and parts of Utah and Colorado

stickball: an ancient game that requires many of the same skills and rituals as war; stickball historically settled disputes between towns and sometimes between tribes; today the game is played with teams of 10 players, each using two wooden sticks similar to lacrosse sticks. The object of the game is to score goals with a ball; forerunner of lacrosse.

Stommish: annual gathering of canoe nations of the Pacific Northwest; a celebration held on the Lummi reservation to welcome servicemen and servicewomen home from war

syllabary: a set of written symbols that represent syllables that make up words

Thanksgiving Address: an address, with ancient roots dating back over a 1,000 years, which greets the natural world; the address opens and closes all ceremonial and governmental gatherings held by the Six Nations; based on the belief that the world cannot be taken for granted and all life must be respected

tipi: a conical tent with a pole frame usually covered with buffalo hides; typical dwelling of the Plains Indians; also spelled tepee

Tlingit: a nation of Native people, many of whom live in Southeast Alaska

Tohono O'odham: a nation of Native people with various bands that live on reservations in southwestern Arizona and in Mexico; formerly called the Papago; Tohono O'odham means "people of the desert"

totem pole: a tall post carved and painted with a series of sea and land figures and symbols that tell a story; carved by artists from the Northwest Coast and Alaska

tribe: a term applied to a group of Native people who share a common ancestry, language, culture, and name; usually composed of a number of bands or villages/towns; preferred term is *nation*

Tsimshian: a nation of Native people, many of whom live in Metlakatla on Annette Island Reserve in Southeast Alaska; originally from Canada

Unangan: the original name for the Aleut people of Alaska

Ute: a nation of Native people, some of whom live on reservations in Colorado and Utah

Wabanaki Confederation: an alliance of five nations, the Abenaki, Penobscot, Maliseet, Passamaquoddy, and Mi'kmaq of Maine and Canada; created during the 18th century; the five tribes remain close allies

Wampanoag: a nation of Native people in Massachusetts, some of whom live either in Mashpee on the mainland (Mashpee) or on a reservation in Aquinnah on Martha's Vineyard

Washoe: a nation of Native people, some of whom live on reservations located in Nevada and in California; also a Washoe community located within the Reno-Sparks Indian Colony of Nevada

wigwam: a cone- or dome-shaped dwelling with a pole frame covered with bark, animal skins, or woven mats; typical dwelling of the Wampanoag and Anishinaabe

Winnebago: a nation of Native people, some of whom live on a reservation in Nebraska; the Winnebago of Wisconsin now call themselves the Ho-Chunk Nation, their original name that means "people with the big voice"

Wyandot: at one time an important nation in the Ohio Valley, it was removed west of the Mississippi River; today there are four Wyandot nations: the self-governing tribe of the Wyandotte Nation of Oklahoma; the Wyandot of Anderdon Nation in Michigan, Wyandot Nation of Kansas, and the Huron-Wendat Nation in Canada

Yup'ik: the name indigenous people call themselves in southwest Alaska; formerly called Eskimo

Yurok: a nation of Native people, some of whom live on the reservation in northwestern California

Native American Museums and Cultural Centers

Alaska

Alaska Native Heritage Center
8800 Heritage Center Drive
Anchorage, AK 99504
(907) 330-8000
www.alaskanative.net

The center elebrates contemporary Alaska Native cultures (Athabascan, Aleut, Alutiiq, Iñupiat and Yupik, Eyak, Tlingit, Haida, and Tsimshian) while the outdoor facilities and sites explore ancient traditions and present stories from the past and present.

Alutiiq Museum & Archaeological Repository
215 Mission Road
Kodiak, AK 99615
(907) 486-7004
http://alutiiqmuseum.org

The Alutiiq Museum preserves the ancient and contemporary cultural traditions of the Alutiiq people as well as all the indigenous societies of the Alaskan Gulf coast.

Anchorage Museum of History and Art
121 West 7th Avenue
Anchorage, AK 99501
(907) 343-6139
www.anchoragemuseum.org

The largest museum in Alaska has exhibits that show the history as well as the changing cultures of Alaska Native peoples.

Alaska State Museum
395 Whittier Street
Juneau, AK 99801
(907) 465-2901
www.museums.state.ak.us/list.html#Juneau

The Museum features extensive ethnographic exhibits on the cultures of Alaska's Native people.

Inupiat Heritage Center
5421 North Star Street
Barrow, AK 99723
(907) 852-4594
www.co.north-
        slope.ak.us/departments/planning/IHCsite/
        index.html

The Inupiat Heritage Center features Iñupiaq culture, history, and language.

Arizona

Arizona State Museum
Arizona State Museum, University of Arizona
1013 East University Boulevard
Tucson, AZ 85721
(520) 621-6302
www.statemuseum.arizona.edu

The museum features the Native cultures of Arizona, the Greater Southwest, and northern Mexico.

Heard Museum
2301 North Central Avenue
Phoenix, AZ 85004
(602) 252-8848
www.heard.org

The Heard collections focus on cultures of the greater Southwest as well as American Indian fine art from throughout North America including drawings, paintings, and sculpture.

Hopi Cultural Center
P.O. Box 67
Second Mesa, AZ 86043
(928) 734-2401
www.hopiculturalcenter.com

The Hopi Cultural Center includes a gallery and museum.

Huhugam Heritage Center
Gila River Indian Community
4759 North Maricopa Road
Chandler, AZ 85226
(520) 796-3500
http://huhugam.com

Through interactive exhibits and educational activities, the center's museum tells the stories of the history, culture, and language of the peoples of the Gila River Indian Community, Akimel O'odham (Pima), and the Pee Posh (Maricopa) and honors the ancient Huhugam.

Navajo Nation Museum
Highway 264 and Loop Road
Window Rock, AZ 86515
(928) 871-7941
www.navajonationmuseum.org

The museum collections feature Navajo culture, language, and history.

San Carlos Apache Tribe Cultural Center
US 70 Milepost 272
PO Box 760
Peridot, AZ, 85542
(520) 475-2894
www.sancarlosapache.com/San_Carlos_
    Culture_Center.htm
    The center feature history, arts, and educational programs and demonstrations.

California

Agua Caliente Cultural Museum
219 South Palm Canyon Drive
Palm Springs, CA 92262
(760) 778-1079
http://accmuseum.org/page21.html
    Agua Caliente Cultural Museum interprets the history and culture of the Agua Caliente Band of Cahuilla Indians and other Cahuilla peoples.

Museum of the American West
4700 Western Heritage Way
Los Angeles, CA, 90027
(323) 667-2000
www.autry-museum.org/maw.php
    The museum (at the Autry National Center) explores the myths and realities of the American West and its diverse populations.

Barona Cultural Center and Museum
1095 Barona Road
Lakeside, CA 92040
(619) 443-7003
www.baronamuseum.org

The Barona Cultural Center and Museum is dedicated to preserving Kumeyaay/Diegueño culture and history in San Diego County.

Hoopa Tribal Museum
Hwy 96 Hoopa Shopping Center
P.O. Box 1348
Hoopa, CA 95546
(530) 625-4110
www.hoopa-nsn.gov/departments/museum.htm
    The museum displays one of the finest collections of Hupa, Yurok, and Karuk artifacts in northern California.

Malki Museum
The Malki Museum and Cultural Center
P.O. Box 578
Banning, CA 92220
(951) 849-7289
www.malkimuseum.org
    The oldest nonprofit museum founded by Native Americans on a California Indian reservation, the Malki Museum has inspired the creation of several other Indian museums. It preserves the cultural traditions and history of the Cahuilla Indians and other southern California Indian tribes.

Palm Springs Desert Museum
101 Museum Drive
Palm Springs, CA 92262
(760) 322-4800
www.psmuseum.org
    The museum has collections of Native American historic artifacts and contemporary art.
Sierra Mono Indian Museum
33103 Road 228

North Fork, CA 93643
(559) 877-2115
www.sierramonomuseum.org/contact.html
    The museum preserves tribal history and lifestyle today of the Mono people through exhibits and a living history experience.

Colorado

Denver Art Museum
100 West 14th Avenue Parkway
Denver, CO 80204
(720) 865-5000
www.denverartmuseum.org
    The museum's American Indian art collection represents the heritage of all cultures and tribes across the United States and Canada.

Ute Indian Museum
17253 Chipeta Drive
Montrose, CO 81401
(970) 249-3098
    The museum features one of the most complete collections of Ute Indian artifacts, history, and culture in the nation.

Connecticut

Institute for American Indian Studies
38 Curtis Road
Washington, CT 06793
(860) 868-0518
www.birdstone.org
    The institute focuses on stewardship and preservation, education, and research. A longhouse classroom and an outdoor replicated Algonkian Indian village draw school children.

Mashantucket Pequot Museum and Research
    Center
110 Pequot Trail
Mashantucket, CT 04339
(800) 411-9671
www.pequotmuseum.org
    The museum presents the history of the
Mashantucket Pequot Tribal Nation with a
16th-century woodland Indian village and a
17th-century Pequot fort. It also shows contemporary life, as well as the histories and cultures
of other tribes.

District of Columbia

Smithsonian Institution/National Museum of
the American Indian (NMAI)
4th Street and Independence Avenue, S.W.
Washington, D.C. 20560
(202) 633-1000
www.nmai.si.edu
    NMAI, part of the Smithsonian Institution,
is dedicated to the preservation, study, and
exhibition of the life, languages, literature, history, and arts of Native America.

Florida

Ah-Tah-Thi-Ki Museum
HC-61, Box 21-A
Clewiston, FL 33440
(863) 902-1113
www.semtribe.com/museum
    Ah-Tah-Thi-Ki ("a place to learn") features
the largest display of the life and culture of the
unconquered Florida Seminoles through
exhibits, rare artifacts, and cultural displays. It

offers a field trip into the rich swamp lands of
the Big Cypress Reservation.

Hawaii

Bishop Museum
1525 Bernice Street
Honolulu, HI 96817
(808) 847.3511
www.bishopmuseum.org
    The museum features millions of artifacts,
documents, and photographs about Hawaii and
other Pacific island cultures.

East Hawaii Cultural Center
141 Kalakaua Street
Hilo, HI 96720
(808) 961-5711
www.ehccircaorg
    The center is a coalition dedicated to preserving cultural, creative, and traditional arts in
Hawaii.

Illinois

Field Museum of Natural History
1400 South Lake Shore Drive
Chicago, IL 60605
(312) 922-9410
www.fieldmuseum.org
    The Field Museum has exhibits, educational programs, and special events for families.
It features information on Arctic and Northwest Coast Indians and ancient Americans, as
well as a full-scale reconstruction of a traditional Pawnee earth lodge that brings to life the

traditional ways of this Great Plains tribe and
contemporary Native cultures.

Mitchell Museum of the American Indian
3001 Central Street
Evanston, IL 60201
(847) 475-1030
www.mitchellmuseum.org
    The Mitchell Museum focuses exclusively
on the history, culture, and arts of the North
American Native people. The museum's collections range from ancient times to the present day.

Indiana

Eiteljorg Museum of American Indian and
    Western Art
White River State Park
500 West Washington St.
Indianapolis, IN 46204
(317) 636-9378
www.eiteljorg.org
    Eiteljorg's Native American art and artifacts come from all regions of North America,
from the Southeast to the Arctic.

Maine

Abbe Museum
P. O. Box 286
Bar Harbor, ME 04609
(207) 288-3519
www.abbemuseum.org
    The history and cultures of Maine's Native
people, the Wabanaki, are showcased through
changing exhibitions, special events, teacher

workshops, archaeology field schools, and craft workshops for children and adults.

Penobscot Indian Museum
12 Downstreet Street
Indian Island, ME 04468
(207) 827-4153
www.penobscotnation.org/museum/Index.htm
The museum houses collections that span thousands of years of Maine Native American history as well as contemporary Wabanaki art.

Massachusetts

Aquinnah Cultural Center
Edwin DeVries Vanderhoop Homestead
35 Aquinnah Circle
Aquinnah, MA 02535
(508) 645-7900
The center is dedicated to the preservation of Aquinnah Wampanoag history and culture.

Boston Children's Museum
Museum Wharf
300 Congress Street
Boston, MA 02210
(617) 426-6500
www.bostonkids.org
The museum showcases cultural objects from the Wampanoag community.

Minnesota

Mille Lacs Indian Museum
43411 Oodena Drive
Onamia, MN 56359
(320) 532-3632
www.mnhs.org/places/sites/mlim
The museum's exhibits tell the story of the Mille Lacs Band of Ojibwe Indians in northern Minnesota.

Montana

Museum of the Plains Indian
124 2nd Avenue N.W.
Browning, MT 59417
(406) 338-2344
www.browningmontana.com/museum.html
The museum exhibits the creative achievements of Native American artists and craftspeople of the United States and presents the diversity of historic arts of the tribal peoples of the Northern Plains.

People's Center Museum
53253 Highway 93 West
Pablo, MT 59855
(406) 883-5344
www.peoplescenter.net/contact.htm
The museum uses oral history to introduce visitors to the Salish, Pend d'Oreille, and Kootenai tribes.

New Jersey

Montclair Art Museum
3 South Montclair Avenue
Montclair, NJ 07042
(973) 746-5555
www.montclairartmuseum.org
The museum features a Native American collection that includes objects from the Northwest Coast, California, Southwest, Plains, Woodlands, Southeast, and the Arctic.

New Mexico

A:shiwi A:wan Museum and Heritage Center
Pueblo of Zuni
02 East Ojo Caliente Road
Zuni, NM 87327
(505) 782 4403
http://ggscircawnmu.edu/mcf/museums/
ashiwi.html
Visitors can experience Zuni history that spans over five centuries.

Haak'u Museum
Pueblo of Acoma
1-40, Exit 102
Acoma, NM 87034
(505) 252-1139
http://museum.acomaskycity.org
The Haak'u Museum houses both permanent and traveling exhibits which present the 1,000-year cultural pathway of the Acoma people.

Indian Pueblo Cultural Center
2401 12th Street NW
Albuquerque, NM 87104
Phone: (505) 724-3533
www.indianpueblo.org
   The center offers a firsthand look at the 19 Pueblos of New Mexico through history, art, culture, and the continuing lives of New Mexico's oldest inhabitants.

Institute of American Indian Arts Museum
108 Cathedral Place
Santa Fe, NM 87501
(505) 983-8900
www.iaia.edu/museum
   The IAIA Museum houses over 7,000 works of art and has been referred to as the "National Collection of Contemporary Native American Art."

Museum of Indian Arts and Culture
Museum Hill
710-708 Camino Lejo
Santa Fe, NM 87504
(505) 476-1250
www.indianartsandculture.org/index.html
   The Museum of Indian Arts and Culture tells the stories of the Native people of the Southwest from ancient through contemporary art.

Walatowa Visitor Center and Jemez Pueblo
   Museum
Pueblo of Jemez-Walatowa Visitor Center
7413 Highway 4
Jemez Pueblo, NM 87024
(575) 834-7235

www.jemezpueblo.org
   The visitor center and museum teach about Towa culture and traditions.

Wheelwright Museum of the American Indian
704 Camino Lejo
Santa Fe, NM 87502
(505) 982-4636
www.wheelwright.org
   The Wheelwright Museum of the American Indian hosts changing exhibitions of contemporary and historic Native American art with an emphasis on the Southwest.

New York

Akwesasne Museum
321 State Route 37
Hogansburg, NY 13655
(518) 358-2461
www.akwesasneculturalcenter.org
   The Akwesasne Museum includes over 2,000 photographic objects and over 700 ethnographic objects of various kinds, related to the Mohawk community of Akwesasne.

Iroquois Indian Museum
324 Caverns Road
Howes Cave, NY 12092
(518) 296-8949
www.iroquoismuseum.org
   The Iroquois Indian Museum, designed in the shape of a longhouse, fosters understanding of Iroquois culture using Iroquois art as a window to that culture.

National Museum of the American Indian
George Gustav Heye Center
One Bowling Green
New York, NY 10004
(212) 514-3700
www.nmai.si.edu
   The Heye Center serves as the National Museum of the American Indian's exhibition, education facility, and performance center in New York City.

Nitchen Center for Native Cultures of the
   Americas
550 West 155th Street
New York, NY 10032
(212) 694-2240
www.nitchenchildrensmuseum.org
   Nitchen, Inc. presents Native cultural programs for school, camp, and youth groups that enhance classroom curriculum.

Seneca-Iroquois National Museum
814 Broad Street
Salamanca, NY 14779
(716) 945-1760
www.senecamuseum.org
   The Seneca-Iroquois National Museum preserves and presents Seneca history and culture.

Shinnecock Nation Cultural Center and
   Museum
100 Montauk Highway & West Gate Road
Southampton, NY 11969
(631) 287-4923
www.shinnecock-museum.org

The only Native American–owned-and-operated museum on Long Island, it presents both their ancient and living Eastern Woodland cultures.

North Carolina

Museum of the Cherokee Indian
589 Tsali Boulevard
Cherokee, NC 28719
(828) 497-3481
www.cherokeemuseum.org
The museum tells the story of the Cherokee people and their ancestors from 12 thousand years ago through the present.

Oklahoma

Gilcrease Institute: The Museum of the Americas
1400 Gilcrease Museum Road
Tulsa, OK 74127
(918) 596-2700
www.gilcrease.org
The museum features a collection of Native American art and artifacts, as well as historical manuscripts, documents, and maps.

Osage Tribal Museum and Library
627 Grandview
Pawhuska, OK 74056
(918) 287-5441
http://osagetribe.com/museum
The museum, the first tribally owned museum in the United States, is dedicated to educating the public about the history, customs, and traditions of the Osage people.

Southern Plains Indian Museum
715 East Central Boulevard
Anadarko, OK 73005
(405) 247- 6221
www.doi.gov/iacb/museums/museum_s_plains.html
The Southern Plains Indian Museum displays richly varied arts of western Oklahoma tribal peoples including the Kiowa, Comanche, Kiowa-Apache, Southern Cheyenne, Southern Arapaho, Wichita, Caddo, Delaware, and Fort Sill Apache.

Oregon

The Museum at Tamástslikt Cultural Institute
72789 Highway 331
Pendleton, OR 97801
(541) 966-9748
www.tamastslikt.org
Tamástslikt celebrates the traditions of Cayuse, Umatilla, and Walla Walla tribes with dramatic exhibits, renowned artwork, and fun events year-round.

The Museum at Warm Springs
P.O. Box 909
Warm Springs, OR 97761
(541) 553-3331
www.museumatwarmsprings.org
Through educational exhibits and programs the museum features a collection of Plateau Native American artifacts.

Pennsylvania

University Museum of Archaeology and Anthropology
University of Pennsylvania
33rd and Spruce Streets
Philadelphia, PA 19104
(215) 898-4000
www.museum.upenn.edu
The museum has extensive collections of artifacts from Native peoples of the Americas.

South Dakota

Red Cloud Heritage Center and Museum
100 Mission Drive
Pine Ridge, SD 57770
(605) 867-5491
www.redcloudschool.org/museum/index.htm
The center, one of the early successful museums located on an Indian reservation, offers a collection of Native American fine arts and Lakota tribal arts, located on the main campus of Red Cloud Indian School.

Sicangu Heritage Center and Museum
Sinte Gleska University, Antelope Lake Campus
P.O. Box 675
Mission, SD 57555
(605) 856-8211
www.sintegleska.edu/heritage_cntr
The museum collects, preserves, and interprets the objects that tell the history of the Rosebud Sioux Tribe and its members from earliest times until the present day.

Sioux Indian Museum at The Journey
   Museum
222 New York Street
Rapid City, SD 57701
(605) 394-2381
Rapid City, South Dakota
www.doi.gov/iacb/museums/museum_
   sioux.html
   The Sioux Indian Museum displays an
extensive array of historic clothing plus horse
gear, weapons, household implements, cradleboards, and toys.

Washington

Burke Museum of Natural History and Culture
University of Washington
17th Avenue NE and NE 45th Street
Seattle, WA 98195
(206) 543-5590
www.washington.edu/burkemuseum
   The museum has a renowned collection of
Native American art and artifacts, especially
from the Northwest Coast and Alaska. It also
has collections from the Western Sub-arctic,
Plateau, Plains, Great Lakes, and Southwest.

Makah Cultural and Research Center
P.O. Box 160
Neah Bay, WA 98357
(360) 645-2711
www.makah.com/mcrchome.htm
   The museum welcomes visitors to experience the life of pre-contact Makah people.

Yakama Nation Museum
CC Administration Office
100 Spiel-yi Loop
Toppenish, WA 98948
(509) 865-2800
http://yakamamuseum.com/showpage.php?pag
   eid=904f27cb
   The Yakama Nation Museum features life-
size dwellings of the Plateau people and
unique dioramas and exhibits that tell the story
of the Yakama People.

Wisconsin

George W. Brown Jr. Ojibwe Museum and
   Cultural Center
603 Peace Pipe
Lac du Flambeau, WI 54538
(715) 588-3333
www.rhinelanders-morningside.com/
   activities/george.htm
   The museum celebrates Ojibwe culture
with exhibits depicting the four seasons of
Ojibwe life as it has been lived for centuries in
Wisconsin.

Milwaukee Public Museum
800 West Wells Street
Milwaukee, WI 53233
(414) 278-2702
www.mpm.edu
   The museum's Indian Country exhibit features a modern powwow grand entry scene
with 37 life-sized figures dressed in colorful
dance attire. Various aspects of contemporary

American Indian life, reservation and urban,
are shown in conjunction with the powwow.

Wyoming

Plains Indian Museum
Buffalo Bill Historical Center
720 Sheridan Avenue
Cody, WY 82414
(307) 578-4072
www.bbhcircaorg/pim/index.cfm
   The majority of the museum collection
comes from the early reservation period, 1880
to 1930, and features objects primarily from
Northern Plains tribes.

Native American Festivals and Powwows

Powwows, which occur all over North America, are Native cultural events that feature
dancing and singing for people of all ages, arts
and crafts, food, and other activities like
rodeos. They are a way of sharing, reinforcing,
and expressing Native heritage.
   Dozens of powwows are held each year.
Some are large; others are small gatherings.
Some are strictly traditional; others are contest
events in which dancers compete for prize
money. Most are open to the public. Some
powwow dances are only for people who dress
in the correct regalia and know the dances.
Each Native community sets its own rules
about which events are open to the public.
Most powwows are held during summer

months, usually outdoors. Some are held in sports arenas.

Many tribes and organizations publicize powwows that are open to the public through Web sites and Native publications.

Northeast

Schemitzun: Feast of Green Corn
www.schemitzun.com

The Mashantucket Pequot Tribe of Connecticut hosts *Schemitzun*: Feast of Green Corn, one of the largest in the nation. It takes place in North Stonington, Connecticut, in August.

Southeast

Coushatta Powwow
http://coushattapowwow.com

The Coushatta Tribe of Louisiana hosts the Coushatta Powwow, an annual gathering of tribes from across the United States and Canada. It takes place in Kinder, Louisiana, in October.

Midwest

Meskwaki Annual Powwow
www.meskwaki.org/special/powwow/mapa.html

The Meskwaki Tribe of Iowa hosts the Meskwaki Annual Powwow. It takes place near Tama, Iowa, in August.

Plains

Crow Fair
www.crow-fair.com

The Apsaalooke Nation in southeastern Montana hosts Crow Fair, one of the largest in the nation. Held near Billings, Montana, every August, it is called the "Tipi Capitol of the World."

Great Basin/Plateau

Wildhorse Powwow
www.wildhorseresort.com

The Confederated Tribes of the Umatilla Reservation host the Wildhorse Powwow. It takes place in Pendleton, Oregon, in July.

Southwest

Navajo Nation Fair
www.navajonationfair.com

The Navajo Nation hosts the Navajo Nation Fair. It takes place in Window Rock, Arizona, in September. It showcases Navajo agriculture, arts and crafts, and cultural entertainment.

Pacific States

Traditional Gathering and Annual Pow-Wow
http://sycuan.com/pow_wow.html

The Sycuan Band of the Kumeyaay Nation of California hosts the Traditional Gathering and Annual Pow-Wow which features Kumeyaay Bird Singing and Dancing and Hand games. It takes place in El Cajon, California, in September.

Stillaguamish Festival of the River and Pow Wow
www.festivaloftheriver.com/festival.htm

The Stillaguamish Tribe hosts the Stillaguamish Festival of the River and Pow Wow. It takes place in Arlington, Washington, in August. The Festival of the River celebrates the Pacific Northwest environment.

Alaska

Midnight Sun Intertribal Powwow
www.midnightsunpowwow.net/aboutus.html

A group of Alaska Natives, American Indians, and First Nations People of Canada host the Midnight Sun Intertribal Powwow. It is a traditional (versus contest) powwow designed to enrich the lives of all Native people, educate the general public, honor elders, and share our similarities and diversities. It takes place in Fairbanks, Alaska, in July.

Hawaii

Hilo Powwow
www.hilopowwow.com

The Federation of American Natives and others host the Hilo Powwow. It takes place in Hilo, Hawaii, in May.

Suggested Reading List for Kids

Alexie, Sherman. *The Absolutely True Diary of a Part-Time Indian.* New York: Little, Brown, 2007.

Ancona, George. *Powwow.* New York: Harcourt Paperback, 1993.

Belarde-Lewis, Miranda. *Meet Lydia: A Native Girl from Southeast Alaska.* Hillsboro, OR: Beyond Words Publishing, Inc./National Museum of the American Indian, 2004.

Braine, Susan. *Drumbeat...Heartbeat: A Celebration of the Powwow.* Minneapolis: Lerner Publications, 1995.

Broker, Ignatia. *Night Flying Woman.* St. Paul: Minnesota Historical Society Press, 1983.

Bruchac, Joseph. *Code Talker: A Novel About the Navajo Marines of World War Two.* New York: Dial Books, 2005.

Bruchac, Joseph. *Eagle Song.* New York: Dial Books for Young Readers, 1997.

Bruchac, Joseph. *Navajo Long Walk: The Tragic Story of a Proud People's Forced March from Their Homeland.* Washington, DC: National Geographic, 2002.

Caduto, Michael J. and Bruchac, Joseph. *Keepers of the Animals: Native American Stories and Wildlife Activities for Children.* Golden, Colorado: Fulcrum, Inc., 1991. Also *Keepers of the Earth: Native American Stories and Environmental Activities for Children* (1988); *Keepers of Life: Discovering Plants Through Native American Stories and Earth Activities for Children* (1994); *Keepers of the Night: Native American Stories and Nocturnal Activities for Children* (1994). Teachers' Guides available.

Carlson, Lori Marie., ed. *Moccasin Thunder: American Indian Stories for Today.* New York: Harper Teen, 2005.

Crum, Robert. *Eagle Drum: On the Powwow Trail with a Young Grass Dancer.* New York: Four Winds/Simon & Schuster, 1994.

Dennis, Yvonne and Arlene Hirschfelder. *Children of Native America Today.* Watertown, MA: Charlesbridge, 2003; Also *Children of Native Today Activity and Resource Guide* (2003).

Ekoomiak, Normee. *Arctic Memories.* New York: Henry Holt, 1988.

Erdrich, Louise. *The Game of Silence.* New York: Harper Collins, 2005.

Griffin-Pierce, Trudy. *The Encyclopedia of Native America.* New York: Penguin, 1995.

Harrell, Beatrice O. *Longwalker's Journey: A Novel of the Choctaw Trail of Tears.* New York: Dial, 1999.

Hirschfelder, Arlene and Beverly Singer, eds. *Rising Voices: Writings of Young Native Americans.* New York: Charles Scribner's Sons, 1992.

Hoyt-Goldsmith, Diane. *Lacrosse: The National Game of the Iroquois.* New York: Holiday House, 1998. Also *Potlatch: A Tsimshian Celebration* (1997).

Hunter, Sally. *Four Seasons of Corn: A Winnebago Tradition.* Minneapolis: Lerner Publications, 1996.

Juettner, Bonnie. *100 Native Americans Who Shaped American History.* San Mateo, CA: Bluewood Books, 2003.

King, Sandra. *Shannon: An Ojibway Dancer.* Minneapolis: Lerner Publications, 1993.

Lacapa, Kathleen and Michael Lacapa. *Less Than Half, More Than Whole.* Taylor, AZ: Storytellers Publishing, 2001.

Left Hand Bull, Jacqueline and Suzanne Haldane. *Lakota Hoop Dancer.* New York: Dutton, 1999.

Lourie, Peter. *Everglades: Buffalo Tiger and the River of Grass.* Honesdale, PA: Boyds Mill Press, 1994.

Maher, Ramona. *Alice Yazzie's Year.* Berkeley, CA: Tricycle Press, 2003.

Messinger, Carla, Susan Katz, and David Kanietakeron Fadden. *When the Shadbush Blooms.* Berkeley, CA: Tricycle Press, 2007.

Ochoa, Annette Piña, Betsy Franco, and Traci L. Gourdine. *Night Is Gone, Day Is Still Coming: Stories and Poems by American Indian Teens and Young Adults.* Cambridge, MA: Candlewick Press, 2003.

National Museum of the American Indian/Smithsonian Institution. *When the Rain Sings: Poems by Young Native Americans.* New York: Simon & Schuster, 1999.

Monture, Joel. *Cloudwalker: Contemporary Native American Stories.* Golden, CO: Fulcrum Kids, 1996.

Nicols, Richard. *A Story to Tell.* Minneapolis: Lerner Publications, 1998.

Ortiz, Simon. *The People Shall Continue.* San Francisco :Children's Book Press, 1988.

Peters, Russell M. *Clambake: A Wampanoag Tradition.* Minneapolis: Lerner Publications, 1992.

Regguinti, Gordon. *The Sacred Harvest: Ojibway Wild Rice Gathering.* Minneapolis: Lerner Publications, 1992.

Roessel, Monty. *Kinaalda: A Navajo Girl Grows Up.* Minneapolis: Lerner Publications, 1993. Also *Songs from the Loom: A Navajo Girl Learns to Weave* (1995).

Santiago, Chiori. *Home to Medicine Mountain.* San Francisco: Children's Book Press, 1998.

Secakuku, Susan. *Meet Mindy: A Native Girl from the Southwest.* Hillsboro, OR: Beyond Words Publishing, Inc. in association with National Museum of the American Indian, 2003.

Shemie, Bonnie. *Houses of Adobe: Native Dwellings of the Southwest; Houses of Bark: Native Dwellings of the Woodland Indians; Houses of Hide and Earth: Native Dwellings of the Plains Indians; Houses of Snow, Skin, and Bones: Native Dwellings of the Far North; Houses of Wood: Native Dwellings of the Northwest Coast.* Plattsburgh, NY: Tundra Books, 1995.

Smith, Cynthia Leitich. *Indian Shoes.* New York: HarperCollins, 2002.

Smith, Cynthia Leitich. *Jingle Dancer.* New York: Morrow, 2000.

Sneve, Virginia Driving Hawk. *High Elk's Treasure.* New York: Holiday House, 1995.

Steltzer, Ulli. *A Haida Potlatch.* Seattle: University of Washington Press, 1984.

Swamp, Jake. *Giving Thanks: A Native American Good Morning Message.* New York: Lee and Low Books, 1995.

Swentzell, Rina. *Children of Clay: A Family of Pueblo Potters.* Minneapolis: Lerner Publications, 1992.

Tayac, Gabrielle. *Meet Naiche: A Native Boy from the Chesapeake Bay Area.* Hillsboro, OR: Beyond Words Publishing, Inc. in association with National Museum of the American Indian, 2003.

Tapahonso, Luci. *Songs of Shiprock Fair.* Walnut, CA: Kiva Publishing, 1999.

Tingle, Tim. *Crossing Bok Chitto: A Choctaw Tale of Friendship & Freedom.* El Paso, TX: Cinco Puntos Press, 2006.

Waldman, Carl. *Encyclopedia of Native American Tribes.* Revised Edition. New York: Facts on File, 1999.

Wittstock, Laura Waterman. *Ininatig's Gift of Sugar/Traditional Native Sugarmaking.* Minneapolis: Lerner Publications, 1993.

Yamane, Linda. *Weaving a California Tradition: A Native American Basketmaker.* Minneapolis: Lerner Publications, 1997.

Yazzie, Evangeline Parson. *Dzání Yázhí Naazbaa': Little Woman Warrior Who Came Home: A Story of the Navajo Long Walk.* Flagstaff, AZ: Salina Bookshelf, 2007.

Yue, Charlotte and David Yue. *The Igloo.* Boston: Houghton Mifflin, 1988; *The Pueblo,* 1986; *The Wigwam and the Longhouse,* 2000.

Web Sites

Canku Ota: A Newsletter Celebrating Native America: www.turtletrack.org

Canyon Records: www.canyonrecords.com

Cradleboard Teaching Project: www.cradleboard.org

Cynthia Leitich Smith's literature resources: www.cynthialeitichsmith.com

Indigenous Geography Website: www.indigenousgeography.si.edu

National Museum of the American Indian: www.conexus.si.edu

◈ Index ◈